"…one of the most unique self-help books on anxiety that you'll likely ever encounter. Hatcher and Willard not only know anxiety inside and out through their decades' long clinical experience, but they can't help but relay laugh-out-loud anecdotes of living anxiety-peppered lives. This would be a funny, de-stigmatizing memoir if they stopped there. But these anxiety gurus provide the reader with sound, evidence-based coping tactics for our crazy world that are designed to regulate the skittish brain, calm the anxious mind, and de-stress the nervous body. A must read for virtually all living humans."

–Dr. Matt Hersh

"Hatcher and Willard's *Anxiety Hacks for an Uncertain World* is a welcome addition to the anxiety help-seeker's toolkit. With shame, pain and stigma being so much a part of the anxiety struggle, this book's irreverent, fun angle helps readers gain the separation and perspective necessary to see anxiety, without being lost within it."

–Dr. Mitch Abblett

# Anxiety Hacks for an Uncertain World

*Anxiety Hacks for an Uncertain World* is a highly accessible guide to anxiety disorders. It helps anxiety sufferers regain control by suggesting an array of useful tactics which when applied can be life altering.

Chapters explore topics such as phobias, panic disorders, social anxiety, general anxiety, pandemics, and more. Additional resources are included in the appendix, such as support groups, services, and helplines. Using light humor and examples from their lived experiences the authors relate to readers and offer useful suggestions to overcome anxiety and understand it.

This book will be essential for anyone suffering from anxiety and phobias or professionals working with this population. It can be used on its own or in conjunction with therapy.

**Jon Patrick Hatcher** is a California-based features writer, humorist, and the creator and co-author of *101 Ways to Conquer Teen Anxiety* and *The Teen Anxiety Guidebook*. He also has a self-help humor blog titled "State of Anxiety" on Psychology Today. He loves steel drums and smelling new things.

**Christopher Willard** is a clinical psychologist, author, and consultant based in Massachusetts. He has been invited to more than two dozen countries to speak and has presented at two TEDx events. His thoughts on mental health have been featured in *The New York Times*, *The Washington Post*, mindful.org, cnn.com, and elsewhere. He teaches at Harvard Medical School.

# Anxiety Hacks for an Uncertain World

Jon Patrick Hatcher and
Christopher Willard

Routledge
Taylor & Francis Group

NEW YORK AND LONDON

Cover image: © Getty Images

First published 2023
by Routledge
605 Third Avenue, New York, NY 10158

and by Routledge
4 Park Square, Milton Park, Abingdon, Oxon, OX14 4RN

*Routledge is an imprint of the Taylor & Francis Group, an informa business*

All illustrations by Peter L. Brown.

ISBN: 978-1-032-38502-0 (hbk)
ISBN: 978-1-032-35142-1 (pbk)
ISBN: 978-1-003-34535-0 (ebk)

DOI: 10.4324/9781003345350

Typeset in Sabon
by Apex CoVantage, LLC

# Contents

# Acknowledgments

For Maria Ananchenko.

To JoAnn Hatcher for personifying resilience and gifting me the love of reading and writing, as I fought you grumbling and flailing. And to James Hatcher for a lifetime of love and support. I was not a mild-mannered child.

Emma Hatcher and Terra Hatcher, you are forever cherished. No high jinks or agents provocateur can diminish this fact.

Marian Lamb, you're a mental and emotional lifeguard and a cerebral ninja. There exists no phrase to adequately define your contributions to humanity and the well-being of others. Your restorative imprint reverberates through countless lives.

Thank you Christopher Kelaher for setting this book in motion. It would not exist without you. You're a gentlemen and a friend.

David Becker, thank you for making this work measurably better. I marvel at your eye for the details. And your subtle knowledge of heavy metal music and copy editing.

Christopher Willard . . . what a ride! Thank you for your camaraderie. The words herein bear witness to the tenacity we forged together in trying times. This book is anxiety road tested.

I'm exceptionally grateful to you, Peter L. Brown, for your artistry and allegiance. You'd hide a body for a fella.

Alicia Stancil, you've become a lady-conqueror of anxiety. The struggle bus is not your ride.

And heaps of gratitude to you, Sarah Gore, for breathing renewed life into the manuscript. Your savvy brain, professionalism, and wonderful demeanor set the bar. You're a modern-day editorial Jackie O.

And thank you, Alison Macfarlane, for your production prowess and taking this book across the finish line. You're a savvy wordist and a pleasure to work with.

To our readers, thank you for investing your time with us. I promise some takeaways that will both soothe and help you find your own "why."

I'm sure I missed someone. Which makes me anxious.
Cast all your anxiety on him because he cares for you.
– 1 Peter 5:7

# An Introduction
## Danger – Unchecked Emotions Ahead

The first time I saw a flameless cigarette lighter anywhere but an old car was on an enclosed patio wall of the Oakland, CA, psychiatric facility where my therapist had sent me in my late teens due to anxiety and depression. Smoking was the only vice afforded to us. Though even while despondent, I wasn't interested in adding nicotine to a budding affinity for alcohol. Perhaps I had hope after all.

I left triage a few days later, knowing the next bout of crippling anxiety or profound depression was a breakup or mere bad day away. I had no more coping skills than I did before arriving. Beyond therapy and medication, I needed to find a purpose to get right with the world and somehow thrive. It's not hyperbole to say it was life or death for me.

I began to journal and noticed a subtle pattern throughout my anxious behaviors. *Humor.* Many of my anxiety-related mannerisms are dysfunctional but laughable and cathartic.

### Find the Humor; Find a Cure

Our thoughts affect our body and vice versa. Anxiety in the mind creates a stress response in the body. Conversely, calming the body will yield positive cerebral results. All physiological functions are linked, and the mind-body connection is especially strong. Perhaps most impactful to the sufferer, however, is that humor provides a unique and unrivaled perspective that shifts our thinking away from despair and toward the awareness that a radically different outcome is possible. Friedrich Nietzsche said it himself: "He who has a why to live can bear almost any how."

Humor is the most accessible form of anxiety *and* depression relief. It may initially feel counterintuitive to associate humor with misery. But sourcing the comical manifestations can separate you from your affliction. It's also how I salvaged my own life.

Mental disorders and illnesses aren't as respected as most other physiological screwups. It doesn't help that they're invisible. The brain is an organ that misfires like any other organ in the body. Anxiety and

DOI: 10.4324/9781003345350-1

depression are real illnesses. But because they don't present with an apparent physical ailment like, say, an arrow to the head, they are often perceived as just "a bad day" or a lack of character strength. You can't see diabetes or mermaids either, but they're just as real.

With anxiety comes agitation. And anxiety attacks. And worry, stress, obsessions, compulsions, insomnia, social avoidance, PTSD, and chronic chewing of nails and cuticles. These are all traits that stand in the way of truly living.

> Anxiety: *Okay, but what if . . .*
> Me: *We went over this 100 times already!*
> Anxiety: *I know but hear me out. I've found 20 new reasons you should be worried.*
> Me: *Go on.*

## No One Thing Causes an Anxiety Disorder, and the Contributing Factors Are as Varied as the Anxiety Symptoms Themselves

For each of us, there are certain events, situations, people, and venues that greatly exacerbate our angst, at which time anxiety can run feral and unchecked in a cataclysmic cyclone of cerebral pillage. Such trials might include elevators, giving a speech, pandemics, the Mall of America, pooping at work, breakups/divorce, job loss, moving, serious illness, or the presence of in-laws.

At any given moment, there are approximately 40 million Americans suffering from debilitating anxiety related to one cause or another. For men, women, and young adults, anxiety is an equalizer that affects everyone at some point. Even the ridiculously good-looking.

This book instills the cathartic "I'm not so alone after all" relatability necessary to laugh at your own neurosis, while learning simple-to-use tactics to feel better when anxiety arises. I will lead you toward what works and to scrap what does not. This is provided by chronicling lesser-known comical manifestations of anxiety and then enveloping you in a cozy smattering of the systematic and proven recovery techniques that follow.

## A Note on the Use of Humor

The guide establishes a tone of humor from the start for a reason: to change your relationship to the problem of anxiety. Using humor in trying times causes a mental and emotional shift that yields a new perspective in approaching difficult situations. The use of humor throughout the book is never to make light of mental illness or the associated suffering, rather to instill a lighter, clinically efficacious, and more hopeful attitude and approach regarding mental disorders.

It may seem blasphemous to laugh at our current misfortunes. But finding the humor is precisely what we need to do to cope. When you are overwhelmed by tragic events, humor is a useful defense mechanism. When facing adversity like illness or even death, humor serves as a buffer. Moreover, people who think about death are funnier. The notion is appropriately called terror management theory.[1] The study suggests that humor functions as a natural and often effective means of down-regulating stressful or traumatic experiences.

Humor is embedded in tragedy, pain, and struggle in ways we cannot grasp. And possibly, humor is also what will save us.

The content herein provides insight, perspective, and the targeted bibliotherapy you need to help overcome worry, panic, and anxiety over life's greatest stressors. It is recognizable and actionable relief you need now. No workbooks or pages and pages of reading. The last thing anyone in the throes of anxiety needs is homework.

## What Is Anxiety?

Anxiety symptoms include muscle tension, weakness, poor memory, sweating, confusion, constant worry, shortness of breath, heart palpations, digestive problems, poor concentration, and a strong "What the hell is wrong with me?" sensation. Anxiety leads us to act in a threatening scenario. In a less ominous setting, it motivates us to get important things done like paying bills or getting a colonoscopy.

## Anxiety Is a Bully You've Got to Constantly Stand up to, or It'll Be Your Personal Shot Caller

According to the National Institute of Mental Health (NIMH), "severe anxiety that lasts at least six months is generally considered to be a problem that might benefit from evaluation and treatment." Each anxiety disorder has different symptoms, but all the symptoms cluster around excessive, irrational fear and dread.

Anxiety and depression are at unprecedented levels with mounting numbers. The World Health Organization (WHO) describes anxiety as an epidemic, directly impacting the lives of nearly one in five people and responsible for substantial global suffering and disability. Anxiety, along with depression, cut across all demographics. And though anxiety disorders are highly treatable, sadly only about one-third of those suffering receive treatment.[2]

---

1 Long, C., & Greenwood, D. (2013). Joking in the face of death: A terror management approach to humor production. *Humor*, 26(4), 493–509.

2 *Facts & Statistics | Anxiety and Depression Association of America, ADAA.* (2021, September 19). Anxiety and Depression Association of America. https://adaa.org/understanding-anxiety/facts-statistics

## Simple Ways to Distinguish Between *Stress* Versus *Anxiety*

• Unlike anxiety, stress is a response to daily pressures, while anxiety is more akin to fear and helplessness.
• Anxiety is classified as an actual mental disorder; stress is not.
• Stress is a response to a specific stressor, while anxiety often has no discernible cause.
• Stress typically goes away with the stressor, while anxiety tends to last longer and be more difficult to treat.
• A diagnosis of anxiety requires persistence of symptoms for 6 months or more.

## What Is the Difference Between Normal Anxiety and the Debilitating Kind?

Anxiety is normal or beneficial when it serves our general well-being. Conversely, it is abnormal if it becomes chronic and impairs functioning or well-being. *The main criteria used to distinguish normal anxiety from an anxiety disorder are that it results in significant distress, or impairs social, occupational, or other important areas of functioning* (source: American Psychological Association).[3] When you live in an anxious state of mind, you perceive the world in a vastly different, even threatening, way. Never think that you or a loved one is overdramatic while anxious. When an octopus is stressed, it eats its own arms.

## What Type of Anxiety Do You Have?

There is a history of division in the psychological community regarding how to classify different types of anxiety disorders. Typically, and per the U.S. government (NIMH), there are *three* classifications of anxiety.[4] However, I separately categorized social anxiety disorder (usually included under "phobias") as its own entity. Like all anxieties, it wanted the limelight. It also contains many relevant manifestations that I want to highlight.

You may experience any of the following four anxiety varietals at any given time (and you may have more than one):

1. Generalized anxiety disorder (GAD)
2. Phobias

---

3 American Psychological Association. (2013). Stress in America™ 2013 highlights: Are teens adopting adults' stress habits? www.apa.org/news/press/releases/stress/2013/highlights
4 National Institute of Mental Health (NIMH). (2022, April). Anxiety disorders. www.nimh.nih.gov/health/topics/anxiety-disorders

3. Social anxiety disorder (SAD)
4. Panic disorder

Anxiety loves acronyms, which are used throughout the book. But don't concern yourself now, as you will be reminded at the appropriate times.

## Anxiety Triggers and Recovery Tactics

The *anxiety triggers* and corresponding easy-to-use *tactics* to de-escalate symptoms are the core of the book. Tactics are derived from a creative blend of effective treatment modalities including cognitive behavioral therapy (CBT), dialectical behavioral therapy (DBT), acceptance commitment therapy (ACT), and exposure response prevention (ERP). You will become knowledgeable in understanding your anxiety and be empowered to create new responses that tame and even eliminate its effects.

There is a difference between a **trigger** of anxiety and a **cause** of anxiety. A cause of anxiety is something that caused your anxiety disorder to become a part of you. For example, your upbringing, environment, and genetics might be causes of your anxiety, whereas triggers are problems that make your anxiety worse or more prevalent – like looking at your income taxes or CNN.

This book is designed to be read either straight through or by skipping around as needed. Though the triggers change, the tactics included throughout are relevant to all the triggers. Keep it close and use it as you would a field artillery guide. If you wear it out, I have more.

www.StateOfAnxiety.com

# Part I

# Generalized Anxiety Disorder

Generalized anxiety disorder (GAD) comprises persistent, excessive, and often uncontrollable worry over things. People with the disorder often expect the worst in absence of any real reason for concern. They anticipate catastrophe and may be overly worried about work, money, well-being, family, or other issues.

GAD is diagnosed when a person finds it difficult to control worry on most days, for at least six months, and has three or more symptoms. People diagnosed with GAD suffer from excessive worry, which exacerbates the system-wide experience of anxiety.

Individuals with GAD tend to find it difficult to control their anxiety, worrying about several things at once and commonly experience excessive amounts of anxiety and worry. Sometimes people with this condition worry but are unable to identify what they're even worried about. They describe feelings that something bad may happen or find that they just can't calm themselves down.

Everyone experiences stress and anxiety at some point, and a little is beneficial. It kept your ancestors alive when a saber-toothed tiger crept into their cave while they roasted s'mores and played stone Jenga. Anxiety keeps you sharp and motivated to respond to threats, deadlines, and the like. A problem exists, however, when there is too much stress; it becomes chronic or leads to depression.

DOI: 10.4324/9781003345350-2

# 1 The State of the World

Only 35 years ago, anxiety did not exist as a diagnosis. Today, it is the most common form of mental illness. *Why?* Ours is hardly the first anxious era humans have endured in history. By way of example, our ancestors bore many challenging times such as the Spanish Flu pandemic, World Wars I and II, the Great Depression, slavery, and all those missing dinosaurs – from which no one has heard a word since the Cretaceous Period. So it seems afoul to rob our angst-ridden predecessors by crowning our own epoch the "Age of Anxiety."

DOI: 10.4324/9781003345350-3

## Today's Anxiety Threat: "High"

We live in a culture of alarmism where the glut of bad news yields fear, aggression, and anxiety. And it's a one-two punch because it does this while blocking happiness, peace of mind, and creative thinking. It's not that the world has gotten worse, but that a prolific media is relentlessly reporting it in HD pessimism and push-notifications to your phone. The only winners in this unhealthy arrangement are the advertisers who regularly interrupt the 24-hour news to scare us into buying more life insurance and anti-anxiety meds.

Negative news can quickly spur anxiety and depression. Look no further than the CNN ticker tape at the bottom of your TV screen to create palpable anxiety. Those regular disruptions of "Breaking News" are oftentimes neither breaking nor newsworthy. And there is an increasing tendency for news broadcasters to "emotionalize" their news, and to do so by emphasizing any potential negative outcomes of a story, no matter how low the risks of those negative outcomes might be.

## Breaking: North Korea Strikes U.S. Cultural Site of McDonald's. Kim Jong-un Says Chick-fil-A Is Next

Exaggerating the headlines to give them more emotional flare is part of TV journalists' fight to remain relevant and competitive. With so many journalists covering the same topics, someone is going to up the impact ante by whatever means necessary. This can include scaremongering to sensationalize the impact of a news story, and it feeds right into humankind's natural evolutionary trait to affix more to the bad than to the good. It's how we quickly identified threats in our primitive days. But this can result in symptoms not unlike those that accompany actual PTSD.

Like hairspray and jail tattooing, overexposure to negative news is bad for your health. Bad news affects us physiologically. Bad news triggers the brain's limbic system, spurring a release of cortisol, a stress hormone that deregulates the immune system and inhibits the release of growth hormones and feel-good love hormones. It'll turn you into a cranky toddler running amok in a prolonged temper tantrum. This is likely how you feel after a sizeable dose of bad news: small, angry, and anxious.

### *The Daily News Is Daily Negativity*

I'm not suggesting you shun all worldly updates and remain blissfully uninformed. But ponder the findings of a study by the *International Journal of Behavioral Medicine*.[1] The psychological effects of televised news

---

1 Szabo, A., & Hopkinson, K. L. (2007). Negative psychological effects of watching the news on the television: Relaxation or another intervention may be needed to buffer them! *International Journal of Behavioral Medicine, 14*(2), 57–62.

were studied in two groups of undergraduate students who watched a 15-minute random newscast followed by either a 15-minute progressive relaxation exercise or a 15-minute lecture. Measurements of anxiety and total mood disturbance (TMD), positive affect, and negative affect were obtained before and after the news, as well as following relaxation exercise or the lecture.

The results show that anxiety and TMD increased, whereas positive affect decreased in both groups after watching the news, and 15 minutes later, they returned to baseline (pre-news) only in the relaxation group, whereas they remained unchanged in the control group. These findings suggest that watching televised news triggers persisting negative psychological feelings that could not be protected by attention-diverting distraction, but only by a fixed psychological intervention such as progressive relaxation. Or you could skip sautéing your psyche in the news altogether, and the imbalance of your TMD is then moot.

The people coding online algorithms know that negativity and brain-clinging nonsense drive clicks—not the boring, complex, interesting, or happy stuff. The world is vast and rife with tons of positive things continually taking place. For example, did you know that Border Collies have been fitted with seed-spreading satchels and trained to run through miles of charred lands to restore burnt forests? Or that high pollen counts, though annoying for people with allergies, are amazing for bees?

## Tactics for Relief: How to Remain Hopeful Despite the Headlines and Hopelessness

### The Mainstream Media Does Not Portray an Accurate Picture of Reality

A leading researcher on the connection between media consumption and stress found that the news can lead us to feeling a sense of helplessness while creating cognitive shortcuts that cause us to see the world less optimistically and as a darker place.[2]

### Replace Negative News With a Few Minutes of Uplifting Content

If "no news is good news," is all news bad news? Temper your negative news exposure with regular doses of humor, good news, and

---

2  McNaughton-Cassill, M. E. (2001). The news media and psychological distress. *Anxiety, Stress & Coping, 14*(2), 193–211.

even animal videos. The levity will extend your life. For good news, run a simple internet search using a search string like "sources for good news." You will discover sites like the Good News Network, Tiny Buddha, TED, or the Good News Today Show website.

Reading positive news is not an exercise in denial; it's ensuring you get a well-balanced emotional regimen of media, which resets the negativity bias. Seeing news footage of a lone shoe in the middle of the street from a hit-and-run victim does no good but prompting you to cinch your laces before leaving the house.

You may like being up to date on news, but at what cost to your internal peace? Make a media exposure limit and stick with it, or your mind will be overloaded, and anxiety will take hold. Take solace knowing that the world is not getting worse; rather we are inundated and over-informed. The more visceral and gnarly the news reported, the more viewers. It's hard not to stare at train wrecks and car crashes. Especially celebrity train wrecks.

A deluge of negativity affects the body and the mind. Exposure to regular negativity has nasty side effects, to include becoming a friendless, full-time cynic. Negativity will also make you more sensitive to stress, lowering your immune system so that you become sick. Negativity and the associated stress can also affect stem cells that cause changes to your brain, putting you at risk for mental illnesses like anxiety and depression, while spiking your affinity for drugs, booze, and nuzzling tubs of ice cream to soundtracks by Adele or Slipknot.[3]

### Follow the Trendlines, Not the Headlines

Regularly watching the headlines is like rolling out of bed each day asking for a damage report. You will see that trends are far more encouraging and contrary to the daily news. Your brain is simply more heightened and sensitive to unpleasant news. Research indicates a powerful negativity bias: Negative reinforcement, as opposed to comparable positive reinforcement, leads to faster learning that is more resistant to extinction in both human adults

---

3 Tower, J. (2012). Stress and stem cells. *Wiley Interdisciplinary Reviews: Developmental Biology, 1*(6), 789–802. https://doi.org/10.1002/wdev.56

and animals.[4] This bias is so instinctive that it can be detected at the earliest stage of the brain's information processing. Guard yourself from the word "venom." "Hope" is a verb.

**It is this unrelenting consciousness of every flaw of humanity, combined with a barrage of doomsayers and extremist doctrine commanding our attention, that creates the feeling of a chaotic and insecure world that doesn't exist as portrayed.**

### *"Push Notifications Disabled"*

The randomness of the push notifications on your phone is not random at all. They are carefully designed by behavioral scientists to maximize addiction with what's called a "variable ratio reinforcement schedule" that creates an unrelenting conditioning regimen.

*"Dear Apple, I will always 'Not Allow Push Notifications'."* The instant your smartphone sends a notification, the anticipation phase of the dopamine reward system is activated. It feels like you just *have* to know what the new information is. Media notifications are a virtual dopamine drip. Mankind has survived thousands of years without needing a notification from an app.

### *Confront Vicious "What If . . . ?" Cycles With Cognitive Exposure*

There is often a scenario such as climate change that triggers your worry and anxiety and elicits a "what if . . ." question. Worries are thoughts set in motion by these "what if . . ." queries. Worrying about climate change is a thought process centered on the future where there is uncertainty about the outcome. The future is perceived as a negative one, and the present is one of demoralization and exhaustion, coupled with a gross intolerance of uncertainty. *Will we all dehydrate into human raisins? Will we be forced to colonize a lesser planet? How angry is God that we trashed one of his cosmic marbles?*

---

4 Thorndike, E. L. (1898). Animal intelligence: An experimental study of the associative processes in animals. *Psychological Review, 5*(5), 551–553. https://doi.org/10.1037/h0067373

All this tension can lead you into cognitive avoidance – an expensive term for mentally dodging disaster or a way that we try to avoid thoughts that scare us. But the thoughts we try to avoid keep returning. Trying to not think about something doesn't work. Alternatively, it can increase the frequency of the thought. Research has shown that thought suppression leads to two unfortunate results:

1. **Enhancement:** When we try to avoid a particular thought that same thought tends to intrude our mind.
2. **Rebound effect:** After a period of thought suppression, we think more often of the thought that was suppressed.

Although avoidance yields a sudden decrease in anxiety in the short term, it leads to an increase in fear and anxiety longer term. So what's the antidote? Cognitive exposure!

Exposure techniques are a common and effective method of treating anxiety. Exposure changes your fear by first activating it and then nullifying your unrealistic fears. A skipping heart does not mean heart attack; a crowded concert does not lead to a mass shooting; a freeway drive does not result in a road rage scenario; eating at a cruise ship buffet does not lead to falling overboard with botulism, and so on.

> *Q: Why did the chicken cross the road?*
> *A: Because the chicken's therapist said she should do more things that scared her.*

Exposure can take several forms but typically involves a gradual approach to places, objects, people, or situations that were once avoided, despite being safe. Exposure therapies for various anxieties take on similar forms, with the primary difference being the subject emphasis. DIY exposure therapy is gladiator-level self-improvement.

I underwent exposure therapy for OCD that was memorably impactful. The psychologist began our session by instructing me to leave his office and return to the hospital lobby and then enter the heavily trafficked men's restroom – a grotto of filth both for being a men's restroom and its location within a hospital. My task was to enter, shut the door, and rub my clean hands all over the inner door handle, toilet handle, and faucet knobs. I would not benefit from touchless appliances on this fair day.

I was then to rub my contagion-level hands all over my face, then leave the restroom, and return to his office. I did each of these things, all under duress and a growing swell of record-setting anxiety, panic, and disgust. This form of exposure is called flooding (exposure to the most intense feared stimulus). I wavered between needing to puke or needing to boil my face and pull off my hands by stepping on them.

I returned to his office as directed and sat back down in front of him. Still appalled and overwrought with anxiety. As I sat through it, and we talked about the experience, my anxiety eased until I nearly forgot what I had done. This was my indoctrination into exposure therapy. It was wildly effective for me in subsequent sessions, and today. Even sans a squirty squirt of Purell.

In the case of perceiving the world as far more dangerous than it is, a suitable exposure tactic can include facing the world and seeing it for what it actually is: unpredictable, but not as deathtrap centric as you think. You can do this by changing thought patterns that lead to anxiety, challenging those thoughts that overrate the risks, and lessening the catastrophic thinking. For quicker results, you can lick the waiting room play area toys in your physician's clinic.

---

### Exercises in Fulfillment: Addressing Life's Big Questions With Cognitive Exposure

*Steps for Effective Cognitive Exposure*

1. Identify your core fear.
2. Write it out in a scenario that takes one to 5 minutes to read.
3. Make the scenario as realistic as possible, including sights, sounds, and other sensations that would be part of your fear experience. You want to create a picture in your mind of your worst fear.
4. Read your scenario and try to imagine it as vividly as possible.
5. Make it real enough that you feel anxious while reading it.

6.  Continue reading your scenario repeatedly and until you experience a significant decrease in your anxiety – that is, you experience the exposure curve.
7.  Be sure that you have a quiet, private place to do your exposure, and do it at a time when you won't be interrupted.
8.  Repeat this exercise as often as you need to reduce your anxiety.

**Note:** For those with the discipline and need, psychologists recommend doing this activity 30–60 minutes every day for 2 to 3 weeks, but I present a shorter version here.

### Do Not . . .

*   Attempt to argue with your fear during the exposure
*   Try to neutralize the fear
*   Stop doing the activity while you are feeling anxious, or at least not without consulting your therapist.

One notable caveat is to *begin with a mild to moderate fear*, preferably in tandem with a trusted therapist who knows exposure techniques and knows you. In that way you can build up your emotional muscle to tolerate bigger anxieties and fears over time.

Another key strategy is to *stick with one exposure until you have mastered it before* moving on to a fear that causes increased anxiety. Lastly, this exercise is meant to create anxiety. If you feel uncomfortable, you're doing it right. Your therapist can help you figure out the ideal amount and pace that will be most helpful for you. That's what I call decent exposure.

### Try Tuning Into Gratitude and Positivity

A 2013 study published found that being grateful results in less aches and pains and feeling healthier.[5] Other studies find not just lower anxiety and depression but better physical health, life satisfaction, reduced aggression, increased kindness, and improved

5 Hill, P. L., Allemand, M., & Roberts, B. W. (2013). Examining the pathways between gratitude and self-rated physical health across adulthood. *Personality and Individual Differences*, 54(1), 92–96.

sleep.[6] Gratitude offers a twofold positive punch: (1) It increases the level of upbeat emotion we feel and (2) it lessens the negative energy that fills us with malaise. You can still shout, "*You're welcome!*" to people who don't thank you for holding doors open for them, so they too can learn gratitude.

---

### Modify Your Mindset: Make a Gratitude List

**Thankfulness is a word of action. List three things for which you are grateful at the close of each day, or three things that are going well, no matter how small.** Do it on your drive home or before bedtime. *Three things* – no more, no less. Make gratefulness perpetual. Practice making every day Thanksgiving Day or whatever it's renamed in the future because of those greedy pilgrims.

And gratitude is never lessened by sharing. Count your boons and blessings with a partner or family before bed. Text them back and forth with a good friend, like a friend of Chris who has sent over 10,000 gratitude items back and forth over more than a decade. If you don't have a bliss buddy, email me what you're grateful for, and I'll email you back with candied yams.

---

### *Stay Creative, Stay in Touch, and Stay Active, But Don't Stay Up Too Long*

If you poison your boss a little each day, it's a called a crime. But if you poison yourself with negative news a little each day, it's called a life. One antidote is to tap into your creative side, even if you think you don't have one. Create something artistic and from the heart. Channel your own angst or emotions into something tangible

---

6 Emmons, R. A., & McCullough, M. E. (2003). Counting blessings versus burdens: An experimental investigation of gratitude and subjective well-being in daily life. *Journal of Personality and Social Psychology, 84*(2), 377–389.

whether writing a letter, journaling, painting, picking up an instrument, or cooking/baking something new. It's an ideal time to realize what talents lie dormant within you.

Creativity is a skill you can acquire at any point in life. Even LEGOs have an age range of 4–99. If you don't perceive yourself as a creative person, join an online or onsite creative class, where you can learn to generate creative ideas, choose one or two of your best, and act on them. In absence of creative leaning, you can train yourself to be creative by practicing things that create new neural pathways in the brain. Anxiety and creativity cannot coexist – sort of like Clark Kent and Superman, or humidity and good hair.

### Promote Good Sleep

Anxiety sleep is like regular sleep, but without the sleep. If one of your greatest accomplishments is insomnia, you need to get to bed early and at the same time each night and awake at the same time each morning. Turn off the electronics to turn off your brain. And avoid consuming anxiety-provoking media within a couple hours before bedtime. You don't need to keep pulling your social media feeds for updates, despite your thumb conditioning. Nor do you need to post about your insomnia. Sleep problems greatly exacerbate stress and anxiety. Similarly, adequate sleep is one of the easiest ways to ease or eliminate anxiety.

They say if you can't sleep, it's because you're awake in someone else's dream. You must find this person and wake them. Research indicates that REM sleep may play an especially significant role in maintaining emotional well-being and psychological balance.[7] Anxiety disorders and sleep problems frequently present together. People who are naturally prone to worry are especially vulnerable to the anxiety-producing effects of poor sleep. Good night, sleep tight; don't let the hair-shellacked media journalists bite.

---

7 Walker, M. P., & van der Helm, E. (2009). Overnight therapy? The role of sleep in emotional brain processing. *Psychological Bulletin, 135*(5), 731–748.

### Exercise: The Phenomenal Underused Antidepressant and Antianxiety Tool

You can work out and no one on social media even needs to know. Channel your nervous energy, stress, and even depression into a regular exercise regimen. Anxiety is the best pre-workout supplement available.

*"I haven't seen you since the plague."*

More than the physical upside, there is the social aspect of a fitness program and seeing regulars and future friends – whether a weekly outdoor walking group, a weekday mom-and-baby bootcamp in the park, a live streaming fitness class, or the augmented camaraderie of a sloshball league. Exercise improves *mental health* by reducing anxiety, depression, and stress, while improving self-esteem and cognitive functioning.

**Since the world isn't ending (but this chapter is), let's close with some tactics to thrive.**

Anxious people on other planets probably think their worlds are ending too. Maybe that's why they keep visiting. Yet we've all survived countless predictions of end times scenarios, with the years 2000, 2012, 2020, 2021, and the current year being the most recent. Even "Mad Max" took place in 2021. Surely future apocalyptic forecasts will similarly fall away.

**Your Anxiety-Trigger Toolkit: Eight Tips for Coping With Current Events**

1.  The secret to success lies within small changes to your daily habits and routine. You change your future by changing your habits.
2.  Take breaks from the news and social media. Actively seek out good news or watch cute, funny, or inspirational videos or TV shows instead. #CatVideos
3.  Confront your biggest fears with cognitive exposure by writing down anxiety-provoking scenarios and continuously reading them until your anxiety lessens. Fear is temporary. Regret lasts forever. Or longer.
4.  Create a list of three things you're grateful for or things that are going well in your life. Maybe you dodged a tax audit or a friend's multilevel marketing scheme this year, for example. #NoMLMs
5.  Do something artistic or creative to express yourself, even if it's something you don't feel skilled at or ever share with anyone else. That's how writers and illustrators of books on anxiety start out.
6.  Develop a good sleep schedule by going to bed at a reasonable hour and at the same time every night, despite your brain creating imaginary scenarios that will never happen.
7.  Seek help from your doctor or mental health professional if your anxiety feels especially bad. The chronically anxious are often calm under pressure and anxious when everything is okay.
8.  Stay active and exercise. The key to sticking with it is finding an activity you enjoy. Most of us dress in activewear regularly. We might as well live the attire.

# 2 Awaiting Medical Test Results

DOI: 10.4324/9781003345350-4

Whether it be cancer, strep throat, or diabetes, at some point most of us have to wait around for a medical test, the results of which we dread. It's a period marked by the abnormally slow passage of time and the self-certainty that you've got the worst case of whatever it is, as proven by your all-night internet research and self-diagnosis.

The biggest birthday surprise I've had was peeing blood on my 2016 birthday. That lasted for three worrisome and un-celebratory days before I began my vocation as an internet urologist to sleuth the cause of the malady. Since this particular birthday landed on Labor Day weekend, I had three days to diagnose myself via the internet, all the while convinced I had some form of rare disease not yet seen in the industrialized world.

I envisioned my condition featured as a case study in JAMA, while specialists worldwide weighed in on the array of dreadful symptoms yet to manifest. I entered a phase of invasive hospital exams. As the weeks slowly passed in a heightened state of anxiety, I progressed through each new lab test, scan, poke, prod, and finally a camera up the pee-hole (cystoscopy) into the bladder. Only then was the culprit revealed.

As a nonsmoking athlete, I had succumbed to an older, smoker's cancer of the bladder. I was the youngest of 173 patients at my oncology center in Northern California. My doctors were mystified as to how I joined their patient census. I spent the next few weeks ruminating over my personal health and exposure history to determine the origin. *Glyphosate in red wine? The rare vanilla-flavored hookah in college? Inhalation of phthalates from cubicle office furniture?*

Ultimately, I realized the cause had no bearing on the outcome. Nor would I be curbing my love of Cabernet and secondhand smoke. Instead, I had to find the upside. Somewhere.

## How to Make Use of Suffering That Chance Inflicts Upon Us

Anxiety can come via "anxiety seed-planting" through our parents. I once heard a pediatrician say, "I've seen a lot of anxious kids with mellow parents. But I've almost never seen anxious parents without anxious kids." Most often, however, anxiety is a result of a genetic predisposition combined with environmental factors.[1]

How you arrived at an angst-ridden life is not nearly as important as how you manage one. But anxiety is fickle, in that it can pivot, or at

---

1 Gross, C., & Hen, R. (2004). Genetic and environmental factors interact to influence anxiety. *Neurotoxicity Research*, 6(6), 493–501. https://doi.org/10.1007/BF03033286

least feel less disruptive, simply by using the aforementioned gratitude tactic.

There is no schooling like struggle. Every philosopher, from ancient to present, East to West, agrees that suffering can be the ultimate conduit to empathy and awareness. Adversity yields purpose and refinement that can come only from life trials. Therein lies your advantage. I'm not referring to the "opportunity comes masked as adversity" trope – but the deeply real way we source or cultivate new abilities when facing the seemingly insurmountable.

My dad, a casualty of indecision, often had me second-guessing my own choices or not making one at all. But I strongly rely on his expansive knowledge, impeccable advice, and life guidance. To this day, if he thinks I made a less-than-prime choice, it has me strongly reconsidering – to the point I'm often paralyzed by an Applebee's lunch menu.

With mom, I share the mixed blessing of cancer remission. I'm remarkably gracious to be in remission with her but uncertain how she was hit with a rare stage IV breast cancer called inflammatory breast cancer (IBC), which spread to her brain. I would take hers on if that was ever an option in my regular fantasy where some omnipotent entity grants us the power to switch diseases.

She has suffered daily for years with neuropathy, seizures, loss of speech and cognition, brain surgery, fibromyalgia, the ravaging effects of chemo and radiation, and eventual paralysis. Not once has she revealed the degree to which she hurts. Either because she's a woman or due to Cherokee blood, she lacks the whine genome. But like any son or daughter watching a parent fade, I had to develop an ability to cope with the anger and emotional vulnerability that comes with uncertainty and powerlessness. Skills I would not have otherwise honed.

Suffering is a conduit to empathy and awareness. Hug your family *and* your hardships. They're trying to tell you something.

## Tactics for Relief: How to Manage Potential Medical Ambushes

### *Common Misconceptions About Worry*

People have a lot of wrong ideas about worry. You may have been taken in by some of these fables yourself. It's important to realize what's true and not true so that you can take a healthier approach to dealing with your anxieties.

*"Worry helps me to solve problems."*

Nope. High levels of anxiety interfere with performance and problem-solving ability. Worry is about worst fears, not best solutions.

*"Worry motivates me."*

Nope. Worry leads to demoralization and exhaustion. Worry is not the same thing as caring for or about something or someone. And worry often leads to avoidance.

*"Worry protects me against negative emotions."*

Nope. You can't predict and prepare for everything in life. When faced with adversity, people cope better than they think they will. You will have normal feelings if something bad happens, no matter how much you try to prepare for it.

*"Worry will prevent negative outcomes."*

And, nope. There is no direct relationship between worry and events that are beyond your control. Life is uncertain and you can increase your tolerance of uncertainty. Negative events are going to happen no matter what.

### Thought-Chaining: Facing Your Worst Fears in Your Head

With worry thought-chaining, the key is to chain out the worries related to your primary fear as far as possible. Leave no nuance of the dread untapped, while continuing to ask yourself, "So then what?" until you reach the finite end of your specific dread. What you will likely learn is that things rarely play out as you most fear. And in the rare instance your worst anxiety materializes, you will handle it with the strength and poise you never knew you had.

As I was revising this chapter for my editor, I began seeing a large, black, flying insect on my right side. I live in a remarkably clean townhome in overpriced California. Insects can't afford this place. Continually swatting at it, I couldn't hit or even discern the genus and specie. Eventually I gave up and returned to work, only to see more insects of varying shapes, sizes, and speeds swirling about my right side. When some of the insects took the form of black cats and vertical lines, it hit me: These aren't insects, they're blind spots. I'm having a stroke!

### "Paging Dr. Google . . ."

I convinced myself that I was just tired and stressed from work, so I lay down and took an hour-long nap. I awoke to a complete loss of peripheral vision in my right eye. So I began my Google self-diagnosis. But I moved to my desk, so if I died, I'd eventually be seen through a window. Everything I read said I had already died.

Not wanting to overreact, I did some simple tests for signs of a stroke. I smiled in the mirror to see if my mouth was uneven like a Picasso painting. Then I raised both of my arms in front to see if they were even in pace and elevation. I was symmetrical. I waited to see if I was better by the following morning. I was not. And now the panic kicked in. I took a few hours off work and drove to the hospital. But I first needed to shave, shower, and put on some nice clothes. All dull tasks I was potentially saving an embalmer.

### The Internet Never Says It's Probably Nothing

When a medical scare presents itself, it's natural to get drawn into a panic or mood descent from researching or self-diagnosing via internet. **Do** stop consuming from the source, whether on your phone, laptop, or Alexa. You are stuck in a confirmation bias spiral. If you absolutely must read, refer to reputable sources recommended by your doctor. No more Dr. McDoomsayer's "10 Reasons You Most Certainly Had an Aneurism."

**Do** think through every detail of your worst-case scenario. Research finds that when we think as far through a worst-case scenario (thought-chaining), it measurably helps. Truth is, you are probably only thinking up to the point of the bad news, and not beyond. Try going as far past receiving that news as possible until you can play it out no further.

---

### Exercises in Fulfillment: Thought-Chaining Your Worries

#### Steps for Thought-Chaining

1. Imagine yourself receiving the bad news you're afraid to hear.
2. Ask yourself, "So then what?" and imagine your reaction to receiving that news.

3.  Think of the first worry related to the news you expected.
4.  Ask yourself, "So then what?" again and imagine the result of that outcome, including why your worry might be unfounded.
5.  Ask yourself, "So then what?" again and move onto your next worry, then ask the same question and think of the outcome and why it might be as bad as you think.
6.  Keep asking yourself, "So then what?" over and over and continuing to envision your worst fears and their outcomes, good and bad, until you have covered all your worries.

### Example of Thought-Chaining Worries About My "Certain" Stroke

In my stroke scenario, as I prepped for looming death or a lifetime of partial speech, I leveraged the tactic of thought-chaining to ease my worry. Statistically I was likely going to live long enough to annoy a few more editors. My thought chain took the following form:

*"I can't believe I had a mini-stroke. I wonder how much of my brain is dead . . . What will I do?"*

And so, what if part of my brain is dead? Then what?

*"I won't be able to write more books or post witty Insta memes. So then what?"*

But did I die? So what if I can't write anymore? Look at how many people make social media posts that are written as if they've had a stroke. I'll fit right in.

*"Since I'll only have a partial brain, I'll have to stay at my 8–5 job that I hate while laughing at my boss's lame jokes till retirement (or till I have a bigger stroke). So then what?"*

Is that so bad? I'll be alive! And I can find more meaningful work that I like.

*"Okay, but what if my brain doesn't work the same way, or I have a bigger stroke? Then I'm most certainly doomed to a lifetime of pureed foods and wearing bibs. So then what?*

You haven't heard of physical and occupational therapy? Stroke recovery is legit. Medicine has made great strides in getting people ambulatory and functional again. Also, you don't even know if you had a stroke! Plus, you can take time off of work.

*"Well . . . these aren't untruths."*

The physician determined that I did not have a stroke. I had a torn retina. I would live to finish this book. But I still called into work "stroked."

### Preoccupy Your Mind With Everyday Activities

When worried about a dire, potential medical calamity, your initial gut reaction is likely, *"But, what will I do!?"* Solid question. You think about it. A lot. You might cry. You'll probably have some denial, anger, confusion, and maybe panic. But at some point you stop crying and go to the bathroom, do the laundry, and make a sandwich. And when you think about what you'll do for the rest of the day that you receive bad news, take comfort knowing that research shows we manage it better when we remember there is still laundry to do.[2] It's never as bad as it is in your own mind.

Whenever you have potentially good or bad news coming, imagine the rest of the day that you'll receive the pending news, and suddenly it's less of a focal point, which lessens the emotional impact. Then when you make the follow-up appointment, keep that calendar day full and your anxiety in check. Don't quit anything to pursue anxiety full-time.

You don't need to distract yourself forever. And distraction only helps so much, especially with anxiety. But if you know that the results come back in two hours or two days, you have your coping skills, but you've also got to stay busy. Be around friends; do stuff that's distracting and engaging – whether it's playing video games, visiting a bookstore, or binge-viewing something until Netflix asks if you're still watching.

### Play to Your Strengths

In moments of anxiety, our brains can essentially shut down and stop working properly. One of the things we often forget is how competently we've overcome past anxious situations. If you're anxious, you've been through this before. Think back to the last medical freak-out you had as you waited for news. How did you cope that time? What helped, who helped, and how did you make it through? Take some time to reflect and maybe even write out what

2 Ford, B. Q., Lam, P., John, O. P., & Mauss, I. B. (2018). The psychological health benefits of accepting negative emotions and thoughts: Laboratory, diary, and longitudinal evidence. *Journal of Personality and Social Psychology, 115*(6), 1075–1092.

you did to manage. Not knowing your own strengths is a sign of weakness.

### Sometimes a Thought Is Just a Thought

It's hard, but not impossible, to outsmart your own anxious mind. Like thinking how the word "bed" actually looks like a bed. Positive people have negative thoughts too. They just observe them without assigning any credence. Being positive or negative is a thought habit to which you subscribe. You wouldn't let jerks hang out in your house, so why let them hang out in your head?

### Schedule Your Worry Time Like You Schedule Lunch

Scheduling your worry time is a technique that will help you control distressing thoughts. The idea is to allow yourself a pre-arranged time to get the thoughts out of your system by setting a specific time each day to think about them. Open your calendar to find a 5-minute block each day, preferably followed by something like exercise. Throughout the day, as the thoughts arise, you will identify them as "just thoughts" and then agree to let them pass until the next scheduled worry time. Make that commitment to yourself.

*"I say 'no worries' a lot for a person who is full of worries."*

Focusing on the worries and assigning them too much credibility as they arise serves no purpose and only subverts the rest of your day. As you await your medical results, gently remind yourself to wait until the scheduled worry time. During this scheduled time, you are to focus only on the disconcerting thoughts and worries. Spend those 5 minutes each day reviewing the distressing thoughts and then put them aside as best you can until the next day. And if you're not worried throughout the day, don't worry about not being worried.

For adherence purposes, you might want to set an alarm for a specific time each day to process the medical-related worries. Typically, what happens is that you get bored or distracted and think about something else, like your to-do list, or if plant-based pizza is healthy. Over time, you'll start to see that the worries are less powerful than you might have thought and more easily dismissed. And soon enough, your results will come in that will not match your previous hypochondria.

## Anxiety Toolkit: Scheduling Worry Time

1. Don't try to suppress the thoughts as they surface. Instead, tell yourself, "*I have a distressing thought. I will acknowledge it now and let it pass until my scheduled worry time.*"
2. Set a specific time each day that you can set aside for worry time.
3. Allow yourself 5 minutes per day for worry time.
4. Ensure that you will have no distractions during the worry time.
5. It's normal to feel some anxiety during scheduled worry time, so try to focus on the facts.
6. Repeat the worries over and over until your time is up.
7. If necessary, use deep breathing and progressive muscle relaxation (PMR) to help yourself tolerate the anxiety sensations. The PMR technique is slowly tensing and relaxing each muscle group, one by one, starting from the forehead down, or from the feet upward.
8. You can use facts to help you think through and process your worries.
9. Continue to use facts to talk back to your fears.
10. When you are finished, refer to no. 1 until the next scheduled worry time.
11. When the distressing thoughts pop up during the day, remind yourself that you don't have to think about it right now; it can wait until your scheduled worry time. Or you can tell yourself that you already processed it enough and it's time to let it go.

### Roses Are Red, Running Is Hard

Movement facilitates a healthier mental and physical state despite whatever else might be going on. It also clears your mind to think straight. Whatever the results of the test, your body and immune system will be improved through exercise, allowing you to better manage anything from major surgery to a bunion. Another attribute of exercise is that it tires you out enough to help with sleep and makes you hungry enough to eat, which are both paramount but hard to do when you are anxious. Try to avoid eating any food that has a TV commercial.

### Create a Slow Zone for Stress Management

Find your rest muscle and train it. Slowing down for a few minutes while you are awaiting medical test results is a sound way to reduce your angst. I refer to mindfulness and meditation throughout this book because it's a powerful tactic in managing stress and anxiety. But neither mindfulness nor meditation comes naturally because our default is to project and future-think, particularly during times of heightened worry. Mindfulness prevents the *"Hang on, let me overthink this"* mindset. If you're doing it right, mindfulness feels like blocking someone's number in mid argument while they're still typing. Consider downloading a guided meditation app and even paying the monthly subscription so you're more likely to adhere to regular use and until you make meditation a regular habit. Inner chill is the antithesis of anxiety.

### Stay Well, Despite Your Worries About Being Unwell

*"I like ice cream and I have anxiety"* is a relatable sentiment. But the statement, *"I like ice cream and I manage anxiety like a Trappist Monk"* can be as well. No matter the flavor or outcome of your medical issue, you can vastly lessen your related suffering using simple tactics such as thought-chaining and mindfulness techniques. Depression looks back; anxiety looks forward; serenity looks present.

**Your Anxiety-Trigger Toolkit: Seven Tips for Coping With Health Concerns**

1. Remember: Your worries won't help solve your problems, motivate you, or protect you from or prevent negative emotions. They're empty mental calories.
2. Directly confront your worries via thought-chaining: Envision your worst fear coming true and continuously ask yourself, "So then what?"
3. Temporarily distract yourself from your worries by keeping busy.
4. Think of coping strategies that have worked for you in the past and try them again. Try writing them down so that you can remember them later.
5. Rather than suppressing worries that come up throughout your day, set aside 5 minutes of worry time in your schedule and save your worries for then and only then. Don't do expressos or worry time at bedtime.
6. Exercising within your current range of abilities can distract your mind and improve your sleep and appetite. But allow yourself a little self-indulgence as well. Have the Pop-Tarts® for dinner on occasion.
7. Summon your inner peace. Slow down for a few minutes and approach an activity with mindfulness, whether it's eating, walking, or driving. There's no place like "om."

# 3 Climate Change

DOI: 10.4324/9781003345350-5

Only in America do we accept weather predictions from a rodent but deny climate change evidence from scientists. Dinosaurs didn't believe in climate change either. Things like global warming don't feel as bad with a hefty dose of denial. And who needs all those pesky glaciers clogging our shipping lanes? But how are we supposed to handle the relentless and dire predictions that can make us feel hopeless?

It's high time we focused on saving our own planet rather than how we'll inhabit others. Unless you'd thrive in a Windexed terrarium looking out onto a desolate, desert landscape with sprawling columns of whirling dust reaching heights of 50 miles during global-scale dust storms, you will likely want to stick around here. The views on Mars are epic, but you'll suffocate and die if you go outside your bubble house. Then there's all that space radiation to consider.

Mars is a last-ditch resort location for humanity if life on Earth becomes untenable due to things like climate change. Yet it would require creating an entire planetary atmosphere through a process called terraforming – a way to create a greenhouse effect, in turn making the planet more Earth-like. If it seems asinine that scientists can create an Earthlike, habitable planet out of Mars while others seemingly allow Earth to die, it is.

## Climate Change Doesn't Just Hurt Polar Bears

The impact of climate change is impossible to ignore in California, where our winters have become noticeably shorter and drier and summers hotter and increasingly flammable. Growing up here, we didn't have what's now called "fire season." Moreover, this fire season gets longer and longer each year and is now considered to be year-round.

With months of West Coast wildfires over the summer of 2020 alone, leaving the house meant chewing through the chowder-thick, carcinogenic air. It even crept into the house where I had to regularly rinse my eyes with cold water to stop the burning. The smoke entered the jet stream and was carried thousands of miles to the east coast, impacting millions more people along the way. There was no escape beyond driving south to hunker down in Baja California or Honduras.

I regularly found myself standing in a window searching for the glowing orange orb of a sun through the claustrophobic haze. I traded the great outdoors for brief, masked interactions at Trader Joe's or Petco. With the toxic particulate matter in the air, my hikes were replaced by long, boring, indoor spin bike rides and carpet push-ups. One can only guess the long-term health impacts of living the equivalent of smoking cartons of Marlboros for months out of every year. If only the Earth was flat so we could flip it over to the cool side like a pillow.

## We Are Fueled by Recycled Dinosaurs

Does anyone else have a plastic bag full of plastic bags in their house, or is it just me? Gina, a client of Chris, was recycling incessantly to channel her anxiety. Recycling was her superpower, but her behavior was bordering on the obsessive-compulsive. She was also suffering from panic and insomnia.

Her endless fear and guilt blocked life functioning and crested one midnight as she began arguing with her husband about whether he should put his pencil shavings in the recycling: *"Paper is made of wood, so can't that just get recycled into paper!?"*

That was basically her rock bottom, at which point her husband firmly suggested she raise the issue with Chris in therapy where they worked toward normalizing her anxiety and helping her respond in more reasonable ways. And in fact, it is normal, especially if you've got anxiety already. One study found that one-third of people had channeled their climate fears into OCD and started compulsively checking energy and water use to reduce their carbon footprint.[1]

## You Don't Need a Panic Room; You Need a Panic Plan

Climate change has become more insidious than someone who takes the middle seat and uses both armrests. In 2017 the American Psychological Association published a report defining a "chronic fear of environmental doom" as eco-anxiety.[2] The report described an increase in anxiety and depression caused by an "inability to feel like we are making a difference in stopping climate change" – yes, the very anxiety that you may feel rising as inexorably as the sea level. This can cause you to wonder why bother doing anything. The good news, or the bad news, is that you aren't alone with this anxiety. Most of us have a little Greta Thunberg in us.

Most people worry about rising sea levels, temperature changes, extreme weather, and more. And not just the environmental impacts but the political, financial, and social effects. In some ways, this means we are all living with a new anxiety. In other ways, it's not so different than those who grew up fearing nuclear annihilation in the last century. All of this leads to much suffering and anguish, individually and communally. Decades ago, the great conservationist Aldo Leopold wrote in *A Sand County Almanac: And Sketches Here and There*, "Being ecologically conscious is like living in a world of wounds."[3] Amen, sir.

1 Jones, M. K., Wootton, B. M., Vaccaro, L. D., & Menzies, R. G. (2012). The impact of climate change on obsessive compulsive checking concerns. *The Australian and New Zealand Journal of Psychiatry, 46*(3), 265–270.
2 Schreiber, M. (2021, March). Addressing climate change concerns in practice. *Monitor on Psychology, 52*(2).
3 Charles, G. (2020). "A sand county Almanac and sketches here and there" by Aldo Leopold. Introduction by Barbara Kingsolver [book review]. *The Canadian Field-Naturalist, 134*(2), 195–196.

What we are feeling is a combination of grief (at what we are losing in terms of species and ecosystems), trauma (at natural disasters already happening that you may have survived or images you've seen), and anxiety (about what could still happen). We've got to address climate change so we can all grow old together.

## Tactics for Relief: How to Hug the Planet and Harmonize Your Well-Being

### Use Humor to Talk About Climate Change

One of the worst parts of climate change for those who worry is feeling so alone – like no one else sees signs of it everywhere. But it's not just an anxiety; it's real, and feeling like people belittle you, don't believe you, and minimize or deny the problem can feel both personal and infuriating, all of which will exacerbate your underlying anxiety. One way to lessen your suffering may be to help others understand that concern about climate change is warranted.

*"I'm way past climate anxiety; I have climate rage."*

Conversations about climate change have been stuck for a long time. A new approach is needed that feels less like an apocalyptic lecture. Researchers have shown that gloomily framing information disempowers people who could otherwise be moved by a shrewder approach. Research further illustrates that using humor lowers defenses and meets people where they are.[4] Within a single year, three studies published in the *Journal of Science Communication*, *Comedy Studies*, and *Science Communication* confirmed the efficacy of humor in engaging the public about climate change.[5,6,7]

4 Nerlich, B. (2019). Book review: Maxwell Boykoff, creative (climate) communications: Productive pathways for science, policy and society. *Public Understanding of Science, 29*(2), 248–249.

5 Becker, A., & Anderson, A. A. (2019). Using humor to engage the public on climate change: The effect of exposure to one-sided vs. two-sided satire on message discounting, elaboration and counterarguing. *Journal of Science Communication, 18*(4), A07.

6 Osnes, B., Boykoff, M., & Chandler, P. (2019). Good-natured comedy to enrich climate communication. *Comedy Studies, 10*(2), 224–236.

7 Skurka, C., Niederdeppe, J., & Nabi, R. (2019). Kimmel on climate: Disentangling the emotional ingredients of a satirical monologue. *Science Communication, 41*(4), 394–421.

### A Vegan, Cyclist, and Climate Change Enthusiast Walk Into a Bar

Everyone else leaves.

It's tough to find humor after seeing Rhode Island–sized chunks of glaciers breaking off into the Southern Ocean or starving polar bears roaming the tundra in search of beluga leftovers. It's even tougher if you're surrounded by climate change deniers. The first thing you can do is to avoid immersing yourself with too much bad news. You don't need to know the monthly ppm of carbon in the atmosphere or memorize the names of every summer wildfire. There is no shortage of grim statistics to spew in the faces of the skeptics. If climate change were a bank it would have been saved already.

Consider sourcing the lighter and even funnier side of our current state of climate affairs. There are optimistic climate documentaries like "Kiss the Ground," which impart a hopeful solution to counter the climate crisis in the form of regenerative agriculture. Or run an online search on "climate optimism," "hopeful climate change news," or "climate change humor."

### Make Love, Not Emissions

We are living in the pyrocene era. With emotional stakes this high, humor may seem heretical. Contrarily, it's a way to garner the attention of people not otherwise reached. Our perilously changing climate isn't funny, but oftentimes laughing at our pain leads to finding solutions. Humor shifts perspective just long enough to appreciate that there is hope for a different outcome.

Trivializing climate change with humor may seem risky, but a greater risk would be for people to stop talking about the problem entirely and miss the chance to reimagine and actively plan in their collective futures. And you know things are bad when I and other introverts are at climate change rallies. But the climate is changing, and so are we.

### Collectively Process Your Fears and Grief With Others

Misery not only loves company, but it's also cathartic and healing with others. Some groups are now working with therapists to hold grieving workshops for those anxious about climate change to connect, collectively grieve, and act. One of the best things you can do is spend less time alone with this and more time with others who get it. I'm not suggesting you simply worry with like-minded people, but I do recommend taking real action together or at least supporting each other and validating the shared pain. Otherwise, the world we give our kids will be four to five degrees warmer.

Climate change is and will continue to be a real threat. We can slow it, we can adapt, but we can't stop it altogether. The accompanying fear and grief are real too, and we can manage them as such. Some of the denial, anger, bargaining, depression, and acceptance may not always fall in that order, but we all experience some of these emotions in different amounts at different times. Try to notice where you are with these sentiments on any given day. Then, channel the inertia of those feelings into actionable tasks, such as those described in a later section. Like, if you hate soggy paper straws, just drink faster.

### The Titanic *Probably Wouldn't Have Hit an Iceberg Today*

Remember also that most of humanity seems to be stuck in that first "D" of denial. And know that people are in denial because this is almost too big an issue for the human brain to wrap itself around. It seems huge and impossible and maybe even far off. If you are feeling alone, reach out online and in person to connect with others who share your concerns and find a way to act. While you're at it, remind others that babies don't float.

Younger people in particular feel helpless, embittered, and alone with this issue when they're not terrified. And while you don't need to sail across the ocean in a wind-powered boat made of recycled milk jugs, there are small actions that you can take. And the science bears it out – taking environmental action, even small steps, seems to protect against depression.[8]

---

8 Fritze, J. G., Blashki, G. A., Burke, S., & Wiseman, J. (2008). Hope, despair and transformation: Climate change and the promotion of mental health and wellbeing. *International Journal of Mental Health Systems, 2*(1).

Perhaps consider some grassroots climate change activist groups. You don't have to chain yourself to a legacy oak tree, but you can collectively synergize with others on non-guerrilla but effective tactics to alter consumer behaviors. Click the "Get Involved" tab at 350.org and find or start a group, for example. This has been a phenomenal movement for change. To view the many others, simply do a Google search on "grassroots climate change activism" or something similar. Your new planet-saving friends await.

### Forget Nihilism, Befriend the Moment!

Whenever you feel yourself overwhelmed by the anxieties of climate change, try to focus on a single task and approach it mindfully. The act of mindfulness is the repeated practice of moment-to-moment awareness. Mindfulness requires no special setting or QVC laser cap. You can do it anywhere, any time, and apply it to anything: eating, showering, working, running errands, cooking, being with a friend, or reading this book. A lack of mindfulness is why you must reread pages because your mind drifted to that cute shopper you saw earlier at Trader Joe's buying IPA and couscous.

---

### Modify Your Mindset: Mindful Photography

Consider this simple appreciation of the surrounding nature as a mindfulness counter related to climate worry: mindful photography. Take a photo of a flower or other natural object with a camera or your phone, slowly zooming in and out and studying the subject through the lens, rather than just taking a quick snapshot. Concentrate on all the colors and nuance.

---

There is no additional time requirement for mindfulness. The core requisite is shifting from a multitasking mindset to one where you are tuned in to the moment. Are you fully cognizant of your experience at this moment? It sounds easy, but it's not, especially for the anxious. Think about your last meal, for example. Do you recall what you ate? Did you pay any attention to the smell, taste, and texture? Or were you thinking of work, the weekend, why your cat only vomits on the carpet, and everything else but what you were eating?

Let's stay with eating for a moment, as this is the perfect activity in which to apply mindfulness.

---

### Exercises in Fulfillment: Mindful Eating Is No Snaccident

At your next meal, whether a PB&J sandwich or beef burgundy with potatoes dauphinoise and lemon meringue tartlets, try observing what you are about to eat.

1.  How appealing is it to you?
2.  What do the texture and temperature feel like?
3.  Take note if you have an automatic impulse to chew quickly to get to the next mouthful. If so, consciously slow down.
4.  Before you swallow, notice that you're ready to, and focus on the act of swallowing. It may feel cheesy, but it's an effective exercise in mindfulness that can be leveraged toward other routine endeavors – such as washing those dishes. And potential bonus: The slower you eat, the less you eat; and the less food you consume, the less you are taxing the environment. Follow this process with each consecutive bite and notice how fast and how much you're eating. Focus on your stomach and how you feel. Are you eating because you're genuinely hungry or in response to stress and emotions, or even depression or anxiety? Mindful eating isn't a diet. It's not even about eating healthy. And it's not about eating while staring at your TV or phone. It's about eating with intent and full awareness. It's sort of like yoga meets tacos.

Begin with mindful eating, and then you can apply similar steps and principles to other activities. What else can you apply the tactic of mindfulness toward? Maybe you can do some mindful gardening or even something unrelated to the environment, like thoughtfully blending your aunt's eye shadow.

## *Skip the Drum Circle and Take Action, Whether Big or Small*

There is no plan or planet B. Taking some sort of action can help mitigate the emotional roller coaster. This sense of self efficacy, that you are doing something, can boost how you feel.

- **Attend a 350.org event.** 350.org is an international climate campaign that works in 188 countries around the world with the goal of ending the use of fossil fuels and transitioning to renewable energy through a global, grassroots movement.
- **Limit the amount of meat and dairy you consume.** Animal-derived food production has a much higher greenhouse gas output than grain and vegetable production because of the highly inefficient transfer of plant to animal energy. Humans and dogs aren't the only beings who can express love and emotion. So does hamburger.
- **Eat more vegetables.** It's probably healthier for your brain and body anyway, and is one of the best things you can do.
- **Shun plastic.** Bring your own bags to the grocery store. Avoid plastic water bottles. Buy products with less packaging and avoid disposable products. The amount of plastic waste going into entombing tiny gadgets is abhorrent and often requires pruning shears to remove. Also, humans went thousands of years without using plastic straws. You can too.
- **Use greener transportation options.** Consider alternatives to air travel, which represents a growing percentage of the world's greenhouse gases. Buy the carbon offsets when you travel by air or have your employer buy them. You can walk and bike more instead of driving; it will give you some exercise to keep anxiety at bay. Or consider the subway or bus. Also think about an electric vehicle, which aren't all socially repellant trapezoids.
- **Contribute financially and politically.** Donate time or spare cash to organizations dedicated to the fight against climate change. Vote or campaign for legislation and politicians that aid against the detrimental effects of climate change.
- **Plant trees.** It's one of the most concrete things you can do and see the impact of. You can't throw shade if there are no trees.
- **Get a free home energy audit** through your energy service company or utility program.

- **Go solar.** Many localities and areas offer enough incentives that the startup costs are minimal. Give solar panels rather than coal to your naughty kids.
- **Shop your values and shop local.** Know the companies with whom you do business. Support businesses that share your values and tell your friends about them. Mother Nature endorses shame and peer pressure for the greater good.
- **Be more conservative with your own energy use.** Wash your clothes in cold water and turn the thermostat a little lower than usual in the winter and a little higher in the summer, or buy a smart thermostat for your private jet.

### Put Your Talents to Use

You can't fix it all, but you can do your part to help. You can also consider what you're good at outside of these suggestions. If you're artsy, you can create art to inspire people to action or design signs or shirts. If you write, you can write blog posts or snarky social media posts. If you teach, you can inspire kids to get outside and appreciate nature and to act. If you're an attorney, you can volunteer your legal prowess. And if you're an engineer or a scientist, you can leverage that expertise to train others. We *all* have skills that we can contribute. Let's keep "hell on Earth" a hyperbole.

### Climate Change May Be Bad, But You Can Still Feel Good

Some people believe in chemtrails and WWE but not climate change. Remember when the only climate change we had was the changing of the seasons? Climate change is yet another problem that can trigger anxiety about the state of the world, which I covered in Chapter 1. If you're still feeling anxious, try some of the tips I reviewed in that chapter. Also, remember that good things are coming. Renewable energy sources like solar and wind are catching on and receiving huge investments. Electric vehicles are expected to dominate the market in coming years. Airplanes are getting more efficient with lower carbon footprints. And global population growth is slowing. While meat consumption is up in some regions, so too is plant-based food. Eating animals is so passé.

**Your Anxiety-Trigger Toolkit: Five Tips for Coping With Climate Change**

1. Use humor when talking to others about climate change, particularly the deniers – like how every disaster movie begins with a government ignoring a scientist.
2. Find others you can commiserate with regarding the anxiety of climate change. Search for groups online using sites like 350. org. Climate crises love company.
3. Become more attuned with the environment through techniques like mindful photography, mindful eating, and other activities that can be performed mindfully. A day without mindfulness is a day distracted.
4. Taking concrete steps to lessen your carbon footprint can also lessen your anxiety. You don't have to drive a donkey to work, but apply grassroots efforts. Burning fossil fuels to get rid of them is not a cure.
5. Everyone has talents they can lend to the cause. Think of something you're good at and how you can apply it to fighting climate change.

# 4 Receiving Bad News

A clinical study by researchers at the University of Cincinnati found that 85% of what subjects worried about never occurred. Of the 15% that materialized, 79% of subjects discovered they could handle it well.[1] The universe is on your side.

> *Q: What travels faster than the speed of light?*
> *A: Bad news.*

It seems that whenever I've experienced a hardy setback, it has occurred along with one or two other sternum punches. For example, I concurrently went through my worst breakup at the same time as a major shoulder surgery. I hit my low during that phase while sitting on my kitchen floor in a sling unable to tie my shoes with one hand, and because I don't yet wear Velcro shoes. I never felt so alone than in that moment, and I broke down sobbing because I missed my ex and a practical arm. The benefit to hitting rock bottom is that you can bounce upward. But I was a medicine ball.

People often say, "Bad things occur in threes." That's B.S. Good, bad, and neutral things occur in ones, threes, eights, and tens. There are no inevitable groupings. This is another instance where humans seek patterns, in this case quantifiable, to feel an element of control over our fate. No one suffering a divorce or a layoff also wants to scan the vista for the other two predictable setbacks of the "bad things come in threes triad" crashing toward them at the speed of fate or karma.

For Chris, it was the year that his mom called to say she had cancer an hour before he was about to speak at a conference. The good news was that there were 4,000 therapists wandering around the hotel grounds in downtown DC. The bad news was that he had no desire to share his mom's diagnosis with a strange therapist. That was the start of a year with both of his parents breaking bones, fertility challenges surrounding his second child, and a time where his 2-year-old broke his leg, all while buying and selling a home.

## Welcome to Perspective 101

But so goes the wholly subversive aura of receiving bad news. It can arrive in droves and permeate every cell in a cataclysmic upheaval of the sanities until you are reduced to basic survival, with only the bleakest disposition left to guide you. It's not uncommon to feel like you've lost everything, no matter the gravity of the situation, while what's left hardly matters. This is why the notion of "perspective" is so crucial. Think of perspective as the measuring stick by which everything in your life is

---

1 Leahy, R. L. (2006). *The worry cure: Seven steps to stop worry from stopping you* (Illustrated ed.). Harmony.

gauged and whereby you determine the relativeness of anything against the grand scheme of things.

Perspective has indispensable potency. There's no disputing that a negative outcome sucks. But, measured against the evening news or an episode of "Dateline," it often feels somewhat paltry. All I'm asking is that you keep the bad news appropriately stack-ranked against the litany of potentialities.

### *Now Entering: State of Denial. Population: 1*

But perspective is an acquired benchmark. We measure things against that which we know. Your setback may be the single worst incident you've encountered thus far. Consider my story from Chapter 2 where I revealed passing blood in my urine for three days while staunchly refusing medical testing. It takes egregious amounts of denial to discount such an obvious ailment.

> *"You can still hope for the Disney ending while prepping for a Stephen King finale."*

Even though it was clearly a serious condition, I tried to will it away. I told myself it was nothing serious, and probably a UTI, cystitis, kidney stones, or pent-up anger. Nevertheless, I continued to live life in denial as I was peeing out pieces of my insides.

I implemented some self-triage in the form of cranberry juice, saw palmetto, and urinary probiotics, hoping I could homeopathically remedy whatever ailed me. As a gender, men avoid most timely medical care. It's one reason we die much younger than women. Further denial and distraction would have resulted in a diaper-clad death.

### Tactics for Relief: How to Redirect a Negative Result Into a Righteous Response

#### *The Brain's Four Fs of Self-Preservation: Fight, Flight, Freeze, and Forget*

"Fine" is an f-word. In shocking moments, our brains shift to a self-preserving form of denial where the logic-loving prefrontal cortex can shut down. This allows the amygdala, the blaring alarm system part of the brain, to take over. It's the part that gives us the big feelings. These feelings are so big, in fact, that the blood rushes there and away from the rest of our brain where we logically think things through, leading to mental paralysis (aka, "freeze"). We also have fight and flight, which you may already know about. "Forget" rounds out the fourth F and entails a kind of giving up – like when you tell yourself, "*I'm too full for dessert.*"

A Summation of the Four Fs:

1. **Fight** to make it go away (makes us more aggressive in the long-term, however).
2. **Flight** to avoid (adds to more anxiety later).
3. **Freeze** to dissociate, hide, and shut down.
4. **Forget** is simply giving up and is an unhealthy, unhelpful response.

### Immediately Implement Some Radical Acceptance

Consciously maintain awareness of your current situation as a transient state in which you are *not* helpless. Normal acceptance is like saying, "it is what it is" over life's trivialities and not letting them upset you further. Radical acceptance requires a bit more mental vigor. It's akin to accepting that your spouse just cleared out the bank accounts and ran off to Ibiza with your pool boy, Brock – 'cause he's rad.

"You want me to do *what* with my anxiety?" Radical acceptance turns the unbearable into the ordinary. Radically accept that when big news hits, you cannot mentally process it all at once because it's often too much to handle. It's a mental Slip 'N Slide. Reach deep within yourself and tap into the only form of acceptance that will lessen your suffering. Sit with what's happening without trying to deny or control the outcome. Acceptance is your only way out and through.

Accepting something is not the same as labeling it good or even okay. It's an intentional mind shift that requires an act of choice, where you turn your focus toward acceptance and skip past rejection and denial of the reality. And it requires an internal commitment – not once, but relentlessly. Oftentimes you must ruthlessly commit to this level of acceptance every minute until it begins to take hold. Blind acceptance is tough, but fighting something ominously painful is harder. Challenge radically accepted.

*Reflect on and Process Your Reactions to Bad News*

My dad has the habit of prefacing bad news with some anxiety-spiking intros. These include top hits like "*I've got some bad news*," "*Are you sitting down?*," or his go-to bad-news breaker, "*I don't know how to tell you this, but . . .*" I've repeatedly asked him to work on his delivery, and that igniting someone's anxiety just before imparting bad news is not the same as stretching before deadlifts.

*Always Preface Bad News by Reminding People They*
*Can Eat Frosting Straight From the Container*

Chris recalls going with his mom to get updates about her cancer treatment. Even as a psychologist, he did not anticipate how much his brain would freeze and shut down. The questions he had for his mom's doctor were in there somewhere, but he lacked access and felt blank. The result was that he walked out of that meeting feeling terrible that he'd recalled no questions for her or himself and gleaned little information.

He reflected on what had happened. Simply put, his thinking brain (prefrontal cortex) was off, and his memory acquisitions were offline because he was in fight-or-flight mode. The next time he went back he was better prepared. Remember when you are in that mode your brain is not getting the blood flowing to the parts that think rationally. But know that you are still "okay."

In fact, the negativity bias (which I explained in Chapter 1) is an issue for all humans, but particularly anxious ones. It can kick into overdrive for your protection, only hearing and sensing danger and bad news. You are literally perceiving different frequencies of sounds and sights to confirm that everything is now crap and that your only options are to freeze or try some reckless abandon, like cheating on your partner or diet. Every pizza is personal size if you're anxious enough.

What's more, when the body and brain prepare for short-term survival, it messes with our digestive and immune systems, which is why we get sick, diarrheal, or nauseous when we are anxious. Yet short-term survival also means we crave certain foods to help us to fight or take flight. Hint: It's not low carb. When we are stressed or anxious, we crave high-energy foods loaded with sugar and fat so we can fight harder or flee faster. And you don't get that kind of quick energy from Brussel sprouts.

*"Give me your tired, your poor, your huddled masses . . . and your anxieties."*

---

### Modify Your Mindset: Tactics to Help With Radical Acceptance

Continue to practice radically accepting the moment and situation for what it is. You can do this with specific mindsets and behaviors such as the following:

- **Observe your breath** by focusing your attention on the inhale and exhale. Observe it in a way that mindfully grounds yourself in the moment, rather than fighting reality. You can set an Apple Watch to remind you to breathe so that each time you receive a reminder alert you can be disappointed that it's not a text.
- **Hold a serene face** as a means of accepting whatever is happening. Reduce tension and anxiety by tensing and then releasing the muscles in your face, neck, and shoulders. Try to adopt a serene facial expression. Practice in front of a mirror. If it feels more familiar, you can make an Insta-selfie duck face, then release and repeat. Remember: Your body communicates to your mind.
- **Maintain awareness of your body.** This can be done anytime, anywhere. Observe your breath as just described and be aware of your body position, whether you are moving or still. Be aware of the purpose of your position, even if there is no intentional purpose. Don't concern yourself with how you could fall off a roof unhurt as a kid, but are wracked with body pain at 40 after "sleeping weird."
- **Grounding.** When working with electricity or anxiety, always ground yourself. Sit or stand up straight and feel your feet underneath you. Depending on where you are, it's best if you can remove your shoes. Relax your shoulders and breathe slowly and deeply. Feel as if you are absorbing the electrons from Earth's surface through the soles of your feet, which is a technique called earthing. Gently press your feet into the ground, aware of the textures and sensations. And check in with other

senses, noticing and counting things around you that are red, or green, or any other color. Maybe tune into sounds for a few moments, noticing the ones furthest away and each sound that seems closer and closer to you. As you bring your awareness to your senses, you bring them away from your worries, at least for a few moments at a time. Don't forget your shoes.

### Practice Self-Compassion

We're often the last ones we're nice to. Self-compassion can help considerably, which might sound trite but is rigorously researched. The topic is also mentioned in the following chapter since it's an often neglected and valuable self-preservation tactic. There are multiple ways to practice self-compassion, several of which are quick and easy. **Simply place a hand over your heart for a few breaths and enjoy the gentle warmth.** This gesture alone can shut down the four F's and turn on what researchers call "rest and digest" where our bodies and brains chill out and reset themselves. This kind of gentle touch is also helpful with falling asleep. Or reciting the Pledge of Allegiance. As self-conscious as it may feel, give it a try while alone.

### What Would Oprah Say to You?

Consider the words and tone with which you speak to yourself when you receive bad news. Are you self-critical and demeaning, and do you blame yourself for the outcome? The more anxious you are, the more likely that is the case. Can you try offering yourself supportive words in a reassuring tone, the very same you might offer a friend or even child who is similarly awaiting news? It's not the job of others to love and care for you. It's yours. Talk to yourself the way you would a puppy you just met.

### Exercises in Fulfillment: See Yourself as a Kidult

How would you treat a child version of yourself if they were the one receiving the bad news? **One of the best methods to develop self-compassion is to think of the vulnerable, child version of yourself and extend that same compassion toward your adult self. It's** palpably easier to extend compassion and understanding when you perceive yourself in this younger context. Follow these instructions to begin showing yourself more compassion:

1. **Think about your current difficult situation or a recent one.** How would you respond to the child version of yourself in this scenario? Consider writing out what you would say, paying close attention to your voice, style, and tone.
2. **Now think about how you typically or are currently respond-ing to yourself in this or a similar difficult situation.** Write out how you typically respond, including what you tell yourself and the tone you use.
3. **You should be able to notice a difference. Ask yourself why this difference exists.** Does this current version of yourself not war-rant the same compassion and empathy? What causes you to treat today's "you" with less kindness and understanding?
4. **Lastly, ask yourself how things could change if you responded to your adult self as you would your child self when you're suffering.** You would likely be far more lenient with the child version of yourself. Correct your sense of self and stop clogging your reality.

*Calm Your Brain With Regulated Breathing and Touch-and-Go Meditation*

Never in the annals of calming down has anyone calmed down by telling someone to "calm down." It's like trying to baptize a bear. One thing that does work is flipping the switch on the amygdala with some regulated breathing. Here's a quick one Chris did with his mom that helped as they were walking together into a later meeting with her doctor. It's called 7/11 breathing.

## Anxiety Safety Briefing: Touch and Go

**Breathe in for a count of 7 and then exhale while counting to 11, and you will immediately begin to think more clearly.**

When most of us are stressed, the brain feels like a colander where all the important information drains out and leaves you with a tangle of noodle-like thoughts. Practice what meditation teachers often call "touch and go."

Lean in and feel the pain, the fear, the doubt, and the anger for about a minute, or as long as you can tolerate, and then lean back to your breath doing 7/11 breathing to counter the rising emotions and "amygdala hijacking" from taking over.

### Shake It Till You Make It

Several years ago, researchers started to notice that animals, whether in the wild or domesticated, would shake themselves out after getting into a fight. What's more, animals don't seem to develop anxiety disorders and PTSD the way humans often do.[2] Scientists began wondering if there was a connection between this semi-voluntary shaking behavior and staving off anxiety.

Several theories exist as to the reason for the post-brawl shimmy and, while they are still being researched, there are some promising leads regarding the benefits of deliberately shaking our bodies to manage stress. The rationality for it is being studied at such places as the Veteran's Administration. The emerging evidence for making your body shake has led to growing popularity of tactics like trauma and tension release exercises (TREs) and trembling therapy to help the body release deeply held stress, tension, and trauma. Or you can subscribe to my personal trauma-coping technique, *"How will I make this funny later?"*

*"Doves don't shake. This is why doves cry."*

Recall that when under stress, your body goes into a fight, flight, or freeze mode that affects every component of your body. This response often remains within you long after the event. Intentional shaking can reset and soothe your nervous system by using the body's natural response to lower anxiety. It does this by intentionally activating the involuntary shaking to release the stress you experience during instances of extreme anxiety or fear. It's the full-body version of "SMH."

2 Levine, P. A., & Frederick, A. (1997). *Waking the tiger: Healing trauma* (Illustrated ed.). North Atlantic Books.

### Modify Your Mindset: How to Shake to Regulate Your Body's Fight-or-Flight Response

Panic can make you shake anyway, so why not do it on your terms? The next time you're hit with a stressful situation, try physically shaking it off. If anyone questions you, tell them you just walked through a spider web.

**Note:** If you have severe trauma or medical/physical limitations, only do as much as you are able to and without discomfort. If the exercise becomes overwhelming, stop and do a breathing exercise to calm yourself down.

Here's how SMB (shaking my body) works:

1. Begin by standing still, just noticing how your body feels in this position of stillness. Take a few breaths and then swing your arms up over your head.
2. With arms above you, begin just shaking out your hands for a minute or so.
3. Add in arm movements, shaking your arms, shoulders, and hands all at once.
4. Next add in your head, shaking it lightly, but using safe movements that won't strain your neck. You're not a PEZ dispenser. If you can imagine yourself as a big spoonful of Jell-O being lifted toward someone's mouth, then you're doing it right.
5. Move the shaking down through your body to include your hips. #Twerk
6. Lastly, add in your legs, shaking each one and then your feet as well. "You do the Hokey Pokey and you turn yourself around. That's what it's all about!"
7. Now just let your entire body become still. Notice any changes in how your body and mind are feeling. You may now rejoin society.

### Empower Yourself With Self-Competence and Support From Others

Lastly, do something you enjoy and have some mastery over. When you're feeling powerless, do something at which you feel competent. That is how you source empowerment. Nothing makes the bad go away, or makes you feel better completely, but small tactics add up. It's like that feeling you get with tons of social media likes on a recent selfie with your new bangs or biceps, except that self-empowerment is *internally* generated and genuinely matters.

Empowering yourself doesn't need to be a grandiose feat of measure; it can entail nearly anything. Maybe you'd like to reach the next level of a video game where you slay the dragon, achieve knighthood, and get the gold or whatever knights are into. Maybe it's learning to master a glazing torch while brûléeing the perfect crunchy top on a crème brûlée. Or maybe it's baking Tater Tots without starting a kitchen fire.

There are support groups where people laugh and cry and care for each other, and where everyone feels awkward the first time they go and are later glad they went. There's a group for every addiction, malady, disease, compulsion, and adversity imaginable. From ataxia and anxiety to SIDS and sex addicts, there's an assembly of supporters who know what you're going through and want to welcome you. Especially the sex addicts.

To find a support group, ask your physician or therapist (if you have one) for suggestions. Also check with local hospitals and medical clinics, which often sponsor a variety of groups. Consider online resources such as Support Group Central (www.supportgroupscentral.com/) or the seemingly countless support groups found on social media.

### If You Think Things Can't Get Better, You're Not Using Your Imagination

People receive negative news every day. Some even get cancer news at a conference, or can't be near a dying loved one due to a pandemic. They get hopeless, panicky, enraged, and tearful, and then they must do homework, take their medicine, make dinner, and have unwanted conversations with loved ones. You may not feel like you can "move on," but you can and do need to "move forward" with the basics of self-care like eating, working, and disagreeing with people on the internet.

### Your Anxiety-Trigger Toolkit: Eight Tips for Coping With Bad News

1.  Try not to give into the four F's – fight, flight, freeze, or forget – in response to bad news. You now have many helpful tactics from which to choose.
2.  As soon as bad news arrives, practice radical acceptance by accepting reality on its own terms without trying to control or change it. Remember: Be will*ing*, not will*ful*.
3.  If you react to bad news with one of the four F's, that's fine; it's only natural. If you receive future negative news, be mindful of your breathing and posture and maintain a serene, Putin-like face.
4.  Practice self-compassion by gently touching your heart and taking a few breaths to feel your own inner warmth. It also works on the cold-hearted.
5.  Develop self-compassion by seeing the vulnerable, child version of yourself and extending that same compassion toward your adult self.
6.  Calm your yourself by using 7/11 breathing. Inhale while counting to 7 then exhale while counting to 11.
7.  Intentionally shake out your anxiety.
8.  Empower yourself by doing something fun that you're good at, or finding a supportive group of people going through the same thing you are. "*Hello, my name is Jon and I'm addicted to lo-fi hip hop and essential oils.*"

# 5 Depression

DOI: 10.4324/9781003345350-7

Depression is anxiety's bae. Anxiety and depression often occur concurrently. They're the Jay-Z and Beyonce of mental health disorders. But you also need to distinguish if what you're feeling is actual depression or just sadness.

### How Do You Know If You're Depressed or Just Sad?

Is your two-day Netflix binge a bout of laziness and apathy, a case of "the melancholies," or clinical depression? Maybe you think you're depressed, or you're just using depression as an excuse to be lethargic only to realize this itself might be a symptom of depression. *It's tough trying to figure out your head with your own mind, right?*

The brain is an organ that can malfunction like any organ. Mental illnesses are illnesses of that organ. Brain scans show that there is a physical difference between a healthy brain and a sick brain. Telling someone with anxiety or depression, *"You don't have an issue, it's all in your head"* is as absurd as telling someone with diabetes, *"You don't have an issue, it's all in your pancreas."* Any organ is susceptible to disease or disorder.

> *"You look depressed."*
> *"Thanks, it's the depression."*

When you're feeling down, it's imperative to distinguish feelings of sadness versus depression because confusion can lead you to avoid evaluation and treatment of a serious condition. Alternatively, you might overreact to a normal emotional state of sadness.

Here's why the distinction is crucial: If you are depressed, it has consequences for your long-term mental health, physical health, and longevity. Sadness is a *normal* emotion that usually fades when you've gotten over the hurt or triggering event, whereas depression is an *abnormal* emotional state; a mental ailment that affects your thinking, emotions, perceptions, and behaviors in persistent and chronic ways.

So what's the primary difference between a case of the sads and depression? In the simplest of terms, sadness is about *something*, and depression is often about *nothing*. Depression can occur in absence of any of the triggers that cause sadness. Depression also typically happens nearly all day every day and has a greater impact on your life, whereas sadness is more transient. I can get sad just by someone asking me what I do for fun, whereas depression must basically screw up your life, work, and relationships.

The symptoms also can't be from substances or medical issues, though these can make someone with depression feel much worse, so check your thyroid and go easy on the sauce. After all, a bottomless mimosa brunch or bucket of beers is enough to spur a days-long bleak spell.

## Anxiety Can Feel Like Worrying You Might Die. Depression Can Feel Like Wanting To

It's tough to find patients who are depressed and who also don't have anxiety. It's equally hard to find people with anxiety that don't have some depression. So don't beat yourself up if you're feeling anxiety on top of everything else. It's more likely than not to occur. An untreated anxiety disorder can lead to depression. Conversely, having a diagnosis of depression can manifest symptoms of an anxiety disorder to include edginess, irritability, and insomnia. However, each disorder has its own causes and symptoms. No evidence exists that one disorder causes the other, though it's common for people to suffer from both disorders. It's a mental smorgasbord.

> Therapist: *Are you struggling more with anxiety or depression?*
> Me: YES.

And though signs of depression, anxiety disorder, and even bipolar disorder have similarities, each requires different treatments right down to the therapy and medications used. This is why a professional diagnosis is vital to get the best help.

## Depression Presents Differently for Each Person

Most people aren't depressed 100% of the time. But tricking people into thinking you're not depressed is draining. There are few things worse than chronic "smiling depression." The constant attempts at concealing one's mental pain only increase the overall burden. And by avoiding others, we avoid their judgment and the barrage of armchair psychiatry by well-wishers who dispense platitudes like *"But you have nothing to be depressed about,"* *"Things aren't that bad!"* or the timeless pejorative, *"Just snap out of it!"*

### Tactics for Relief: How to Feel Better When the Depression Memes Aren't Enough

#### Seeketh the Joy Again

Think of things that you enjoy, big or small, and go do them. It can be anything from listening to music or walking a dog, to spending time with a friend. Don't overwhelm yourself with a plan. Keep it simple so you don't feel like bailing later. You may have to push yourself at first, but it will help you to feel better, and you won't have to hear anyone ask, "*Who was crying in the bathroom last night?*"

Put a few good things into your calendar. Planning a vacation, whether you take it or not, let alone could ever afford it, can boost your mood. Go online and Google "best affordable vacations." I just did it, and now I'm wondering how many books I must sell to write the next one on Moorea Island in French Polynesia.

Put smaller things into your calendar that you can look forward to this weekend. Maybe just meeting a friend for coffee. Put one small thing in your calendar for the end of the day, even if it's watching your favorite show on the couch, texting with an old friend, or mac and cheese for dinner.

### Crack a (Half) Smile

Rather than trying to smile through anxiety and tension, which tells the brain you are masking something, try half-smiling instead. A half smile is slightly turned-up lips with a relaxed face, like one you might see in a celebrity mug shot. The originator of the technique, Marsha Linehan, is an American author, psychologist, and the creator of dialectical behavior therapy (DBT). This tactic is proven to be effective in turning around cycles of negative moods such as depressive episodes. Because emotions are a combination of thoughts, sensations, and behaviors, changing just one of these components can result in significantly altering the course of the emotion.[1]

Aim for a serene facial expression, while recalling that your body communicates to your mind. If you don't think this anomaly works, try it now. If you're reading this in a public space, just stare blankly at this page and commence that half grin. You will instantly signal to the brain a feeling of levity. That's assuming you don't break out laughing, which you might do while donning this serial-killer smirk.

1 Linehan, M. M. (2014). *DBT® skills training handouts and worksheets* (2nd ed., Spiral-Bound Paperback ed.). The Guilford Press.

## Modify Your Mindset: Take a Moment to Half-Smile

There are many opportunities throughout the day where you can
**hold a half smile for at least three gentle breaths,** slowly inhaling
and exhaling, to quickly improve your mood.

- ☺ **Half-smile when you first awake in the morning.** Hang a sign or
  a post-it on the wall or bathroom mirror so that you see it when
  you first awake. Use these seconds before you arise to breathe
  mindfully. Inhale and exhale three breaths gently while maintaining a half smile. Even on Mondays. Especially on Mondays.
- ☺ **Half-smile during free moments.** Anywhere you find yourself
  sitting or standing while waiting for a restroom, in a check-out
  line, or in traffic, crack that half-smile. Look at an animate or
  inanimate object, like a DMV "now serving" number display,
  and half-smile for the count of three inhale/exhale breaths. It's
  the same smile you'll need for your photo.
- ☺ **Half-smile while enjoying music.** Listen to a song for a few minutes,
  while paying close attention to the lyrics, music, tempo, and feelings. Avoid songs with words you'll need to make up, like "Work"
  by Rihanna, any version of Auld Land Syne, or all of "Cotton Eye
  Joe." Half-smile while noticing your inhalations and exhalations.
- ☺ **Half-smile when annoyed.** Whenever you realize, "*I'm both-
  ered,*" immediately half-smile. Inhale and exhale gently and
  non-murdery, while holding a half smile for three breaths.
- ☺ **Half-smile while lying down.** Lie on your back on a flat surface
  without a pillow or support. Arms should be loose by your
  sides and legs straight and slightly apart. Then, you guessed it:
  maintain a half-smile. Let yourself relax, maintaining attention
  solely on your breath and quirky half-smile. Your state of mind
  should be equal to winning an award for laziness and sending
  someone to pick it up for you.
- ☺ **Half-smile while pondering someone you despise.** This one is last
  for a reason: It's the hardest but wildly effective. Picture someone
  who has caused you great suffering. Think on their features you
  most loathe or find vile. Now imagine what might make them
  happy and what causes suffering in their own life. Have they possibly been influenced by any biases, ignorance, hatred, or anger?
  Continue until you feel compassion arise within you, and anger
  and resentment fade. Practice this tactic repeatedly on the same
  person as you shift from revulsion to empathy for them.

*"Change your face, change the world."*

### Avoid Alcohol, Caffeine, and Drugs and Maintain a Healthy Diet

Caffeine is less aggressive than an EpiPen®, but it sets unrealistic expectations for your daily productivity and can measurably spike anxiety. When you're tired and you caffeinate yourself, you increase your heart rate while remaining exhausted.

At low doses (50 mg) caffeine improves cognitive performance.[2] It's how I wrote this book. However, studies reveal higher anxiety levels in moderate- and high-caffeine consumers versus their less twitchy peers. Moreover, reports indicate that mania can result from high intakes of caffeine such as energy drink consumption – so can diabetes and urine that looks like antifreeze.

Alcohol often makes for a good distraction or stress intervention, but it's temporary and a depressant that slows down the brain and the processes of the central nervous system. It can also cause feelings of anxiety and depression and interfere with prescribed medications. Ultimately, it makes stress harder to deal with. Oftentimes people aren't addicted to drugs or alcohol; they're addicted to escaping reality. The key is to change the reality.

You can't spell "salad" without "sad," but there's a direct link between a healthy diet and a healthy mind. Stress can lead you to consuming comfort, fast, and junk foods, which will slow you down and make you less capable of managing stress. Not only can unmitigated stress raise blood pressure, but unhealthy foods increase serum cholesterol levels increasing risk of heart attack. The first pizza slice may cure depression, but the last 11 bring it right back. I talk a lot about pizza for a guy suggesting that you avoid too much pizza.

Studies show that both stress-related endocrine changes and behaviors can cause people under prolonged stress to gain weight over time. It's why Winnie the Pooh wore crop tops and no pants. But you can improve cognitive function and prevent stress-related mental disorders by consuming antioxidant-rich fruits and vegetables, aka brain food.

2 Smit, H. J., & Rogers, P. J. (2000). Effects of low doses of caffeine on cognitive performance, mood and thirst in low and higher caffeine consumers. *Psychopharmacology*, *152*, 167–173.

*Eating "Healthy" Is Actually Eating Normally*

One psychological trick to modify your behavior is restructuring your environment. This is designer-speak for moving junk food out of your line of sight. Make unhealthy or highly processed foods less visible and harder to reach. Tuck those Double Stuf® Oreos in the back of the highest pantry shelf. Nothing slows a craving like having to retrieve a ladder to down some hydrogenated fats. Make the healthier foods more front and center. Keep a fruit bowl readily available on the counter. "Out of sight, out of belly."

When you can recognize it's your stress craving the junk food and not your body wanting it, your mood loses some of its power over you. Also remember some of the basics, like not shopping when hungry and making a list before you go to the market. Oftentimes we eat junk because we don't know how to cook healthfully. Consider taking a cooking class. You'll only need a few good recipes to get started on a better path. You might also meet some good people at the same time. And you'll need people to help eat those Oreos.

Remember, you don't have to change everything all at once. Start small by upping the vegetable-to-carb ratio and work your way green. But be realistic. Don't eat a McDonald's Double Quarter Pounder™ with Cheese combo today because you had a side salad yesterday.

Eating your emotions doesn't usually include broccoli and chard. Food can distract from pain, but unhealthy foods only create more pain. Emotional eating doesn't heal emotional issues. And you may not give a damn today or tomorrow, but you will again soon. And you won't be happy that your past few days were fueled by Domino's and Häagen-Dazs.

## Anxiety Safety Briefing: Sow Some SEEDS

- **Sleep:** Get enough of it – 8 hours a night if possible – and maintain a regular sleep schedule. But don't exceed 9 hours, and don't nap. Depression is exhausting and loves napping.
- **Exercise:** Do something to get your blood pumping (stimulate your body). Emotions can be heavy. Squat them.

- **Educate:** Teach yourself something, whether a skill or learning some cool new information (stimulate your mind). Mastery of a new skill, talent, or hobby is a fearsome antidepressant that instills immeasurable self-confidence.
- **Diet:** Eat a healthy diet with lots of fruits and vegetables and not too much caffeine or alcohol. Nothing tastes as good as healthy feels.
- **Socialize:** Interact with people even though you don't want to. *Especially* if you don't want to. You may need to preface your interactions by letting others know you're tired, stressed, <insert preferred excuse>, so they don't keep asking you what's wrong and trying to cheer you up.

### *Your Anxieties Are Made for Walking*

Walk as a mental and emotional tactic with purpose. Walk and try to notice the beautiful stuff out there while you're walking. Start small and try to notice one nice thing on your commute to work, or maybe from your office or residence window every day. Eventually, your perspective can shift a bit. Look at the trees if any are within your line of sight. If none are available, change your purview.

### *Today Is National Treat Yourself Day.*
### *Tell the Others*

Dost thou pamper thy self? Self-care is a vital part of the treatment for depression. What follows are some basic self-care tactics, building on the idea of "behavioral activation." Essentially, behavioral activation is **acting** your way into a new way of thinking by deliberately choosing to do things that shift your mood or perspective, even slightly.[3] Over time, these actions start to add up to new habits and new moods. It is said that "behavior goes where reinforcement flows," even if it's sitting in your car alone outside your house as a means of escape.

3 Nagy, G. A., Cernasov, P., Pisoni, A., Walsh, E., Dichter, G. S., & Smoski, M. J. (2020). Reward network modulation as a mechanism of change in behavioral activation. *Behavior Modification, 44*(2), 186–213. https://doi.org/10.1177/0145445518805682

**Exercises in Fulfillment: Behavioral Activation**

Plan daily activities and goals, whether small or large, that are meaningful to you and are achievable without being overwhelming. Also work in some downtime where you don't have to worry about accomplishing anything. This isn't easy when you're depressed, so set small goals and objectives. If it feels like too much, break those goals down even smaller. No shame. Struggling like this is itself a symptom of depression.

- **Plan.** Set a daily schedule for sleeping, personal hygiene, eating, work, and so on. You need some structure, and more is better when you're depressed. For best results, and to avoid the general avoidance that comes with anxiety or depression, schedule things from easiest to hardest. Maybe start with opening the mail and work your way up to opening your home to a new pet.
- **Set a pleasure goal.** Increase pleasurable activities. Each day commit to one pleasure goal for the following day. Read, partake in a hobby, watch standup comedy, or blow pet-safe bubbles for your dog or cat. It's a thing (check online or at your local pet store).
- **Set a productivity goal.** Each day commit to one productivity goal for the following day. With depression comes avoidance, and your creditors don't get depressed. You're going to have to get things done despite your state of mind.
- **Schedule downtime and reward yourself.** Taking regular mental breaks affords you a litany of upsides to include increased productivity, replenished focus, and fostering creativity. Online shopping, scrolling, or apathy is not rest. Unless you're a writer.

*Take a Forest Bath*

About 20–30 minutes of activity like walking (even slow walking) can be about as good as medication for moderate depression. And, if you're surrounded by nature during your walk, even better! Remember to bring your phone or GPS. It's awkward when you must eat other hikers because you got lost.

According to a Stanford study, there is quantifiable evidence that walking in nature can reduce stress and lead to a lower risk of depression. Published in the *Proceedings of the National Academy of Science*, the study found that people who walked for 90 minutes in a natural area, versus participants who walked in a high-traffic urban setting, showed decreased activity in a region of the brain associated with a key factor in depression.[4] In an unrelated study, watching "Man vs. Wild" on the couch in a North Face® jacket had no benefits whatsoever.

With increasing urbanization, more people are exposed to risk factors such as poverty, noise, and pollution, contributing to increased stress, which in turn has negative impacts on mental health.[5] That said, cities provide better access to health care, employment, and education. There is a continued need for increased understanding of the interaction between city living and mental health.

There are a lot of pros and cons to city living, but the mental health benefits of nature are clear. So city folk should find a way to get out and enjoy nature every now and again. If you live in an urban setting, find the greenest, most tree-laden plot of land available and then hike or walk it. If you see signs that read "Missing wheelbarrow" or "Thank you for returning my wheelbarrow," then you've arrived.

The hardest part is forcing yourself out. Take it one task a time. Get dressed for your outdoor saunter. Grab your water bottle and quinoa-mint bark bar and head out the door. Drive, Uber, or ride to the park or trailhead and then walk and don't return till you're bejeweled in the sweat of serenity and achievement.

### Laugh at Your Pain

You can watch a comedy special tailored to anxiety and depression like Gary Gulman's *The Great Depresh*; Maria Bamford, who shares about her battles with extreme OCD; Chris Gethard's *Career Suicide*; or Neal Brennan's *3 Mics*, which covers mental illness. Comedians are aces at conveying truths in their mental health experiences while leveraging humor and compassion.

4  Bratman, G. N., Hamilton, J. P., Hahn, K. S., Daily, G. C., & Gross, J. J. (2015). Nature experience reduces rumination and subgenual prefrontal cortex activation. *Proceedings of the National Academy of Sciences, 112*(28), 8567–8572.
5  Gruebner, O., Rapp, M. A., Adli, M., Kluge, U., Galea, S., & Heinz, A. (2017). *Cities and mental health*. Deutsches Ärzteblatt International.

### Don't Fake Well-Being or Being Well

No matter your flavor of anxiety, depression, or both, they can be managed, and you *can* lead a happy and meaningful life. Oftentimes additional suffering is incurred due to the invisible nature of the disorders. Just because you leave the house, do your job, and run errands doesn't mean you aren't suffering. People love to assuage your emotional pain because they often don't understand it, they can't see what's happening with your brain chemistry, or they simply don't know how to help.

As someone who has spent a lifetime managing both anxiety and major depressive disorder, I used to find it easier to blame my mood or behavior on *anything* but a mental illness. This is largely because so many people don't understand chronic mental health conditions, and I grew tired of the trivial and peppy clichés offered if I shared my feelings with others. Be good to yourself. Whatever you do today, let it be enough.

**Your Anxiety-Trigger Toolkit: Eight Tips for Coping With Depression**

1.  Sadness is temporary and can usually be tied to a specific cause, but depression is more pervasive and can often be triggered by nothing – kind of like clear air turbulence.
2.  Cracking a half smile while slowly inhaling and exhaling for three gentle breaths can quickly improve your mood, especially while feeling irritated.
3.  Avoid caffeine, alcohol, and self-medicating, which could exacerbate your depression in the long run. Focus on eating healthy foods. You can't spell Funyuns® without "fun," but you're less likely to need an angiogram from bags of carrots.
4.  Sow some SEEDS: Sleep, Exercise, Educating yourself, eating at a healthy Diet, and Socializing with others.
5.  Walk with a purpose and be aware of the beauty that surrounds you. If nothing else, find a tree to gaze upon. Trees know how to turn sunshine into growth better than anything.
6.  Set at least one *pleasure* and one *productivity* goal for each day. Smash goals. Clap for yourself. Stay humble.
7.  Bathe yourself in nature by going for a walk in a park or anywhere with trees, flowers, bushes, or whatever natural surroundings you can find and immerse yourself in them, leaving your troubles behind. Lather copiously.
8.  Find comedians or funny shows that make fun of anxiety and depression and laugh along with them at your shared experiences with pain and misery. It's almost never a bad time for humor.

# Part II

# Phobias

Phobias are like mental allergies. A phobia is a type of anxiety disorder that causes a person to experience extreme, irrational fear. If you are holding this book, you may have already experienced this. Phobias are the most common psychiatric illness among women and the second most common among men.

Childhood phobias occur most commonly between the ages of 5 and 9 and tend to be short-lived. Longer-lasting phobias begin later in life, particularly in people in their 20s. Adult phobias tend to last for years, and they are less likely to go away without treatment. Phobias can increase an adult's risk of other types of mental illness – especially other anxiety disorders, depression, and substance abuse.

Phobias typically arise from an irrational fear of something where one feels powerless and not in control. In some cases, symptoms can escalate into full-blown panic attacks. The most common phobias typically involve the environment, animals, fears of injections and blood, as well as specific situations. I have a phobia of telling other people my specific phobias, in the event that someone uses one of my fears against me. You never know who might have a huge spider or anchovy pizza in their pocket.

Self-help methods for the treatment of phobias are often overlooked by the medical profession. Not to worry, I've got your anxious back.

*It's not a fear of heights; it's a common sense of gravity.*

DOI: 10.4324/9781003345350-8

# 6 Fear of Living Creatures

DOI: 10.4324/9781003345350-9

You're more likely to be killed by a cow in the United States than a shark or crocodile. Each year 20 people die from being stepped on by cows, and 450 die while falling out of bed. More people die on their couches watching "Shark Week" than being bitten by them. We fear the wrong things. It's the monsters that lurk in our minds that truly invoke fear.

I avoid any insect that makes an audible crunch upon crushing it. I rely on two indoor housecats, Thelma and Louise, to handle all pest control in my home. I regularly find my felines torturing an array of spiders, flies ("flying raisins"), silverfish, and even grasshoppers that they drag in from the patio. They rarely kill anything; they just play with them – to death.

> *"Oh, I'm sorry. I didn't know you were going to put your feet in these shoes again."*
>
> *– Spider*

I once moved from my condo after 6 years when I overheard my new downstairs neighbor talking to pest control personnel about the bedbug infestation she had knowingly brought from her last residence. When I learned that this was the third professional attempt in unsuccessfully ridding of the pests, I had to balance my anxiety with common sense. I leaned toward reason and swiftly packed and moved to where I'd never again share common walls.

## Fear Is a Liar

Truth is that our fear of animals is rooted in the stories we've told ourselves or stories others have told us. For instance, movies and TV often depict all snakes as venomous murder coils, whereas, at least in the United States, most wild snakes are nonvenomous reptiles that eat insects and rodents. They don't care about humans and would rather slither away than attack us. But such chill creatures would make for dull antagonists in "Snakes on a Plane," "Snake Island," and the lesser-known "Snake Outta Compton" (2018). So their danger level is hyped for effect and to sell more theater popcorn and Red Vines.

Animal phobia is one of the most common forms of what are called specific phobias. It is an anxiety disorder defined by a remarkable and irrational fear resulting in avoidance behaviors, where the fear far exceeds any real threat. One of the most effective treatments for animal phobia is exposure therapy, where the individual is increasingly and recurrently exposed to the feared stimulus until it no longer causes a fear response.[1] What does this mean for you? It's time to face your critter fears. Gradually.

---

1 Hemyari, C., Dolatshahi, B., Sahraian, A., Koohi-Hosseinabadi, O., & Zomorodian, K. (2020). Evaluation of the effectiveness of one- and multi-session exposure-based treatments in reducing biological and psychological responses to rat phobia among students. *Psychology Research and Behavior Management, 13*, 665–679.

# I Got Buzzed

Spring is the time of year where I triple the money spent on hospital copays. This is due to my mind's struggle to focus on any one thing while simultaneously performing feats of amateur athleticism as the days grow longer and lighter. I inaugurated one such season on a Tuesday evening with an unusual circumstance. I was 3 miles into a 6-mile trail run in the hills of Palo Alto, CA, after work. I was running through some tall weeds when a large insect barreled down into my throat, as if waiting in the flora to ambush my trachea. It somehow bypassed my lips and tongue, going straight to the cheap seats past my tonsils.

Of all the wide-open, beautiful places to fly within the blossoming hills of the peninsula, this six-legged bullet flew roughshod into my larynx. It's not like I run with my mouth agape while eating bugs like a filter-feeding baleen whale. I was running uphill, and I have tiny nostrils. If I can't spit out an object, I simply swallow and tell myself that my immunity will defend me. However, this pest would not budge. He was a brawler with an agenda contrary to my own – chiefly his survival at my discomfort.

Upon ingestion, I went into a flailing spasm. I was shocked that something much larger than a gnat had made it into my mouth. I bent over and gagged like a college frat boy on pledge night. Yet the tenacious throat miner didn't nudge.

I tried swallowing, but it barely moved. Instead, it met my attempt by stinging me. It was then that I was able to cough up the waspy invader and spit him to the ground. As my throat began to swell, I had four solitary miles back to my truck – a trek that would prove challenging in possible anaphylactic shock.

I didn't want to go missing this way. Plus, I had clothes in the washer. And who would hide the tube of apricot exfoliating scrub and lemon-butter cuticle creme from my bathroom counter?

I was knocked out of my daydream when the ER doc managed to pull the stinger out from a few inches down my throat. When I arrived home, I gargled Listerine for a few minutes, then took a Percocet for the pain and passed out. I now run with my mouth closed, despite my need for more air. You'll know it's me by the nose whistle.

While it's reasonable to fear a freak incident like this, even if you ran through an active beehive with your mouth open like a windsock, your chances of swallowing one and having it sting you are slim. Yet these extreme stories are the ones we remember. We forget or don't hear about all the animal encounters where nothing bad happened, which is the great majority of them.

Yet so many of us have unfounded fears. Consider anatidaephobia, for example. This is the baseless fear held by subjects that somewhere a duck or goose is watching them, not necessarily to attack or harm, but just observing like a Marxist waterfowl.

## Tactics for Relief: Using Exposure Therapy to See the House Spider as Your Friend and Roommate

### *Don't Run From Your Fears, Confront Them (Slowly)*

The usual response to being afraid of a living creature is flight: avoid and hope it goes away or sell your house and move somewhere with perceptibly friendlier critters. But you can't avoid everything. Do you have a crippling fear of encountering an albino pygmy Sunda pangolin? Good news, you likely won't see any unless you're vacationing in the Lesser Sunda Islands west of greater Timor. And though black widows and brown recluse spiders are more prolific, I've run into both countless times within California garages and have yet to be harassed or asked to dinner.

Phobias can feel weird and even embarrassing. That's why they can fester and get worse. Take birds, for instance. Chris has had many clients over the years with bird phobias. This phobia is unavoidable since birds are most everywhere. Such clients practice avoidance by doing things like never going to the beach, never eating at restaurants outside, avoiding vacations, and not cutting through the park on the way to the subway.

For the most part, their friends don't know it's a thing because one can casually avoid some of these scenarios unbeknownst to others. At some point, however, the people close to you figure it out, especially your avian-loving friends and those of us who gift marshmallow Easter Peeps.

This book is not going to eliminate a major, life-disrupting fear or phobia overnight, but it will detail what you need to do on your end, which should probably include the help of a great cognitive behavioral therapist who does exposure and response prevention (ERP). You can also do this on your own in the form of graduated exposure to the organism you most fear.

For the sake of this chapter, and because it's the most common phobia Chris has come across in his work, let's focus on birds. But you can insert whatever critter is most relevant to you – whether dogs, spiders, or politicians.

Exposure therapy, a gradual process of slowly exposing yourself to your fear incrementally, is one of the most common methods of overcoming phobias. Using a "fear ladder" (aka, exposure hierarchy), you incrementally and repeatedly face the fear until you feel less anxious each time. You begin first with gradual mental and emotional exposure. Then, once you feel comfortable, move on to gradual physical exposure. Use the fear ladder until you never distress over another bird smaller than what's in a KFC Extra Crispy™ bucket again.

*Mental and Emotional Exposure: Start by Thinking About, Reading About, and Looking at Images of the Feared Creature*

Become as informed as possible on the creepy crawly that freaks you out. It is essential that at the end of graded exposure you feel in control of the animal, rather than the other way around. You don't need to buy a pet tarantula, but you can confront an indoor spider without a lighter and hairspray. Understanding your phobia is the first step to overcoming it.

Start by exposure to the target fear and increasing it as tolerable. When you learned to ride a bike, you started with training wheels and then worked up to riding a two-wheel bike. You didn't start on a Kawasaki Ninja H2R unless you had rich, sadistic parents, or your last name was Knievel or Pastrana.

The mental and emotional exposure portion requires that you take your time. It involves four levels of increasing exposure, and you should stay at each level for as long as you need until you feel comfortable enough to progress to the next level. You can move through these steps in a week for a mild phobia if you're motivated, or you can take a month or more for an intense fear. What's important is that you continue the exposure progress. Being brave isn't the absence of fear. Being brave is having that fear of birds but volunteering to carve the Thanksgiving turkey anyway.

---

**Exercises in Fulfillment: Mental and Emotional Exposure**

1.  **Think about birds.** Practice breathing or relaxation until the mere thought of birds doesn't result in a pounding heart and sweaty palms.

2. **Read about and look at pictures of birds,** maybe in a book or online. Keep doing this for a few days until you no longer have much of a reaction.

3. **Watch videos of birds online.** Start with the sound off and in black and white and small images if needed. This is what a lot of people find creepiest – the way birds move in somewhat quirky and unpredictable ways. Notice your emotional reaction and practice some breathing or relaxation to keep yourself calm. This is the "response prevention" portion of ERP (exposure response prevention) where you are trying to activate a response and then prevent it from taking over by regulating your emotions.

4. **Gradually move toward videos with more close-ups of birds in larger onscreen windows or places where birds are present** (pigeons on the sidewalk near a restaurant or seagulls at a beach). You can leverage YouTube, or a supportive partner or friend can shoot some footage for you. Nature documentaries about birds are also a good option. Start with a finch, not an emu.

---

*Physical Exposure: Get in Touch With Your Feathered Frenemy*

The next task in the hierarchy is building not just mental and emotional resilience toward birds, but physical encounters with them in real life. It involves five levels and, like the mental and emotional portions, you should progress through each one at whatever pace feels most comfortable to you. Don't make it hawkward.

---

**Exercises in Fulfillment: Physical Exposure (Continued From Mental Exposure)**

5. **Visit a pet store and check out some birds.** Just walk past them at first in the cages or behind glass. Notice your heart rate and other potential signs of anxiety and wait for it to reduce. Give yourself a specific amount of time to spend there while knowing that you are free to leave. Even if it'll hurt the bird's feelings.

6. **Ask to handle a bird at the pet store.** Another option is if an employee can remove it from the cage and see if you can

**manage that.** Again, this is probably best done with a friend or a professional, not a falconer.

7. **Walk through an area with birds,** like the park, a shoreline, or another bird-centric locale you've been avoiding. And not somewhere in spring with geese.

8. **Face the birds on your home turf.** Get a birdfeeder or birdbath for your yard. Maybe start with it at a distance from the house and gradually move it closer to a window. If it flies into your window, remember that they have tiny brains.

9. **Live your normal life,** even if you've mastered your bird phobia. That doesn't mean buying a macaw or starting a bird-watching blog, but it does mean saying "yes" to long walks around the city rather than avoiding places you might see a bird. Don't celebrate your newfound success by watching "Bird Box."

### Is That a Komodo in Your Pocket?

Certain animals are avoidable or ones you'll likely never encounter. A Komodo dragon attack is unlikely outside of Komodo or the Rincon islands in Indonesia. But others you might want to work on exposure toward, at least up to the amount that the phobia no longer interferes with your life. You don't need to jump into a pit of vipers like Indiana Jones or hug a wasp's nest naked. You need only extinguish the *disruptive* part of the fear, not the fear altogether. A healthy fear is still useful.

For animals like bees or spiders you can, perhaps with the help of a therapist or friend, check out bigger spiders at a pet store or talk to a beekeeper if you want to get more up close and personal. Throwing a shoe at a harmless bug on your bedroom wall is so pre-phobia.

Also, keep in mind that these creatures are just trying to live their lives. When you're cold, they're cold. And they don't want to share a room with you either. Sometimes a little compassion can help shift our perspective and diminish our fear response as well. Fear no weevil.

### What Are Great Whites Scared Of?

I surf in Northern California, but I'm afraid of Great Whites. It's a rational concern since their population is growing in the area, and the six- to nine-foot juveniles swim the shallows. I absolutely love sharks, but it's a love unrequited. Despite knowing that they're largely uninterested in human soft tacos in neoprene, there are enough accidental bites in the news to keep me frosty. I face my fear regularly on weekends by paddling out to practice, knowing full well that I'm an uninvited guest in their home. I bet I taste like chicken.

Whatever your specific fears, the odds are proven in your favor that whatever worst-case scenario you've mentally and emotionally conjured is not only unlikely, but irrational. Ironically, humans are statistically the scariest animal of all.

---

**Your Anxiety-Trigger Toolkit: Ten Tips for Coping With a Fear of Living Creatures**

1. Slowly expose yourself to your feared animal, taking as long as you need with each level of the exposure hierarchy, and monitoring your thoughts and emotions along the way.
2. Begin with mental and emotional exposure by just imagining the animal. Long ago you dreamt of a having pony. It's kind of like that.
3. Educate yourself by reading about the animal and looking at photos of it. We fear what we don't understand. That's why celebrities and taxes are scary.
4. Watch videos of the animal, maybe with the sound muted at first.
5. Switch to videos that show the animal up close and that depict locations where the animal is present. Keep your research rooted in likelihood, however. You're never going to encounter a honey badger on the London Underground on your way to work.
6. After you feel comfortable with mental and emotional exposure, move to gradual physical exposure with a friend or supporter. Start by going to a location where the animal is in a cage or behind glass, and just observe it like the new kid at school.
7. Ask a handler or a pet store clerk to take the animal out of its enclosure and show it to you. Preface that this is an observational visit, not a heavy petting session.
8. Walk around an area where the animal is roaming freely.
9. Face the animal or insect at home, whether in your yard or in the house. Gradually move closer to it. Tell it you come in peace.
10. Move on with the rest of your life and know that you won't panic whenever you run into this creature again. Not on the street, not in the Serengeti.

# 7  Fear of Taking on a New Challenge

DOI: 10.4324/9781003345350-10

Whether designing a less-repulsive form of crocs, remodeling your home, or launching your own AI nacho and margarita drone service, new challenges or performances are rife with angst. Being successful requires an ability to leverage fear.

## Challenge Considered

Taking on a new challenge can mentally feel like subscribing to a new world order. We live in a society obsessed with achievement and success where the notion of failure is minimized, denied, or avoided out of fear. Meanwhile, the world remains affixed to the belief that due to competition, success falls to only the few. In truth, so many never achieve success because fear-based behaviors minimize the risk of failure at the cost of potential success.[1]

There are many facets that attribute to fear of failure, including underlying intrapersonal and interpersonal fears. The intrapersonal aspect of fear resulting in shame or embarrassment, for example, has been linked to avoidance of achievement goals, while aspects of interpersonal nature have been linked to maladaptive success motivation such as socially prescribed perfectionism.[2] The question is not "Does anal retentive have a hyphen?" It's "Why does it matter?"

## Devil in a Blue Sweater: A "Challenge Unrequited" Tale

On a personal front, I have left many opportunities on the table in the past due to my anxiety and "challenge aversion." But there is one noteworthy encounter that bedeviled me. It was a regular workday afternoon in Silicon Valley when a few colleagues invited me to sushi for lunch. For the sake of time, we collectively acquiesced on a place known for its tepid and mediocre fish.

The layout of this venue was such that the sushi chefs were in the center of the room with a large sushi bar surrounding them. The bar, half the size of the restaurant, was surrounded by chairs crammed close together. Encircling the sushi prep area and bar was a slow-moving moat of water that facilitated the journey of a clunky fleet of wooden sushi boats gently chained together. Word on the street was to avoid the moat altogether and order directly from the disgruntled sushi chefs. Angry fish tastes better.

After being seated at the bar, my concentration went from imminent foodborne illness to the gorgeous, professional brunette in a royal blue sweater directly across the sushi bar from me. Reminding myself of my

1 Rothblum, E. D. (1990). Fear of failure. In *Handbook of social and evaluation anxiety* (pp. 497–537). Plenum Press.
2 Bartels, J. M., & Ryan, J. J. (2013). Fear of failure and achievement goals: A canonical analysis. *Journal of Instructional Psychology, 40*(2), 42.

new decree to never let a good opportunity pass – or whatever I had recently decreed – I decided to create a tactic that would allow me to meet this woman, unbeknownst to both my colleagues and the other patrons in the packed restaurant. It did not take me long to craft a scheme of which any Lothario would be proud.

Since I was sitting to the far right of my co-workers at the bar and the circuitous water also flowed to the right, I would draft a slightly perceptible note addressed to "Hottie in Blue Sweater" with a quick introduction and my contact information, then fold it into a standing triangle, and place it on one of the empty wooden boats while letting the flowing aqueduct carry my vulnerable declaration.

Upon receipt, I would discreetly nod so she could identify her maritime suitor. Why I didn't think of sending a sashimi platter or Tiffany's tennis bracelet with a private introduction via the server, I don't know. I soon learned that the downside of avoiding future regret was the regret that comes much, much sooner.

I stealthily placed my note on the next empty boat between some discolored unagi and salmon-roe schooners and watched it drift from me toward my brief paramour. As the dinghy wafted away to the right, my heart crept into my throat. I quickly realized the error in my way. But it was too late. Like a drunk middle manager spewing sexist jokes at a company holiday party, my fate was sealed at the speed of a clumsy sushi canal.

Then, the unexpected happened: The memo floated right past my intended recipient unnoticed. My excitement and trepidation turned to dread. This scenario never crossed my mind, nor did I have a contingency plan. My note-on-a-boat was now completing one full bar rotation, passing another ten diners as it came left around the bend toward my colleagues on its shameful homeward stretch.

One by one, each customer noticed the passing message and then chuckled while scanning the bar for the courier. Further committing to my novel "no regrets" mantra and fueled by the positive reactions of my newfound audience, I no longer hid my participation. I was all in and pushed my anxiety aside by letting everyone know that I was serious in my quest to meet this woman. In my mind, if nothing else wooed her, self-deprecation would do it.

Two of the girlfriends flanking her saw the note and prodded her to grab it despite stares from gushing gawkers around the sushi bar. Annoyed, she begrudgingly snatched the little paper triangle from the wooden boat, glanced at it, and stashed it somewhere – most likely the soy sauce–tinged floor, without so much as a grin or chortle. She appeared disgruntled at being the center of attention.

This was clearly not the lunch she had envisioned when she left her own beige tech office. I had annoyed her, humbled myself, but provided impromptu theater for all. This was love kamikaze style. And happily, without the burning aftertaste of regret.

## Tactics for Relief: How to Channel Your "Challenge Accepted" Mindset

### *Take the Long View: Look Five Years Into the Future*

Chris has a close friend, a professional artist, who while fresh out of college had been invited to be a photographer at one of those opulent billionaire events somewhere in the Caribbean. She arrived to find lots of crusty old dudes tossing back pirate-themed drinks and talking about world domination, the size of their stock portfolios, and how many divorces each had earned.

A few drinks in, they all started talking and flirting with her, while assailing her with useless inquiries like, *"What's your 5-year plan?"* By this they didn't mean Stalinist purges of the peasantry, or I guess they didn't mean just that. But where did she see herself, or what was she planning, since the fine arts could not possibly fulfill a person past their 20s.

The story always stuck with Chris, not because of the financial implications the blue-haired, billionaire boys club tried to drive home, but because taking the long view can sometimes help us find the courage we need to book those tickets, make that call, or try to meet that person in the blue sweater.

When we are young, we often have a lot of time but little money, whereas when we are older the opposite becomes truer. **Think in terms of five- and ten-year perspectives when it comes to decisions. Don't just ask yourself, "How will I feel in five years if I do this?"; ask, "How will I feel in five years if I *don't* do this?"** Consider Chris's own past potential regrets to bolster this point:

- *"It's unlikely that in five years I'll regret spending the summer backpacking across Southeast Asia, but there's a chance I'll regret not doing it and will probably not get another chance."* Chris started traveling for pleasure and discovered a passion in visiting over 50 countries, and has now traveled for work to over 25 more.
- *"It's unlikely that in five years I'll regret telling Olivia's best friend I have a crush on her, but I might regret not saying something."* Olivia and Chris are now married with two beautiful kids.
- *"It's unlikely I will regret sending a book proposal out to publishers in 10 years, but it's likely that, if I don't, I'll regret doing*

*all that work on my dissertation to have it just collect dust in my basement.*" This is the 15th book Chris has been a part of, and his dream of being a writer has come true. An underpaid writer, but still.

Take a current challenge, wish, or desire and examine it in this way. How will you feel if you just try it? Moreover, how will you feel if you *don't*? How much will you care in five weeks, five months, or five years? The worst thing that could happen is a solid lunch story about sushi boats and no regrets. And the best?

### Be a Goal Digger: Set SMART Goals

Tap into your inner shot caller by setting SMART goals: *s*pecific, *m*easurable, *a*ctionable, *r*ealistic, and *t*imely. You greatly increase your chances of success by approaching your specific challenge or goal using this model because sucking at something is the first step to becoming sort of good at something.[3] Dreams are free. Idleness is free. Goals are paid in sweat equity.

---

**Anxiety Safety Briefing: Be SMART About Setting Goals**

Make sure the goals you set are specific, measurable, achievable, relevant, and timely.

- **"Specific" answers the question "What is to be done?" and describes the results of the event or activity to be done.** Write it out in such a way that anyone reading your objective will construe it the same way. To be specific, it also needs to be observable – meaning that someone can see or hear you taking on this feat or challenge, but not as if you're visibly straining or muttering profanities.
- **"Measurable" answers the question "How will you know you met expectations?"** It refers to the extent to which your goal

---

3 Doran, G. T. (1981). There's a S.M.A.R.T. way to write management's goals and objectives. *Management Review, 70*, 35–36.

can be evaluated against some standard such as a quantifiable measurement (e.g., time, points, distance), a quality measurement (e.g., "best in class," second place, gold medal), or a frequency measurement (e.g., you gave six stellar presentations over a three-day conference and drank only one vodka tonic).

- **"Achievable" answers the questions "Can you do it?" "Is this a realistic expectation of yourself?" and "Do you have the experience, knowledge, or capability to achieve this?"** Is this goal appropriately timed and rooted in realism, or are you simply trying to impress your boss, significant other, or YouTube? It's okay, even preferred, if it's slightly out of reach and requires practice and training to achieve. There's nothing wrong with achieving numerous small goals on your way toward a large one. It's one of the best strategies to goal attaining. You then also obtain some dopamine from the achievement, however small, which builds momentum and reinforcement going forward.

- **"Relevant" answers the questions "Should it be done?" "Why?" and "What will be the impact?"** You must ensure that your current goals will help you meet your primary challenge and long-term objectives. Make certain that how you're spending your time and efforts are preparing you for the big day and moment. If you're preparing for a marathon for example, you probably want to avoid doing squats at the gym two days prior to race day. Interestingly, seemingly irrelevant goals can help you maintain some direction and discipline and serve as an early warning sign when they don't get done.

- **"Timely" answers the question "When will it be done?"** This refers to the fact that an objective has an end with midway checkpoints built into it. A challenge or activity has several milestones to help you assess how well you're doing so that corrections or modifications can be made as needed. If you're preparing for your first big public speaking engagement, and you just train-wrecked leading your child's third-grade class in the Pledge of Allegiance, you'll want to ramp up the practice gigs.

---

### *Do an Anxiety Pivot: Turn Anxiety Into Excitement*

Instead of trying to quell your anxiety, reframe the feelings as excitement and channel the performance-related anxiety into challenge-conquering energy. To successfully do this, first accept that you're feeling anxious rather than trying to fight or avoid it. Then, channel your focus by disconnecting from anything needlessly sapping your vigor, like your phone and the internet.

I realize that only bots never go offline but fight the FOMO. Moreover, fight the NOMO (phobia): the fear of being without a connected mobile device. The zombie apocalypse likely started when we all began shuffling around while staring into phones. Your need to be constantly connected to others can skew priorities. Unplug for a while. Your mental and emotional health should not depend on your ability to get online. Instead, nurse your JOMO ([joh: moh] • *noun*: joy of missing out – e.g., your friends in line at the club and you're in soft pants on the couch). It's a sense of contentment and disconnecting as a form of self-care.

### *"Notify Anyway"*

Tech companies try to make things frictionless, with one click sending a person or machine to your door with whatever you want. Add friction back in. Leave your phone at home when you go out. Okay, maybe just in the trunk of your car turned off, but not in your pocket or hand. Alternatively, set up the operating system to "do not disturb" or "notifications silenced" during certain hours of the day. It will also show people that you're enigmatic and unavailable.

### *Practice and Training Make You Competent, Which in Turn Makes You Confident*

Practice your intended feat mentally, emotionally, and physically until you can't get it wrong. For example, when getting ready for a specific event, put that practice time in your daily calendar leading up to it, and practice for it until you feel a sense of mastery over whatever it might be: asking someone out, giving a wedding toast, or playing that big, vertical violin thingy on stage. The better prepared you are, the less chance that stress and nerves will have a negative impact. But practice mindfully. Productivity does not equate to performance. Practice doesn't make anyone perfect. Practice makes progress, moving you in the direction you want to go.

### *"911, What's Your Emergency?" Don't Push Yourself Too Hard*

Sometimes just getting dressed for a challenge is too much for your current state. That's okay! Forgive yourself along the way when necessary. None of the previous tactics will work unless you first accept the normalcy of anxiety's presence. It's unrealistic and unlikely to expect that you'll completely stop the fluttering in your stomach. But keep directing that anxious energy into attaining the small goals toward your larger challenge.

### Be Your Own Swolemate

Some people only jump out of bed because they're late for the couch. There is scientific evidence that the physically active have lower rates of anxiety and depression than the sedentary. It is believed that exercise enhances mental health by helping the brain to better manage stress. It's not always about fitness or building muscle. It's just therapy. Take a walk every day. Or at least briefly consider it.

You can't do ten crunches and just wait for your abs to show up. Researchers in one study found that regular exercisers were 25% less likely to develop anxiety or depression over the subsequent five years.[4] But you may need to ease your way back, particularly if you're recovering from an injury.

> . . . *when your running injury feels healed for 30-seconds*
> *"I don't want to tempt fate, but I think everything is going to be totally fine forever."*

### How Does Exercise Help Ease Anxiety?

Until panic attacks count as cardio, tap into exercise as a distraction and countermeasure to feelings of anxiety. Movement decreases body tension and anxiety. And increasing your heart rate positively changes brain chemistry by boosting anti-anxiety neurochemicals like serotonin, gamma aminobutyric acid (GABA), brain-derived neurotrophic factor (BDNF), and endocannabinoids.[5] Exercise also increases resilience to unregulated emotions. Lastly, exercise assists

4 Otto, M. W., Church, T. S., Craft, L. L., Greer, T. L., Smits, J. A., & Trivedi, M. H. (2007). Exercise for mood and anxiety disorders. *Primary Care Companion to the Journal of Clinical Psychiatry*, 9(4), 287–294.
5 Heijnen, S., Hommel, B., Kibele, A., & Colzato, L. S. (2016). Neuromodulation of aerobic exercise: A review. *Frontiers in Psychology*, 6, 1890.

in our reactions to both real and imagined threats by activating the frontal regions of the brain such as the amygdala.

## But There Is a Caveat

The effects vary depending on the individual. While some gain noticeable benefits, others find no discernable mood enhancements. That said, the positive effects of exercise on both physical and mental health are irrefutable, and staying physically active should remain a priority.

## When Life Gives You Lemons; Make Them Lululemons

Exercise is what happens when we leave our computers. Exactly how much exercise will ward off bouts of anxiety? A meta-analysis in the anxiety-depression journal found that those participating in high-level physical activities were less likely to develop anxiety symptoms than people exhibiting low-level physical activities.

Yet other research reveals that a single session of exercise can lessen anxiety.[6] Take from that what you will. But take it with a protein drink and some commitment because it's important to regularly attempt enjoyable activities.

I've noticed when contending with some of my most anxious periods that I feel just as good with a long walk outside as I do after being tossed around by a bunch of weights. I've done three-hour weight workouts and three-hour trail runs in the throes of anxiety, and I've found that a simple nature walk will treat what ails me. Again, the key is to let the negative and/or nervous energy of anxiety fuel your exercise and the related physical response. Activity burns calories and anxiety. So does sex – in case that's an option.

## Be a Pelican Not a Pelican't

Before YOLO and carpel tunnel there was carpe diem. If you truly believe the task is currently insurmountable, then take manageable steps toward your goal. But also consider the inevitable setbacks and failures that will ensue. Failure isn't the biggest risk. Regret is the biggest risk.

6 Wipfli, B. M., Rethorst, C. D., & Landers, D. M. (2008). The anxiolytic effects of exercise: A meta-analysis of randomized trials and dose – Response analysis. *Journal of Sport and Exercise Psychology, 30*(4), 392–410.

**Your Anxiety-Trigger Toolkit: Six Tips for Coping
With a Fear of Taking on a New Challenge**

1.  New challenges scare us partially because of societal pressures to succeed that make us fear failure. Regularly visualize success knowing that failure is a prerequisite.
2.  If you are hesitant about taking on a particular challenge, imagine yourself five years from now and ask yourself "*What does my future look like if I don't do this?*"
3.  Set SMART goals for yourself that are *s*pecific ("What needs to be done?"), *m*easurable ("How will I know I've met expectations?"), *a*chievable ("Is it realistic?"), *r*elevant ("Why should I do this?"), and *t*imely ("When will I be done?").
4.  Turn anxious energy into positive excitement. Turn your worries into exciting challenges to overcome. When you were a teen it was called "angst," and you wielded it with abandon.
5.  Keep practicing and preparing yourself mentally, emotionally, and physically until you feel competent and in control over the outcome, but do so mindfully. Rehearse daily in your mind, with your body moving, and tracking your emotions as you do.
6.  Don't overwhelm yourself trying to overcome a challenge. Be forgiving of your mistakes and setbacks and allow yourself to take a break. Try going on a short walk outside or relax for bit without trying to accomplish anything to clear your head.

# 8 Fear of Serious Injury

DOI: 10.4324/9781003345350-11

There are injuries and illnesses that wreck us while reminding us that nothing else matters when we or a loved one lands in an ICU, a cancer center, or loses our favorite limb. It helps to remember that a broken bone hurts less than a paper cut, and radically accepting that much of life is completely out of our control. So much suffering comes from trying to control or resist rather than to accept and embrace a life wholly lived. Your fear of living should never exceed your act of living.

I've destroyed an impressive array of body parts, starting at age 5 with a cracked chin from a fall that I credit to Dr. Seuss's original *Cat in the Hat* book. This was lesson one regarding the uncompassionate nature of gravity, as I fell from atop a ball and landed chin first on a concrete patio, cracking the bone and sustaining a large gash requiring 12 stitches.

Along the way, I've garnered a notable list of injuries that I attribute to bad decisions and a lack of appreciation for physics. They include 13 sports-related orthopedic surgeries, a punctured lung, an orbital fracture of the eye, a concussion, a broken nose, and many fractured and broken bones.

But the sum of my worst injuries came as a cataclysmic crescendo late one night at age 21. At some point during sex with my girlfriend at the time, I ended up on my back with her on top. This was purely acrobatic sex, despite being a monogamous couple in love. She went up and down like a jockey riding a steed through an inflatable bouncy house. But I missed a beat and came out as she sprung up and bore down with full body weight, pubic bone first, on my erection like a game of Whack-a-Mole.

I heard an alarming "crack" followed by a combination of numbness and intense pain throughout my penis, as it turned a shade of purple reserved for eggplant. She cautiously dismounted and we stared together in shock at my broken, deflated penis. I had a pit in my gut as I realized the magnitude of my situation, knowing full well it would require a memorable ER visit. I had once read about the dreaded penile fracture and knew it resulted in great pain, followed by corrective surgery.

I gently cupped my cracked appendage in two hands, like George Milton delicately holding his dead puppy in *Of Mice and Men*. I was swarming with anxiety. I had no idea what Frankenstein urologist would be on call at 1:00 a.m. With limited options, it wasn't the time to Yelp penis docs. Despite the novelty of a boomerang-shaped penis, I voted for surgery.

All men should know that a penile fracture can't be treated with ice, Tylenol, or whiskey. Surprisingly, it's considered a minor injury in that it's repairable and men can go completely back to normal after surgery. The pain, however, may linger for a long time. Interestingly, there are reports in world literature that include cases of penile fractures resulting from banging an erect penis against a toilet, masturbating into a cocktail shaker, or placing an erect penis into tight pants – also known as "the 80s."[1]

## Tactics for Relief: How to Fear Nothing, Including Fear of the Hurts

I once took a beach stroll in Santa Barbara with a girlfriend. She was walking a couple of feet directly in front of me, as I blissfully sauntered barefoot behind her. My gaze was fixed skyward on something colorful when I rammed my foot into a partially buried rock. I tripped and fell forward with absurd force, slamming my head into the center of her back, causing her to lunge face-first into the sand. As we both lay semi-dazed, I could hear her drone on about my lack of coordination. I looked at her and muttered, "*Kite . . . so pretty . . . tripped.*"

Maybe I'm not so good at functioning upright and better suited to another anthropological era – Paleolithic perhaps. What's important is that I didn't let my history of toe stubbing get in the way of enjoying a casual walk. When a person with a current or previous injury is exposed to a situation where injury can again occur, they begin to experience extreme sensations of terror (breathlessness, sweating, dry mouth, feeling sick, shaking, heart palpitations, an inability to think clearly, a fear of dying, or a full-blown anxiety attack).

### Exposure Through Education

The newsroom cliché of "if it bleeds, it leads" ties into our anxious need to affix more attention to the negative for survival and shows that people are drawn to stories of misery and trauma. Exposing ourselves in controlled doses to scary things helps us learn to cope by leaning in. It's called exposure therapy, and it works. I implement this one daily. If I didn't, I'd roll myself in bubble wrap and lock myself in a bunker full of weed gummies.

Exposure therapy involves exposing yourself to the anxiety source or its context without causing harm. Learning about a

---

1 Jack, G. S., Garraway, I., Reznichek, R., & Rajfer, J. (2004). Current treatment options for penile fractures. *Reviews in Urology, 6*(3), 114–120.

feared activity before doing it is the least harmful way of exposing yourself to it. The result is a lessening of the anxiety through repeated practice and an ability to overcome the distress. Exposure therapy is pretty much the plot of Dr. Seuss's *Green Eggs and Ham* where the narrator relents and eats the green eggs and ham only to love it.

If you're afraid of a concussion for example, pick up a head trauma memoir written by someone who has experienced one. Visit a rehabilitation unit or a residential treatment facility and look for the veiled sources of happiness, survival, and perspective. Talk to the staff and nurses about how people cope and be moved by their responses. As an aside, if most of your conversations start with, "*Did I tell you this already?*" or "*What was I gonna say?*" then you're normal, not concussed.

You can also interview a paraplegic who literally lived life in the fast lane and discover that most people with chronic injury or trauma are no more unhappy than the rest of us. In fact, after a traumatic event you are just as likely to experience post-traumatic *growth* as post-traumatic stress.

From a clinical perspective, exposing yourself to post-injury education is important, to a degree. It's equally important to avoid overexposure or fixating on any anxiety trigger or provocation since this can yield increased anxiety or fear. The difference in enough and too much exposure is a fine line that can be crossed as easily as reading too much regarding the subject on the internet. You don't want to become a personal injury conspiracist who cuts your own hair after inundating yourself. Wiki with caution.

### Face Your Fears Through Graded Exposure

You can avoid reality, but you cannot escape the consequences of doing so. Avoidance of your fear may feel good short term, but it counteracts the realization that your fear isn't as scary or crushing as you think. Avoidance yields bigger, scarier fears while never allowing you to feel that you're the one in control.

*Avoidance* is adding insult to injury anxiety. *Exposure* is more like insulting the anxiety injury. Slowly and continually expose yourself to the feared activity or behavior at your own pace. You will feel your anxiety and fear of injury flow, crest, and ebb like worry waves upon the shores of your mind until it inevitably passes.

With regular cumulative exposure, you'll feel more confidence and control, and a realization that consistent, metered training is the best way to avoid injury. The anxiety and fear then begin to lose their effect over you. A pulled muscle is just a muscle that wasn't ready.

They say we attract what we fear, but I never feared debt or sensitive gums. It's critical to start with an activity that you can tolerate and develop self-confidence as you ascend the "fear ladder." Another term for this is "graded exposure,": gradually exposing yourself to the feared situation in a way that allows you to control your fear at each step. It is important to feel the fear, acknowledge its weight, and then gently move forward. That's when you'll realize your fears are bigger in your mind than in reality.

---

### Exercises in Fulfillment: Climb a Fear Ladder to Reach Your Goal

This graded exposure tactic is like the exposure hierarchy in Chapter 6 but follows a slightly different process. Think of an activity or a goal you want to accomplish but are nervous about doing because of injury, like running a mile or driving on the highway. Come up with a fear ladder made up of smaller goals and activities that will allow you to slowly build up to your ultimate objective. A fear ladder is like a corporate ladder, sans the backstabbing.

1. **Build your fear ladder.** Create a list of steps that you can take to gradually build yourself up to a goal or activity you're anxious about. Organize the actions from the least to the most fear provoking. When making the ladder, focus on your end goal (to run a 5k without panicking, for example) and plot the steps accordingly.
2. **Gradually ascend the fear ladder.** As you start the first step, work it until you're comfortable and without anxiety. Try to mindfully remain in the activity. The longer you expose and immerse yourself in your fear, the more you will acclimate, and the less fear you'll have during the next exposure. Only when you can continually complete a step without fear or anxiety, should you move to the next. Any step that feels too hard can be further broken down into smaller activities and done more slowly.

3. **Practice.** You will progress more quickly with more practice. That said, don't be hasty. Stick with a manageable pace that fosters mastery without feeling overwhelmed. Keep in mind that your anxiety will temporarily increase as you confront your fear. Stick with it, and the anxiety will fade. Even doctors are still "practicing medicine."

4. **Know when to stop.** If pain appears, however, get checked out. Phantom and real pain are both valid, common, and anxiety provoking. It's important to understand which pains are normal and which might be a sign of doing too much, too soon. When in doubt, log off Painhub and consult your physician for reassurance.

*Sample Fear Ladder for a Fear of Driving*

1. Stare at your parked car as you hold the keys.
2. Get into the car and position yourself in the driver's seat. Peacefully visualize yourself driving the vehicle for up to 5 minutes.
3. Start the ignition and take a short drive around your neighborhood, making right and left turns.
4. Navigate to a main city street and practice making left turns at intersections.
5. Proceed to the nearest highway and spend time driving in the right lane for a few exits or major intersections.
6. On the same highway, drive in the far-left lane for a few exits or intersections.
7. Lastly, driving on the same highway, change lanes multiple times over the course of a few miles. Use your turn signal because you're courteous and awesome.

When working to alleviate anxiety due to an accident or injury, it's important to note that if your fear is chronic, you can work to make exposure a consistent part of your activities until it becomes habitual. And if you feel ashamed because of your fear, remember that plenty of others are having the same thoughts about the same fears. Helen Keller once said that *"Avoiding danger is no safer in the long run than outright exposure. The fearful are caught as often as the bold."* Grow some bolds.

**Anxiety Safety Briefing: Additional Considerations for Climbing Your Fear Ladder**

When using a fear ladder, there are a few important things to keep in mind:

- Find someone who can support you during your graded exposure exercise if needed.
- Consider the environment – time, location, and so on – in which you confront your fears and how they might make things easier or harder for you.
- Stick with it! You'll eventually have to confront your fear, so may as well do it now.
- If you start feeling overly anxious, try performing a quick mindfulness or relaxation exercise to calm down, like diaphragmatic breathing (inhale through your belly for 4 seconds, hold the breath for 2 seconds, exhale through your nose or pursed lips for 4 seconds, wait a few seconds, and then repeat 4 to 6 times or as needed) or PMR.
- Seek training, guidance, and education in the activity you're undertaking to make you feel more competent and less anxious.
- If you subscribe to the "we attract what we fear" tenet, then fear the Olympic trials.

Here is an example of how to apply these special considerations to driving:

1. **Have a copilot.** Try to take **short trips with someone else in the vehicle** to keep you relaxed. If you find that being a passenger is too difficult or anxiety provoking, replace driving with riding as a passenger on empty streets with someone you trust. You might also find that it's less taxing to sit in the backseat. Once you acclimate to riding along, progress to riding with others on more triggering drives, such as busy freeways or anywhere in Southern California.
2. **Get back on that metal steed.** Many of us are extra anxious to get back in the car and drive after an accident. But you never know when you will need to drive somewhere in an emergency. Furthermore, the longer you wait, the harder it's going to be for you to lose the fear.
3. **Create some ohm in the car.** Create a relaxing setting within the car before you start driving. Calming music helps considerably. Music can sometimes be a negative distraction, but typically

only at high volumes or if it's bagpipes. If you're listening to **soothing music at a low volume, it will help to keep you relaxed** while driving. You're more likely to become uneasy while listening to "Seek & Destroy" by Metallica than while hearing Beethoven's "Moonlight Sonata."

4. **Start with daytime driving.** When you're ready to drive solo, try to avoid driving **anywhere at night** if you're able. Potential hazards are easier to see in daylight. So are "garage sale" and "free puppies" signs.

5. **Take a defensive driving course.** One of the main reasons people are afraid to drive is because they're unsure of their driving skills. You can further your driving game by attending high-performance driving courses that enable you to hone and sharpen your skills behind the wheel of one of the most powerful production cars. In the meantime, don't block the fast lane.

6. **Factors of control.** Oftentimes we must come to terms with the many things entirely outside our control. With driving, for instance, you can't control other drivers or environmental factors such as weather, road conditions, or if your car realizes it's out of warranty and stops rolling. This is the time to challenge yourself to control your response to what's happening. "Jesus, take the wheel."

## Challenge the Negative Thoughts

With fears and anxiety, there's a tendency to overestimate the negative outcome of being exposed to our fear and to underestimate our coping ability. Anxious thoughts that activate and feed fears are typically negative and unrealistic. They often fall into the following categories:

- **Fortune telling.** "This bridge I'm driving across is going to collapse." "I'll get concussed if I try snowboarding again." "If I attend the rock concert, I'll be hurt by a pyrotechnics mishap."
- **Overgeneralization.** "That dog lunged at me. All dogs are toothy beasts." "I got sick once after eating sushi. I'll never be able to eat it again without nose-puking." "This book is the most self-helpy book I've ever read. All self-help books are great."

- **Catastrophizing.** "The pilot said we're about to pass through turbulence. The plane is going to disintegrate, and I'll free-fall into a Kansas wheatfield!" "I'm alone in the house and heard something downstairs. I'm going to be tickle-murdered." "The guy in front of me at the airport is yelling at TSA. I bet he has a machete!"

---

### Modify Your Mindset: Question Your Negative Thoughts

Once you've recognized the specific bad thoughts, analyze them by asking yourself four questions:

1. What evidence is there that opposes your negative thought(s)?
2. What could you do to solve your feared scenario if it does happen?
3. Is your thinking or thought process harming you?
4. How would you advise a friend or loved one who has this same fear?

Here's an example of how to apply these questions to the negative thought, "This bridge I'm driving across is going to collapse."

- **What evidence is there that opposes your negative thought(s)?** "This bridge has never collapsed, nor do many bridges that are in current use. In fact, most of us don't know anyone who knows anyone that's been on a bridge that has collapsed.
- **What could you do to solve your feared scenario if it does happen?** "I could keep my seatbelt on and windows down for the best possible outcome."
- **Is your thinking or thought process harming you?** "Yes. I'm fortune-telling, as there is no evidence to suggest that the bridge can or would collapse, even in an earthquake. I'm not in a Godzilla movie."
- **How would you advise a friend or loved one who has this same fear?** "I would tell a friend that the chances of this or most any bridge collapsing are exceptionally low, especially during the short duration you are actually driving across it. Unless there is in fact a giant, Japanese fictional dinosaur."

### Sometimes You Can Have Gain Without Pain

As a kid, I was adept at backflips off the elevated diving boards at our community pool. Every summer my best friend Shawn and I would sprint barefoot to the pool around the corner and spend the long days swimming and flip-flying from the boards. One afternoon, I didn't spring myself far enough outward, and when I bounced up from the end of the diving board, I went into my reverse flip and came straight back down, head-first onto the board before ineptly falling into the water like a bag of oranges.

### Be a Swan and Dive . . . or Backflip

I wasn't badly hurt, but it rattled me enough that I never tried anything beyond simple jackknifes and cannonballs again. It was a shame because not only did my fear fester and grow over subsequent years, but I spent countless summers after that largely benign incident regretting that I gave in to my injury anxiety. Had I shaken it off that day and returned to the board, I would have continued to excel at the recreational endeavor. Instead, I sidelined myself and remained a lifelong spectator to something I once greatly enjoyed.

One who falls and gets back up is measurably stronger than one who quits – less coordinated and temporarily more awkward, obviously, but stronger.

**Your Anxiety-Trigger Toolkit: Seven Tips for Coping With a Fear of Serious Injury**

1. Learn about the activity you fear will cause injury by reading about it or talking to people who have done it before. Both are effective forms of exposure.
2. Use a fear ladder (aka, graded exposure) to create a list of smaller steps and activities that will slowly build toward your goal. The first step should make you feel somewhat anxious but not overwhelmed, and each later step should gradually build in intensity.
3. Find a supportive partner who can accompany you as you gradually face your fears. Also consider environmental factors like time and location when doing an exposure exercise. Crawling, tears, and apprehension are acceptable. Quitting is not.
4. Always keep in mind the many factors outside your control. Your own hair is a reminder of this fact. You can only do so much in the best of circumstances.
5. Challenge your negative thoughts, whether you're fortune-telling, overgeneralizing, or catastrophizing, by asking yourself four questions: "*Is there any evidence that contradicts my negative thought? Could I do anything to resolve this situation if it does occur? Am I thinking in an unhelpful way? What would I say to a friend who has this fear?*"
6. If you find yourself getting nervous during an exposure activity, try relaxing yourself through diaphragmatic breathing.
7. Recognize when your fear of injury is too much to handle on your own and talk to your doctor or find a mental health professional who can help. Even therapists need therapy.

# 9    Homesickness

DOI: 10.4324/9781003345350-12

Occasionally, I'll Google-Street-view former residences of mine. I don't know why other than it feeds my reminiscence belly. But it's not always a sage activity for me. It can trigger feelings of simpler times with people who are no longer around. Also, California real estate is so egregiously priced, it serves to remind that I'd long ago be retired if I'd bought and held a prior home. Real estate regret is one of my many muses.

Being comfortable with the past or familiar present is not nearly as growth inducing as expanding your world through exploration. Homesickness isn't just for unhappy campers. Being away from home is disorienting and stressful for anyone and is completely normal. But it can also get in your way, become life limiting, and turn into paralyzing anxiety.

Homesickness is a form of anxiety. In small doses, homesickness is a sign of your healthy attachment to loved ones. In more chronic cases, it can be associated with depression, anxiety, and loneliness. It's important to first note that the nostalgia and wistfulness of homesickness is common. It's not a disorder, rather a normal feeling and reaction that fluctuates over time. Moreover, it isn't bound by any timelines. It waxes and wanes and can be short or long lasting, but rarely what anyone on "Gilligan's Island" suffered.

But what is homesickness, exactly? The journal *Pediatrics* defines it as "distress and functional impairment caused by an actual or anticipated separation from home and object attachments such as parents."[1] Everyone and all ages experience homesickness in different ways, but the general theme of homesickness is more likely about missing normality and routine because that's what makes a place feel like "home."

Feelings of being homesick exist when militarily deployed, while on vacation, or as in the focus of this chapter: relocating. Then there is the more profound homesickness for a home to which you cannot return – a home that maybe never was or the nostalgia, the yearning, and the grief for the lost places of your past.

My parents tried to ward off future potential homesickness as a child by dropping me off at malls, amusement parks, and soccer practice while I pondered if or when they might come back. We had only payphones back then, so I wasn't e-tethered to home or most anyone I knew. Coddling is the foe of independence.

The only time I felt a strong sense of homesickness was at 18 when I left California for bootcamp in New Jersey during winter. I'm not sure if I missed home or just loathed a real winter and being awakened at dawn by drill sergeants screaming profanities while banging metal garbage can lids together.

Homesickness is nothing new. It's mentioned in the book of Exodus in the Bible and Homer's "Odyssey," and it happens to nearly everyone

1 Thurber, C. A., & Walton, E. (2007). Preventing and treating homesickness. *Pediatrics*, *119*(1), 192–201.

at some point. The type of homesickness we feel as a kid at camp or a sleepover is petty compared to the kind we experience as adults, which can include leaving for college, losing your home to a natural disaster, or being left for hours on the tarmac at JFK Airport on JetBlue.

## Tactics for Relief: When Google Street View Isn't Enough to Ease the Longing for Your Homies

### *What Does "Home" Even Mean?*

Home is where you most like to poop. In absence of doing the opposite of the homesickness phobia, you face the alternative of living a life that becomes smaller and smaller until you feel paralyzed to venture beyond your mailbox. It becomes a self-perpetuating cycle, to the point that complete avoidance of tactics included herein can result in becoming completely housebound with agoraphobia.

The English word "home" is from the Old English word *hām* (not the kind you add to a pineapple pizza), which refers to "a village or estate where many 'souls' are gathered." It implies there's a physical dwelling involved, but the main idea is that it's a gathering of people. Or of a single person and his or her cats.

"The defining feature of homesickness is recurrent cognitions that are focused on home (e.g., house, loved ones, homeland, home cooking, returning home), and the precipitating stressor is always an anticipated or actual separation from home."[2] The report identified four main risk factors for homesickness: (1) feelings of unfamiliarity brought on by a new experience; (2) your attitude toward the new experience (sometimes expecting to be homesick can bring on a self-fulfilling prophecy); (3) your personality and ability to warm up to new people and situations; and (4) outside factors such as how much you wanted to move in the first place and how your friends and family back home are taking it.

*So why leave home at all?* It feels safe there, and existentially it makes sense that we'd want to stay home and miss home when we leave it. But eventually we must travel for work or pleasure,

---

2  Thurber, C. A., & Walton, E. (2007). Preventing and treating homesickness. *Pediatrics*, *119*(1), 192–201.

or because someone willed us a 19th-century Tudor home before passing away.

*"New country, who dis?"*

Whether for amnesty or sanity, most of us have fantasized about starting an anonymous new life in another country. But it takes courage and an ability to withstand tiny airline seats. When most Americans want to move to another country, we move to Florida.

## Turn Nostalgia Into Your Advantage

According to a study published in the *Personality and Social Psychology Bulletin*, nostalgia fosters social connectedness, which subsequently increases self-esteem, which then boosts optimism. In other words, experiencing nostalgia is fundamentally optimistic and portrays a subjectively positive future.[3] Reminisce no further than making mixed tapes and CDs or when Netflix arrived in the mail to support this premise.

Check in with your own nostalgia to note what aspects of home create joy and then use these to seed your present and future. Do this by recreating the positive facets of what you miss and left behind within your new setting. Do you miss mom's meatloaf? Ask her to forfeit the recipe so you can cook it in your own kitchen. Did you love trivia night at the bar on Wednesdays with your friends? Google local trivia nights near you and go make some new friends and memories. And don't worry, "Taco Tuesday's" are most everywhere. If not, start your own and invite new friends to your improvised taco bar.

## Stay in Touch With Your Own Traditions

Some say that tradition is just peer pressure from the dead. Sure, it's that. But it's also open bars at weddings and presidential turkey pardons in America, the scrambled egg festival in Bosnia, and never showing-up on time in Venezuela. Traditions and routines provide a sense of home and keeping them alive in a new location can help

---

3 Cheung, W.-Y., Wildschut, T., Sedikides, C., Hepper, E. G., Arndt, J., & Vingerhoets, A. J. J. M. (2013). Back to the future: Nostalgia increases optimism. *Personality and Social Psychology Bulletin, 39*(11), 1484–1496.

ground us. For example, as an American abroad, you could celebrate "Friendsgiving" or the Super Bowl. Even if your new friends
are vegans opposed to aggressive sports, they might revel in drinking pints and overeating to a risqué halftime show on the tellie.

Many immigrants to the United States maintain cultural ties and
traditions to their homeland and culture; a practice that serves
many purposes, including the easing of anxiety and homesickness.
Read about your planned move, including the fun parts and the
logistics. Consult maps for a sense of orientation, and Trip Advisor
or Yelp for ideas of your future hangouts. Research and plan activities. Start packing and boxing things well ahead of time to allow for
the unexpected so you can adjust as the time nears.

> *"If someone stops me to ask for directions, I give them direc-
> tions to my house. See you in 20-minutes new best friend."*

Get to know where you are going by perusing Google images
and street views of your new area to learn the terrain. Get a sense
of which parks, eateries, theaters, and districts you're curious about
and which to avoid. Homesickness can also be eased by looking for
what is similar to home. Observe and understand how the locals
do things, and look for similarities, not differences, from home
and you'll find yourself more settled and relaxed. Remember: The
Hawaiian manapua is just the original Hot Pocket.

### Network, Because You Can't Be Your Own Squad

You can make new friends while keeping legacy ones. When feeling
lonely or anxious, it's critical to establish a support network in your
new place. Just ask them to brunch and talk about eyebrow thread-
ing or the history of denim. The simplest way to foster new relationships is to find commonalities in others. And the easiest way to
do that is to pursue events and activities you enjoy that also involve
others. Think bocce, bowling leagues, running or book clubs, after
work networking events, or a corgi fan club.

### Maintain Your Routines as Best You Can

If you are feeling disoriented, create routines you can stick with to
ground you. You can't control this new place, but you have control

over how you spend your time. Do you have breakfast at a particular time? Do you exercise in the morning or evening? Do you text hilarious memes or filtered selfies to your friends while working or using the restroom? Keep doing those things. We feel insecure and anxious when out of our routine. This goes for your companions, whether kids, kittens, or ferrets.

### Anticipate There Will Be Bad Days

Know that some days will just suck. Remember that expectations often lead to disappointments. A helpful form of radical acceptance is to just expect – whether you're on a work trip, vacationing, or relocating – that about one day in seven will be one of those days where things don't go right. Just as you budget yourself financially, budget yourself emotionally for tough days so that, when they happen, they won't hit as hard. These are the days to pause and remember that some of your high school friends are still working in the mall food court to support their garage bands.

### Get Help When You Need It

If you start to feel like nothing you're doing is alleviating the emotional pain and anxiety, seek out a therapist with whom to discuss your feelings and obtain additional tactics for help. This could entail a single session or continuing therapy until the symptoms subside. Accessing therapy via app, phone, or online is easier and more prevalent than at any time in history. You may also benefit from medication in the form of an antianxiety or anti-depression prescription or a sleep aid. Do not self-medicate. A liquor store receipt is not the same as a prescription.

### Think "HALT": Don't Let Yourself Get Too Hungry, Angry, Lonely, or Tired

There's a quick acronym that can help in anxious times and with all aspects of life. In fact, it's a common tactic in 12-step and recovery circles. If you're feeling overwhelmed, think "HALT" to remind yourself to avoid becoming hungry, angry, lonely, or tired. If you can manage these four physical and emotional states, you will be in a better position to manage your anxiety and homesickness.

### Hunger: *Eat Before You Get Hangry and Hanxious*

Sometimes your Lunchable will come with one less cracker than you need. The one thing to be sure to always plan is eating. The hungrier you are, the more likely you are to stress, not think clearly, and get irritable or anxious. It can be difficult to plan meals when stressed and disoriented by a big move; especially in a foreign country or somewhere where familiar food is difficult to find. Taki's and Taco Bell might briefly sustain you, but keep high protein and healthy snacks readily available to nourish your body and brain.

Relocating is partly exhausting because the brain is on overdrive, processing new material and making more decisions than usual. Your brain will tire more quickly than you realize, with a correlating impact on judgment and your ability to process emotions like anxiety. Healthy food and maintaining the meals you did previously is key. For some, stress and anxiety yield a lack of appetite, while others eat their anxiety. Note: If your partner or child tells you they're hungry, it's already too late.

### Anger: *Exhale It*

Traveling and moving are fraught with tiny annoyances. And we often slip into anger and resentment while feeling swamped, particularly as we acclimate to a novel environment. This can trigger a "fight" response that isn't helpful when dealing with new people and circumstances. Whether you're frustrated by a new roommate, a moving company, or a communication problem with the cable guy, unchecked anger will only further impair your judgment. Anger is one letter shy of "danger."

Quickly check in with your emotions when you feel negative mood spikes. Ali Ibn Abu Talib once said that *"A moment of patience in a moment of anger saves you a thousand moments of regret."* If you feel a bout of fury or angst arising, take 1 minute to implement this quick breathing exercise. Otherwise, you risk long-term repercussions of your unchecked emotions.

**Exercises in Fulfillment: One-Minute Reset
Breathing Exercise**

Skip the lavender and try this centering activity On the basis of a slow inhalation and an incremental increase in the length of exhalations.

1. Inhale to the count of two.
2. Exhale to the count of two.
3. Inhale to the count of two.
4. Exhale to the count of three.
5. Inhale to the count of two.
6. Exhale to the count of four.
7. Inhale to the count of two.
8. Exhale to the count of five.

**Loneliness:** *Keep in Touch With Old Acquaintances and Find New Ones*

"Should auld acquaintance be forgot, and never brought to mind?" Many of us like to be alone but hate feeling lonely. But being alone and in your head, a common feeling while in a new and foreign place, can make you feel isolated. As the saying goes, "If your mind is a dangerous neighborhood, don't go there alone." Have a plan for reaching out to family and friends, especially if there's a time difference. Still not the time to send an ex a tiger selfie.

*Status: Table for one, drinks for two.*

But don't wait to reach out. The ride in the car or moving truck to your new place of residence is a great time to call friends and catch up. And the time between dinner and sleep is an opportunity to message or text with someone you haven't contacted in a while. And talk to locals. You don't have to chat up everyone you meet like Forrest Gump, but people generally like to talk about their own area and region and will impart advice you'd never otherwise glean, from the best drycleaner to the worst commutes and nosiest neighbors.

### Tiredness: *Foster Good Sleep Habits*

New bedroom sleep. It's like regular sleep, but without the sleep. Sleep is often an unattainable luxury when moving, traveling, or sleeping anywhere but your own familiar room. A different time zone, and a new bedroom filled with strange sounds and skeletons in the closet that aren't yet yours, can lead to fatigue. Being tired impairs your judgment and the prefrontal cortex, while the rest of your brain won't work to manage impulses, make sound decisions, or appropriately manage emotions.

*"If I fall asleep right now, I'll still get 3.25 hours of sleep."*

It's difficult to develop and keep a good sleep routine in an unfamiliar place, particularly if you're staying there for the long haul. But you can develop new sleep habits or maintain healthy former ones wherever you go. Avoid alcohol and raves before bed, and use the bed for only sleep and not a rumination pad. At bedtime, kids turn into dehydrated conspiracy theorists in search of a debate. Be resolute about bedtime rituals, and steadfastly defend bedtime limits versus anything in footed pajamas. Nothing works on too little sleep. Especially you.

### *The Bags Under My Eyes Are Gucci*

Don't be too ambitious about work or sightseeing your new town if you want to keep your brain in shape to manage potential anxiety. Strike a balance and aim for moderation in all regards. Imagine the breakdown of your total time spent as a pie chart, with equal slices spent on work, sleep, self-care, etc. If any one slice gets too big, you'll feel the instability in the form of anxiety, stress, lethargy, or resentment. Remember that sometimes doing nothing is also a form of productivity.

There's no one failsafe sleep remedy for everyone; especially in a new place. But refer to the sleep tips in Chapters 19 and 21 and know it might take some time to find what works best for you and then to acclimate.

### *Don't Give Homesickness a Timeline*

It's not uncommon to begin feeling homesick before closing the door on your old home and starting the journey toward a new one.

In other instances, the emotions don't hit until you've been in a new place for a while, and the novelty of your environment begins to wane. No matter when the feelings arise, it's key to identify and embrace them for what they are.

Sometimes homesickness never fully wanes. In this sense, homesickness is a lot like grieving for the loss of a loved one: You continue reminiscing about them no matter how much time has passed. When it comes to homesickness, there's no right or wrong way to feel, or right or wrong time for it to manifest. Just as you cannot control its onset, don't fixate on controlling when it subsides. Homesickness isn't an illness, it's a state of mind that shifts with time and where your Wi-Fi automatically connects.

Consider inviting friends from your former home to come visit you. Friends may want to come for a getaway and get to know the area with you. They'll be even more inclined knowing they have a free place to stay. Whether a weekend escape or longer adventure, the planning stage will provide a dual advantage of seeding some excitement about seeing more of your host geography, while also thinking and talking less about the things you miss about home.

### Create a New Routine If and When You're Ready

Ask yourself what you want as your new daily and weekly schedule, and then make it. Don't overlook adding fun and interactive activities into the mix like meeting new acquaintances out for coffee or drinks, attending or participating in midweek sporting events, or sunset hikes. Change doesn't always suck. Remember when you hated spankings?

Research shows that exhibiting and feeling in control leads to less suffering from homesickness, which is vital since homesickness can negatively impact your physical, cognitive, and psychological well-being. And though homesickness occurs across all demographics, risk factors including geographic distance from home, perceived locus of control, and race have been linked to a potential increase in vulnerability to it.[4] You can't control your cowlicks or oftentimes geographic distance, but you can absolutely maintain your locus of control.

---

4 van Tilburg, M. A. L., Vingerhoets, A. J. J. M., & van Heck, G. L. (1996). Homesickness: A review of the literature. *Psychological Medicine, 26*(5), 899–912.

### How to Avoid Mood Poisoning: Don't Spend Too Much Time in Your New Digs

Temper the allure of your home as a retreat and refuge, while keeping in mind that too much time there will intensify your homesickness and make you feel worse. Moreover, the isolation and idle time will likely be used to ponder on what you miss about home. Try to keep busy by organizing day trips, volunteering, reading or studying at cafes, vino painting, or trying out extracurricular activities rather than staying in your abode, despite the allure of naps and the metaverse.

### Bring Along Home Comforts, Even Seemingly Insignificant Items

Whether it's your Pokémon blanket, lava lamp, or a leather NASCAR jacket, we all have objects that cheer us up while feeling down. When my parents sold my childhood home in 2020 and gave most everything away, I lacked space in my condo to take anything from our house. This initially spiked my anxiety about losing such a long-term sense of home, as there were so many things I wanted, like my mom's first car, a garaged 1941 Ford coupe.

On the day they left the house forever, I went into the backyard and took only three rocks – one a small stone from atop the memorial of our German Shepherds, another from the rose garden my mom enjoyed for decades, and the last, a small stone in the space below where our tree house had stood. These relics appear worthless to anyone else. To me, they serve as priceless remnants that prompt a flood of memories of "home" upon touch. And rocks are less triggering than social media "you have memories" prompts.

### Keep Healthy and Don't Numb Your Fears

Don't make unpacking a drinking game. Remember that alcohol, shopping, gambling, and so on are ineffective, temporary fixes that won't get you over or through feelings of homesickness. At most, they serve to briefly numb and distract while leading you toward a dependence on useless coping strategies. And you're also numbing the good stuff.

## Make a Bucket List for Exploring Your New Geography

One of the downsides about being somewhere too long is that we often take the atmosphere and all it has to offer for granted. Having been born in San Francisco and raised in Oakland and the East Bay, I'm ashamed of how little I visit some of the countless gems in my immediate area. I haven't been to Angel Island since I was a kid, I've never oyster-shucked in Tomales Bay, and I should know more about Jack London and Jack Kerouac than visiting the same local bars they did.

Research the new area where you live and make a list of places you absolutely must visit that are tied to your interests. These could be hiking or biking trails, the local art scene, or the best architecture. Challenge yourself to do or see all of them as you stay focused on creating adventure and discovery where you are, rather than ruminating on what's going on elsewhere, such as back home. Cattle ruminate, but they still love new pastures.

However, remember to not overextend on your acclimatization. Putting too much pressure on yourself to adapt to your new environment can leave you feeling more anxious and exhausted. Take your time and spread out these activities as much as you need so that you can adapt at a comfortable pace. Even plants and goldfish must slowly adapt to new settings.

## Take Your Cat, Old Doormat, and Showerhead With You

You used to run away from home for attention. Moving is the adult, expensive version. But you can be at home no matter where you are. And feelings of homesickness that remain even *after* adapting are perfectly normal and healthy.

### Your Anxiety-Trigger Toolkit: Seven Tips for Coping With Homesickness

1.  You can still embrace modernity and keep in touch with traditions and rituals from your old home while creating your own (e.g., foosball Fridays, moqueca Mondays, trivia Tuesdays, self-expression Sundays, a day for art and creativity).
2.  Maintain your old routines in a new location to give yourself a sense of stability. If you're used to doing daily activities at a regular time, maintain that schedule.
3.  Adjusting to a new environment is tough, and some days will be harder than others. Accept this as perfectly normal and part of the long-term adjustment, though the process goes quicker in absence of finding a former tenant's hair in your new bathroom.
4.  Think "HALT" and avoid becoming too hungry, angry, lonely, and tired. If you find ways to manage these emotional and physical states, you will be in a better position to adjust to your new surroundings. HALT also works when you're not relocating.
5.  Homesickness has no timeline, so don't force one on yourself. Unexpected feelings can come up at any time, even years after a big transition. Catching feelings is all part of it.
6.  Building new routines when you're ready can help you feel more in control of your new environment. Try something that will give you a sense of mastery and self-competence.
7.  Create a list of places you would like to see and explore by foot, bike, or car. Don't overindulge in unhealthy activities that will leave you less mentally and physically able to cope with homesickness. Binge on your new life.

# Part III

# Social Anxiety Disorder

My brother, Jeff, and I were adopted as toddlers from separate families. After many years, we came to resemble one another, like an owner to his dog. There is one remarkably divergent characteristic, however: Jeff lacks my superpowers of anxiety and neuroticism.

Looking back, I realize that even outsiders saw me as the naturally sensitive one. I recall the anomaly of the first albums we ever owned, which were gifts from our aunt one Christmas. Jeff received Black Sabbath's, "Sabbath Bloody Sabbath," whereas I was the proud recipient of ABBA's "The Magic of ABBA."

Jeff's subsequent albums were from AC/DC and Iron Maiden. *My next two albums?* Barry Manilow and Christopher Cross. Soon thereafter, I joined the city boy's chorus and the Presbyterian Church Hand Bell Choir. I was soon standing in our city park's gazebo clad in polyester pants among other budding child superstars, wailing tunes of enchantment and piety.

*My brother?* He was at home with a self-constructed drum set fashioned from old paint buckets, while bellowing rock tunes in the backyard. I would only look upon him disapprovingly, while crooning, "*Mamma Mia, here I go again . . .* " My lyrics fell dead upon the banging plastic of my brother's improvised drum set.

This prepubescent phase was my totality in the limelight before ending at age 13. I soon hung up my taupe suede vest and tambourine and soothed myself in 80's rock and dodging crowds larger than four people. On those occasions where I saturate myself in other humans, I strive for a recuperative period until I can bear it again. Whereas you can find my brother waiting for his next chance to be pressed against the stage at a rock concert in an urban downtown stadium somewhere. We play to our strengths.

DOI: 10.4324/9781003345350-13

# 10  Going Out

DOI: 10.4324/9781003345350-14

At home and on social media you're an extroverted badass. In public, you become an isolationist dodging eye contact and teethy handshakes, with a tendency toward agoraphobia and a general excitement over cancelled plans.

*"Just go on without me. I'll be here reading into things."*

The most common of all the anxiety disorders, social anxiety is an extreme fear of being scrutinized and judged by others in social or performance situations. A little social worry is normal for everyone. But when social anxiety gets outsized, it's a self-serving narcissist hell-bent on your full attention. Social anxiety is the third largest mental health disorder in the world. But despite the statistics, you don't need to be part of the antisocial club.

## When Your Favorite Party Trick Is Not Going

Social anxiety disorder is an enigma in that it comprises a general distaste for peopling, with an opposing internal need for people. But on your terms, and in limited doses. The upside of social anxiety is saving money on the fun things you would otherwise go out and do. The downside includes a sadistic focus on all the things that can go wrong, nervously blurting everything you never wanted to say aloud to fill conversational lulls, and performing extensive post-interaction analyses to scrutinize your perceived collective flaws.

Perhaps you get anxious during long pauses in a conversation. Even a few moments feel far too angst-ridden, so you fill the void with a non-sequitur about your botched hysterectomy, or you ask your boss how his divorce is going. Your attempts at social stimulus are met with side eyes. And silence.

Or maybe you occasionally freak out when texting someone you like and not hearing back for a while. Your rumination and worry churns into resounding panic, yielding a volley of additional texts, all met with successive silence. Next you concoct a series of worst-case scenarios about why they're not responding to you; not limited to them driving through a guardrail and off a cliff while reading your original text or deciding they don't like you. And just as you're texting a coup de grâce, they finally reply. It's like the heavens opened and gossamer-winged angels descend upon you because it came with a heart emoji.

## How Does One Get Social Anxiety?

Social anxiety is contagious. Sort of. Researchers are learning that anxiety disorders run in families and that they have a biological basis, much like allergies, diabetes, and balding.[1] Anxiety disorders typically develop from a complex set of risk factors that include genetics, brain chemistry, personality, and life experiences.

## Neurosis Loves Company: Social Anxiety by the Numbers

Anxiety is the most common mental illness for adults, and the number one mental health issue in North America.[2] And of all the anxiety disorders, social anxiety is the most common, with 15 million American adults suffering a social anxiety disorder, or 13 out of every 100 people.[3] The malady is equally common among men and women and typically begins around age 13 – the age kids begin needing social skills more than ever. Life is a conflict diamond.

### Tactics for Relief: How to Go Big Instead of Going Home

We live in a time when it's annoying if someone calls rather than texts. And this was before a pandemic arose separating the introverts from the socially anxious and giving us a reason to stay home, rather than forcing us out to dodge conversations by staring at our phones. All of this seemingly supports a rationale for keeping a blank social calendar. However, you no longer need to be a "can't person" or left pondering something embarrassing you did 17 years ago, certain everyone else is still thinking about it too.

#### *Throw a Counterpunch*

Do not give in to what the anxiety is driving you to do. Instead, acknowledge and rebuke it. *"Hey, inner angst, I'm the shot caller and I came to party."* Or at least go out and make your best,

---

1 Telman, L., van Steensel, F., Maric, M., & Bögels, S. M. (2018). What are the odds of anxiety disorders running in families? A family study of anxiety disorders in mothers, fathers, and siblings of children with anxiety disorders. *European Child & Adolescent Psychiatry, 27*(5), 615–624.
2 Mental Health America. (2022, October 20). *Number of people reporting anxiety and depression nationwide since start of pandemic hits all-time high in September, hitting young people hardest.* Mental Health America (mhanational.org).
3 Anxiety and Depression Association of America. (2020, June 18). Facts & statistics. *AADA.* https://adaa.org/about-adaa/press-room/facts-statistics

open-minded attempt. You don't have to lead a conga line or Tik-Tok the Kangsta Wok. Each time you parry your fear, you are "rewiring" your brain and weakening anxiety's hold on you.

Social anxiety leads to isolation, which leads to increased risk for alcohol abuse, depression, loneliness, decreased occupational advancement, and the increased likelihood of remaining isolated. Fortunately, most peer socialization doesn't end like *Lord of the Flies*.

### Expose Yourself

If you test positive for "avoidance," consider that studies reveal the efficacy of exposure-based therapies for anxiety disorders, as summarized in several published meta-analyses.[4]

It's common to put more effort into avoidance than the activity or behavior itself would require. You don't need to drive to the Target two towns away to avoid possibly seeing an acquaintance. Expose rather than avoid by creating an exposure hierarchy. Write down scenarios that cause you anxiety in order of severity. Perform the easiest behavior first and move down the list. Your hierarchy might start with asking a stranger for directions, and end with asking your boss for a raise. It doesn't matter if she laughs you out the door. It matters that you asked. Social anxiety wants you timid. And poor.

### Become an Askhole

Asking questions makes for great social lubricant when you otherwise have nothing to say in a social setting. Ask open-ended questions such as *"How do you know the host?"* or *"What are your favorite books?"* or *"What is the physics formula for social tension?"* Alternatively, try soliciting advice by asking something like *"Does anyone have movie/pet-sitter/Pad Thai recommendations?"* *"How do you typically spend your weekends?"* These are easy ones. Ask follow-up questions that take the conversation deeper, such as *"Oh, I want to hear more about that"* (whether you do or not) or *"What was that like?"* or the therapist default, *"And how did that make you feel?"* Asking where the restroom or bourbon is

---

4 Steinman, S., Wootton, B., & Tolin, D. (2016). Exposure therapy for anxiety disorders. *Encyclopedia of Mental Health*, 186–191.

located or when the party ends doesn't count. But if you panic and your brain blanks on questions, carry a copy of your favorite questions on your phone and steal a glance when needed.

### Give Yourself License to Chill

The more you worry and let anxiety rule your days, the more you literally program your brain to continue worrying and being anxious, while continually linking anxiety to specific events. Instead, consider yoga, tai chi, or visualization to prepare yourself. Incorporate the proven technique of visualization. Create a mental picture of relaxing. It could be at a beach sunset, watching a forest gently sway to a breeze, leaves falling silently in your backyard, and so on. When you visualize, engage your other senses as well. What does the place smell and feel like? What do you hear? Do it every day for long enough until you can approach someone in a long hallway and not panic wondering when to begin eye contact.

Insecurity is part of the human condition. It's texting your partner on your wedding day asking, "*Hey, are we still on for today?*" Your insecurities are also what mean people memorize and use against you in later arguments. A small amount of insecurity or self-doubt is helpful because it leads to introspection and growth. And lacking all self-doubt is a troubling sign, while a complete lack of social anxiety is indicative of psychopathy. But you don't need to live in a maximum insecurity prison.

The most common problem for people with social anxiety disorder is depression, followed by other forms of anxiety disorders such as GAD or panic disorder.

With social anxiety, if you go out, you'll want to come home, but if you stay home, you'll want to go out. The key is to gradually challenge these maladaptive thinking patterns by exposing yourself to social situations often and for longer periods of time so you can see that nothing bad is occurring.

It's tough to be present and enjoy life if while engaging with others you're constantly asking yourself, *Could they tell I was feeling anxious? Did they think what I said was stupid? Did they think I was stupid?* You can never really know what someone else thinks of you. Rather than worrying about it, focus on what you want to convey, such as asking good questions and maintaining sustained self-assuredness. Before you know it, you'll be holding regular rear-view mirror eye contact with your Uber drivers.

### Silence "Boo"

Boo is the cruel cynic in your head relentlessly booing you and filling you with worry and doubt. Dispute boo's negative rants with truths such as (1) you are more than capable of nailing the upcoming marathon/wedding toast/hostage negotiation; (2) there are at least as many reasons things will go right for you; and (3) you are competent, skilled, and deserve to be happy. Boo's a lieclops.

### Stop Giving a #%@! What Others Think

Social anxiety is tied to feelings of being judged. The judgments and opinions of others have no reflection on your worth or talents. Most people are too busy wondering what others are thinking about *them* to be thinking about you. What others think about you is none of your business. Social anxiety treatment includes learning to be flawed, while detaching approval from external sources. Being a perfectionist is fine in quantum physics, but not when bringing Chex™ Mix to game night.

Opinions are not facts. How can other people know you better than you do? According to an American Psychological Association study, we consistently overestimate how much, and how badly others think of us, causing us to be more inhibited and less impulsive and happy than we could be.[5] In 2006 scientists declared that Pluto is no longer a planet. Despite their judgment, Pluto never wavered and keeps revolving around the Sun like it has for billions of years. Be a Pluto.

### Press Lever for Snack

Upvote yourself. Rather than berating yourself in post-interaction analysis, practice self-reward. Commend yourself for attending the event, for being present, and for facing down your anxiety. You are taking back your life one endeavor at a time. A tenet of

---

5 Savitsky, K., Epley, N., & Gilovich, T. (2001). Do others judge us as harshly as we think? Overestimating the impact of our failures, shortcomings, and mishaps. *Journal of Personality and Social Psychology, 81*(1), 44–56.

CBT is the importance of rewarding yourself for exposure to your fears. You deserve the adulation, and you will be more motivated to do it again if there are some self-high-fives or new shoes on the back end.

Recall that your mind and body are inherently linked. There is ever increasing evidence that how you treat your body can have a significant effect on your anxiety levels, your ability to manage anxiety symptoms, and your overall self-assurance. Dopamine is the brain's reward chemical. You hack it by doing some self-care. Get the massage, order the movie in HD, have the cake, buy the thing. Just don't reward yourself with something that will create more future work; like upgrading your lifestyle or residence. Buying an RV as reward for attending a BBQ is skewed and will yield joy until you have to park it. Think smaller rewards more often. Pastries, not ponies.

### Check Your Flow and Redirect Your Field of Vision

"*Hocus pocus, you just lost your focus.*" When you're in a social situation that makes you anxious, your focus is likely on your own anxious thoughts, sensations, and your distorted perceptions that others may have about you. But this inward focus is counterproductive and debilitating. Since you cannot be attentive to two things at once, swap your focus from internal to external to dramatically reduce anxiety. Just observe. Shifting your focus to what's going on around you versus within you will lessen the effects of anxiety. Move your attention to other people, engaging them and establishing connections, rather than on your own thoughts. Truth is, other people are often just as nervous or anxious as you are. You're not the only one who gets spinach in your teeth.

### Stop. Collaborate, and Listen

But listen with intent. Not the kind of listening we do in line at a Walmart while someone is trying to return an 8-year-old mattress. But mindfully listening to what is being said without worrying about your follow-up reply, or how your last statement fell short in some way. You can't listen to your irrational thoughts if you're actively listening to someone else. Focus on the present moment and strive to be genuinely attentive.

*Face It Till You Make It*

If it scares you, it's likely because you need to confront it. The more you avoid social interactions, the more anxiety riddling they become. Also, avoidance prevents you from doing things you'd enjoy, or attaining desired goals, like making new friends or doing improv comedy.

But don't take on your greatest fears straight away. Refer back to the exposure hierarchy and start with a situation that you can handle and increasingly work your way up to more daunting scenarios, while increasing your confidence and technique as you scale the "social anxiety exposure ladder." You can start by accompanying a friend to a small gathering. Once you're comfortable with that step, you might try going solo to an event or attending a larger event like Oktoberfest in Munich or to Costco.

*Plug Your Nose*

Try alternate nostril breathing. This is a simple, natural breathing technique for managing stress and anxiety. I use this often while driving in California traffic, and it works like a sinus charm. According to Ayurvedic medicine, alternate nostril breathing brings the body and mind into a state of balance and neutrality and has been used by elite athletes and authors for decades.

---

### Exercises in Fulfillment: How to Do Alternate Nostril Breathing

1. Close one nostril by placing your thumb gently over it.
2. Breathe out then in through the uncovered nostril.
3. After each breath cycle, switch sides. A breath cycle is one out-breath and one in-breath.
4. Leading with your out-breath, do one out-breath followed by one in-breath through each nostril.
5. Repeat this series, alternating nostrils after each inhalation.

It will likely be easier to breathe through one nostril than the other. You're not deformed; it's normal.

*Pump-up Your Jam*

Pick a mantra, slogan, or verse to rouse yourself prior to an event or performance. To get motivated to conquer a sale or a village, consider AC/DC's "For Those About to Rock." Find your own song or chant that calms or instills confidence as you head to a gathering or performance. Alternatively, Philippians 4:6 is an example calming scripture: *"Do not be anxious about anything, but in every situation, by prayer and petition, with thanksgiving, present your requests to God."* Remember, anticipation of a worrisome social situation is usually worse than the actual event. Unless it's going to prison. Or to Disneyland.

See your doctor or a mental health provider if anxiety disrupts your life or daily activities. You may need treatment to get better. Like a receding hairline, social anxiety happens gradually and initially without much notice. Cognitive behavioral therapy is an effective treatment for social anxiety. Self-medicating is not.

### Your Anxiety-Trigger Toolkit: 12 Tactics to Become Your Own Best Social Chairperson

1. Ask only open-ended questions to spur conversation and allay social awkwardness. No "yes" or "no" types like "*When regular dogs see police dogs do they think, 'Oh no, it's a cop.'?*"
2. Use visualization to relax, by creating a serene mental picture while engaging all of your senses. It's like a mental, scratch-n-sniff coloring book.
3. Challenge maladaptive thinking patterns by exposing yourself to social situations often and for longer periods of time. It's the social equivalent of tanning.
4. Silence your inner critic by recognizing it, then challenging and reframing the twisted chatter. *What evidence is there? Could the opposite of the insight also be possible? Yes!* Convert your inner doomsayer into an inner oracle.
5. Detach from the approval of all external sources. Opinions are not facts. Even when they're yelled.
6. Commend yourself for attending an event, for being present, and for facing down your anxiety. Even if you didn't have fun.
7. Shifting your focus to what's going on *around* you versus *within* you will lessen the effects of anxiety. And the effect will be immediate, like hairspray.
8. When socializing, listen to others with intent and without worrying about your follow-up reply or about your last comment. Anxiety is an internal narcissist.
9. Use the exposure hierarchy while increasing your confidence and technique as you scale the "social anxiety exposure ladder." Little tyke steps are key.
10. Implement alternate nostril breathing to quickly manage stress and anxiety. Start with clean hands.
11. Regularly rehearse and recite a significant mantra to rouse yourself prior to a social event or performance. Remember that the anticipation of a social situation is worse than the actual event.
12. See your doctor or a mental health provider if anxiety disrupts your life or daily activities. If you even wonder if you might benefit from help, get it.

# 11 Social Media

DOI: 10.4324/9781003345350-15

It's called a "selfie" because "narcissistie" is too hard to spell. You are far more than the sum of your followers. And you can do much more with eccentric thoughts than turn them into tweets. There is considerable peace in staying grounded in the offline world.

## The Upside/Downside of Social Media Use

My generation grew up in an era not known for leaps in technological advances. The lack of fun, lithium-ion-powered iThings forced us to engage in odd traditions like going outside, playing with other kids, or reading. Living offline allowed us to keep screwups to limited audiences. Today we often perceive anyone who shuns social media as old or uncivilized. However, they might be the most mentally fit among us.

This is notably true when you consider social media during breakup or divorce recovery, which was far less grueling when the world was offline. Before social media, breaking up was a discrete event. **A split used to occur when phones were dumb** and **tethered to a fixed wall.** Imagine a time when you answered every call hoping it was your ex calling to make up, but it was Aunt Edna asking if you wanted ambrosia salad for Sunday brunch. Today the media crumbs are forever memorialized in the cloud.

*"Maybe if I fall in love with my anxiety, it will leave me too."*

Most people have little awareness of the frequency with which they check their phone. In one 2022 study, Americans were checking their phones an average of 344 times per day.[1] That's once every 4 minutes. This is concerning because several studies and researchers have associated social networking with several psychiatric disorders, including depressive symptoms, anxiety, and low self-esteem.[2] We're prisoners to our phones; that's why they're called "cell" phones.

### *Stop Deleting Your Mental Health to Focus on Social Media*

Social media brings us closer to people who are distant, but distant from the people who are close. But you have options beyond removing all social media to preserve your mental health, only to redownload the apps 3 hours later because of #FOMO or a sense of being cut off from humanity. Years ago, I had an epiphany to delete hundreds of people from Meta and the Gram. It was one of the most cathartic hours of my life knowing I'd never again see their manipulated selfies and banal posts about nothing.

1 Wheelwright, T., Wheelwright, T., Buchi, C., McNally, C., Sandorf, B., & Buchi, C. (2022, January 24). 2022 Cell phone usage statistics: How obsessed are we? *Reviews. Org.* www.reviews.org/mobile/cell-phone-addiction/
2 Pantic, I. (2014). Online social networking and mental health. *Cyberpsychology, Behavior and Social Networking, 17*(10), 652–657.

Hours later, however, an irrational panic set in that I somehow needed those faux chums. I spent the next few hours trying to recall everyone I had unfriended and then awkwardly invite them back to my network as if nothing occurred. "*I was a different person back then. Please come back.*" My memory had my best interests in mind, however, and I could only recall a fraction of those I relegated to the ethosphere. I had to live with my virtual shearing of hundreds of former non-friends, never to see their humblebrags, "*he's my king*" relationship statuses, filtered sunset pics, and barfy "*Thank you for all the birthday wishes*" posts as weak attempts to garner more birthday posts.

> "*How scary would it be if everything that popped into people's heads was automatically posted to social media? Because it is.*"

All research studies and clinical data aside, ask yourself right now how you typically feel during and immediately after scrolling social media feeds. *Happier? Exuberant? Fulfilled? Peaceful? Wiser?* Unlikely. You probably feel like you just mainlined eight sleeves of Oreos into your brain. Since 2008, I've not once felt better after perusing social media. Conversely, it's a nasty habit like chewing my cuticles. It feels good in the moment until I'm left cursing and bleeding for 10 minutes into a platelet-affixed napkin wrapped around my finger. #ThesePeopleArentEvenActualFriends

## Tactics for Relief: How to Digitally Cull and Detox Your Life

Consider these ten lesser-known pro and con stances regarding social media use:

### Pros

1. Messaging on social media sites leads to face-to-face interactions when plans are made via the sites.
2. Social media increases voter participation and facilitates political change.
3. Social media helps reduce loneliness of senior citizens who are socially isolated.
4. Social media allows for quick diffusion of public health and safety information during crisis events.
5. The U.S. military and Department of Veterans Affairs use social media to help prevent suicide.
6. Social media can help disarm social stigmas like anxiety or depression.

7. Crowdsourcing on social media allows people to attain a goal, thereby empowering users to achieve positive change.
8. Social media provides academic research to a wider audience, allowing people access to previously inaccessible educational resources.
9. Social media sites can help improve overall well-being by providing users with a large social group creating a "contagion" effect.
10. Professional networking sites greatly assist companies to find personnel and job seekers to find work.

### Cons

1. Social media posts cannot be entirely deleted.
2. Social media can endanger our military, journalists, and activists.
3. Social media use is associated with personality and brain disorders.[3]
4. Students who are heavy social media users tend to have lower grades.
5. Social media can exacerbate feelings of disconnect and put children at higher risk for anxiety, depression, low self-esteem, eating disorders, and even suicide.[4]
6. Criminals use social media to commit and promote crimes.
7. Social media can be a sunk cost in time that adds up.
8. Advertising practices of social media sites create an invasion of privacy.
9. Social media facilitates sexting, which can lead to revenge porn, criminal charges, and a proliferation of personal images.
10. Social media use can cause personality and brain disorders, ADHD, and self-centered personalities, particularly in youth.[5]

If the preceding review of pros and cons leave you confused as to how often you should thumb-scroll, you're not alone. But know this: Most people experience huge benefits from taking a social media break. The more grounded you are in your identity, the less

3 Pantic I. (2014). Online social networking and mental health. *Cyberpsychology, Behavior and Social Networking, 17*(10), 652–657.
4 Seabrook, E. M., Kern, M. L., & Rickard, N. S. (2016). Social networking sites, depression, and anxiety: A systematic review. *JMIR Mental Health, 3*(4), e50.
5 Sherman, L. E., Payton, A. A., Hernandez, L. M., Greenfield, P. M., & Dapretto, M. (2016). The power of the *Like* in adolescence. *Psychological Science, 27*(7), 1027–1035.

likely you are to be a heavy user of social media and to be negatively affected by it. For example, if you know that you are more
than how many likes and comments you receive to a given post,
then you are probably social media resilient. You probably don't
mind dental deep cleanings or sunburns either.

*Temporarily Closed for Mental Maintenance*

However, if you struggle with feelings of insecurity or find yourself
putting much time and effort into depicting yourself a certain way on
social media, then you are more vulnerable and would profoundly
benefit from regular breaks. This will provide the space needed to
move away from a false self and toward your true self. Start with a
1-week break and take it from there. You'll likely find an immediate
boost in your mental health, better sleep patterns, increased productivity, decreased depression and anxiety, and shorter restroom
breaks. And you don't need to post on social media that you're taking a break from social media.

---

**Anxiety Safety Briefing: When to Take a Social
Media Sabbatical**

1. You check your feeds before falling asleep and upon waking.
2. You scroll unconsciously and near incessantly.
3. You procrastinate completing work or tending to family.
4. You compare yourself or your life to others.
5. You feel worse afterward.
6. You constantly monitor the amount of views, likes, shares,
   upvotes, and so on.
7. You hoard connections.
8. Your thumb breaks off.

---

Limit yourself to 15 minutes of social media each day; less if you
note a mood decrease with usage, which most people do. While it
can be hard to go cold turkey, start small to reduce social media

time, especially on the sites that make you the most miserable/jealous/anxious/depressed/annoyed, and evaluate from there. Offline is peace of mind.

---

### Modify Your Mindset: Shortcuts to Wean From the Social Media Teat

*Simple Tactics to Curb Usage and Feel the Positive Effects*

- Start by putting the worst offending apps at the end of the list or within a less accessible grouping on your phone screen and shut off the related notifications.
- Keep yourself logged out, so it takes more effort to check and isn't as frictionless.
- Use software to block hours on your apps. Chris has his phone and computer set to cut him off between 8 p.m. and 8 a.m.
- Consider taking the social media apps off your phone altogether. If you access them solely via computer, you're far less likely to compulsively check while working, in the bathroom, at the dinner table, in bed, or while reading this.
- If you need to use social media for work, keep your work account active and accessible, but make your personal accounts less accessible.
- Assess how much you truly miss it, while considering the recent benefits, and try a break of a weekend, a week, or longer. Savor your newfound freedom.

---

Track your emotions in real time as you scroll. This can help you notice the effect that social media has on your moods. Seriously, try it. Notice how you're feeling at this moment and then pick up your phone and open one of your social media apps. Consider the little red alerts, which are specifically designed to make you anxious, by the way.

> *"Remember, most social media engagement is done from the toilet."*

Read and review the first few posts or pictures you see within your feed as you scroll and identify and name your initial emotional reaction. Reflect on this feeling a few moments, then close the app and notice how you feel afterward. Usually it goes something like this:

- Photo of someone's cute kid – *Alright lady, that's like the 17th picture of your kid eating spaghetti. It's too much. And gross.*
- Friend at the beach – *Jealousy. I hope it rains.*
- Friends at a party – *Wait, why wasn't I invited?*
- Random person from high school you weren't even friends with, and will never see again, posting a lame meme about your favorite sports team – *What a pud. I'd delete him, but I need to maintain my "friends" count.*
- Depressing news story – *Ugh, I'm sad and worried.*
- Troll-y political post related to bipartisan news story – *Screw that guy for not believing as I do!*

You now close your social media app feeling far worse than when you started. Then you notice red notifications on a different social media app. Repeat process. Feel even worse. Check back in after 2 hours.

### What Can You Do Right Now Instead?

*Why All the talk of "the Now?"* As you may have noticed, there seems to be a focus on "living in the now" (aka, mindfulness) to help with mental health. Sound anxiety relief advice will include "staying in the moment": Don't drift, don't let your mind wander, and stop "what-iffing" about the future. *Do* stay focused, *do* be attuned to yourself and your surroundings, and *do* get intensely interested in the now. If mindfulness was a 1912 band, it would be Wallace Hartley's orchestra playing "Nearer My God to Thee" as the Titanic tilted and sank while people ran wild.

> *"Don't just do something. Sit there!"*

From a logical standpoint you can't be in the "now" all the time. Sometimes you must think about the future. You know, for those eccentric tasks like paying your bills or planning around traffic so you're not late somewhere. So it seems like the advice that is supposed to help you feel better is contradictory to functioning in our daily lives. The nuance, however, is to focus on the now whenever possible and helpful to do so. Planning for retirement? Not the moment to join the "live in the now" movement. Another way to look at it is to become focused on the now when you are feeling overwhelmed and need to take a quick mental break. *Did you just realize that you're part of the last generation whose baby pics weren't taken on phones?* That's a mindful moment to ponder while in the now.

### Why Does It Work?

There is a steadfast method to the way our brains work regarding thoughts. If you think about the past, you become sad or even depressed. If you think about the future, you become anxious. But if you focus only on the present, things feel better. This was abundantly simpler prior to cellphones when people lived in the moment rather than recording it.

Recognizing that you are having a thought gives you greater control over your current emotional state and makes the moment more tolerable. An interesting facet of reading social media posts is that it often leads your thinking into the past, future, or anywhere you aren't right now. Your life is only ever now.

### Get out There IRL and Do Something

Have you ever noticed that doing activities with a friend helps reduce the anxiety that flares up in face-to-face interactions? Running, building, hiking, whatever it might be when we are next to each other, we often relax enough to just let the conversation flow.

Humans, particularly guys, are hardwired to perceive face-to-face interactions as potentially threatening. Chris accentuates this is why therapy with guys is often hard. Things like eye contact can signal a challenge. Get away from directly sitting across from one another and do some side-by-side activities. Think about those male stereotypes of fathers and sons working on the car together, building something, or fishing side by side. Veiled threat averted.

### What Would You Be Doing If You Weren't Feeling Anxious? Do That

When you're feeling anxious, it's helpful to focus on purposeful, goal-directed activities. If you were planning to go shopping or grab coffee somewhere, stick to it. You will feel markedly better if you, not your anxiety, are making the decisions and following through. You might still feel anxious, but you won't be stymied, passive, and powerless.

### Every Day Is Leg Day When You're Running From Your Problems

Don't work out just so you can tell people you work out. Work out because there is copious research proving that working the body greatly benefits the brain. This isn't about vanity; it's about vanquishing anxiety, depression, and self-doubt. Looking better naked is merely a byproduct.

In radical candor, I struggle with the reality that each time I burn 600 calories on my spin bike, I eat 600 calories in my kitchen . . . from riding my spin bike. It's a zero-sum game. I remind myself that I'm working out for my heart and mind and that abs are made in the kitchen. I've also accepted that a one pack is safer in a fall.

Not only is there strong evidence to support that 2–2.5 hours of moderate to high-intensity exercise per week is sufficient to reduce one's risk for the occurrence of chronic disease(s), but numerous epidemiological studies have also shown that exercise improves one's self-esteem, sense of well-being, and slows rates of age-related memory and cognitive decline in comparison to those who are more sedentary.[6] Adults who engage in regular physical activity experience fewer depressive and anxiety symptoms, thus supporting the notion that exercise offers a protective effect against the development of mental disorders.[7] Humans were made for activity and human interaction for survival. We're not koala bears.

### But There's a Caveat

Firstly, a brief lesson in "state" versus "trait" anxiety. State anxiety is a temporary emotional response involving unpleasant feelings of tension and fearful thoughts, while trait anxiety refers to a trait of personality, or the likelihood that someone will experience state anxiety in a stressful situation.

6 Anderson, E., & Shivakumar, G. (2013). Effects of exercise and physical activity on anxiety. *Frontiers in Psychiatry*, 4, 27.
7 Ibid.

Now, back to the exercise stipulation. If you have anxiety and enjoy lengthy or permanent phases of idleness, a study found that distraction techniques such as meditation and quiet rest were as effective as a single session of exercise in reducing state anxiety. Exercise and cognitively based distraction techniques were shown to have *equal* effectiveness at reducing *state* anxiety, but exercise was more effective in reducing *trait* anxiety.[8] Additionally, the anxiolytic (aka, anti-anxiety) effects of exercise are shown to last for a longer period than those produced by therapies on the basis of distraction techniques.[9]

### You Are Your Ultimate Social Chairperson

Anxiety often feels like chilling on an iceberg and suddenly getting "Titanic" Wi-Fi, while social anxiety is nothing more than indulging conspiracy theories about yourself. What's important is that you do something other than ruminate, obsess, or otherwise dwell on what the anxiety is prompting you to do, which is typically to feed your anxious thoughts.

8 Petruzzello, S. J., Landers, D. M., Hatfield, B. D., Kubitz, K. A., & Salazar, W. (1991). A meta-analysis on the anxiety-reducing effects of acute and chronic exercise. *Sports Medicine, 11*(3), 143–182.
9 Stubbs, B., Vancampfort, D., Rosenbaum, S., Firth, J., Cosco, T., Veronese, N., Salum, G. A., & Schuch, F. B. (2017). An examination of the anxiolytic effects of exercise for people with anxiety and stress-related disorders: A meta-analysis. *Psychiatry Research, 249*, 102–108.

## Your Anxiety-Trigger Toolkit: Seven Tactics to Answer Calls Instead of Googling the Missed Numbers

1.  What happens on social media stays in the cache forever. Social media is a great place to proclaim your thoughts to the world before you've considered them yourself.
2.  If you put considerable time and effort into depicting yourself a certain way on social media, then you are more vulnerable and would profoundly benefit from regular breaks. Start with 1 week. Remember: "social media" is an oxymoron.
3.  Track your emotions in real time as you scroll and notice the effect that social media has on your mood. Reflect on this feeling a few moments, then close the app, and notice how you feel a few minutes later. Hint: It will likely be "less triggered."
4.  A key component of anxiety relief includes "staying in the moment." Stay focused, be attuned to yourself and your surroundings, and get intensely interested in the now.
5.  Doing activities, especially side by side with a friend, helps to reduce the anxiety that flares during face-to-face interactions.
6.  Numerous epidemiological studies have shown that 2–2.5 hours of moderate to high-intensity exercise per week improves one's self-esteem, sense of well-being, and slows rates of age-related memory and cognitive decline in comparison to those who are more sedentary. Get to high stepping.
7.  In defense of idleness, however, a study found that distraction techniques such as meditation and quiet rest were as effective as a single session of exercise in reducing *state* anxiety. No gym shower flip-flops needed.

# 12  Dealing With Family

DOI: 10.4324/9781003345350-16

Oftentimes we don't realize how unstable our family is till we start describing them to someone else. But people from dysfunctional families are not destined for a dysfunctional life. We can't choose family, but we can choose antidotes to thrive despite our genetic roots.

## The Trappings of Holidays and Special Events With Family

It's not the holidays without a little emotional scarring. Holidays are a time of constant comparison. We compare how we celebrate, how much we have, how much we give and receive, how happy our families are, all the way down to comparing our own families to those of our partner, and even our own childhood memories and expectations to our current realities.

There's an expression that "expectations are resentments waiting to happen." Expectations can be either positive or negative. "*It's going to be amazing to have the whole family together,*" thinks your mother-in-law. "*This weekend will be an absolute shit-show,*" you mutter to your spouse. And so, our gatherings can become self-fulfilling prophecies on the basis of how we think and act going into them.

Usually, we are comparing them to idealized childhood versions that never existed, or have hazy memories that are half conflated with shmoopy Hollywood movies. For some of us, it's recent family fiascos that maybe aren't quite as bad as we recall that stick out in our minds; neither of which match realities we've lived through or are likely to encounter.

> Aunt: *Why are you wearing so much cologne?*
> Me: *Why isn't anyone eating your scalloped potatoes?*

One recent Thanksgiving, Chris's client Terrence and his wife, Janelle, had just given birth to their first baby. The chaos of packing for three, flying with an infant, and managing simple travel logistics left them mentally underprepared as they headed into the holidays. Things started out well enough, chatting with in-laws and relatives, and proudly showing off the new baby. By nighttime, however, the crib lizard who had been a miracle sleeper since birth decided to show everyone in the small house his displeasure at the new sleeping arrangement in a strange house.

He spent most of the night keeping the entire extended family awake with screams of discontent. This only added to the new parents' exhaustion and humiliation after bragging to all the relatives about what a great sleeper he was. Remember that expectations = resentments thing?

The next day saw an early start, coupled with a heavy dose of exhaustion and crankiness in the mix from everyone. Terrence and Janelle fielded active complaints and passive aggressive comments about the baby's sleep, as if there was much that even a seasoned baby whisperer could do.

Meanwhile, Terrence was flipping between flares of hot shame and blistering anger, on top of the baby fatigue. The conversations dragged on as family stretched topics of common interest to the breaking point and struggled to not repeat whatever anecdotes they had on hand, all while steering away from hot button political issues. Soon, the claustrophobia and boredom of the cold rainy day settled in.

Dinner was set to be mercifully early and short, leaving Terrence and Janelle an open evening with a chance of escape. Relatives offered to babysit while they went out to meet friends and flee the closing walls. Terrence spent the day fixated on the relief of a break away from the parent shaming that the end of dinner would bring.

*"Blood ain't thicker than peace of mind."*

Things further derailed a few minutes into that afternoon when one of the in-laws who was scheduled to babysit poured themselves a promised "just one drink" in the form of an eight-ounce glass of scotch and gulped it down before the dinner's wine came out. Terrence was infuriated by the recklessness of it as he watched the gates of freedom slam shut. He felt ready to snap, not knowing if he was more angry or anxious about the behavior and broken promises.

He soon flipped the anger toward himself. *"What was I thinking? How could I be so short-sighted? We knew this person had a track record with irresponsible drinking. I should have known better than to trust this person with our child. I'm a bad father.*

It serves as another example of having expectations of others, albeit reasonable, that turned into resentments.

### Tactics for Relief: How to Mark Yourself "Safe" From Family Drama

*Get Back to Chilling in an Olive Garden Parking Lot Conversing With Family Members, While Chewing a Toothpick and Holding a To-Go Box Status*

Family doesn't always respect family. Family can gaslight, manipulate, and control. Family can disrespect. Family can abuse. Family can take the most toxic form of relationship you know. In such instances, you don't owe anyone anything but yourself. Some of the hardest people to cut off are family members. Extricate and terminate. Full stop. Even the worst people you know have value: They can teach you how not to act.

One thing that can always help in stifling family visits is having avenues of escape such as creating solid plans in the day to get out of the house, even if it's a feigned errand. Kids are great for this: *"Oh jeez, we're low on diapers and need to drive 45-minutes to the store that sells our favorite organic brand that doesn't cinch or bunch-up, and smells of cedar."*

### Create Time Buffers and Emotional Boundaries Into Your Itinerary

One hour with family can be 7 years on Earth. But there is enjoyment beyond fleeting breaks of scrolling social media in the bathroom. Yet just the right amount of family dysfunction has made some of the most creative and funny people we all know.

Chris and Terrence discussed using the following technique developed by clinical psychologist, Chris Germer, called the self-compassion break during future interactions with family. They also jointly planned how to be more aware of interactions with family and how Terrence felt before, during, and after the inter-actions. They worked out escape plans and moments they can connect with each other and communicate away from the family. Serenity now.

### Try the Self-Compassion ACE

Find some space to yourself (if you're able) and gently place a hand over your heart, your belly, or your cheek. This itself is a caring gesture that instantly soothes and consoles, while releasing the oxytocin that creates feelings of comfort and safety. Try a few short affirming phrases softly aloud or silently to yourself. This can be your **ACE** in the hole during moments of suffering.

> **A:** Acknowledge
> **C:** Connect yourself to the human experience
> **E:** Extend yourself whatever compassion you need in the moment

Chris Germer might suggest the following self-reflection:

> **A(cknowledge):** *This is a moment of suffering.*
> **C(onnect yourself to the human experience):** *We all suffer.*
> **E(xtend yourself the compassion needed):** *May I be kind to myself in this moment.*

Chris and Terrence decided on this version when things inevitably spiral.

> A(cknowledge): *This is a moment of holiday stress.*
> C(onnect yourself to the human experience): *We all experience holiday stress to the point that it's become a cliché of TV dramas.*
> E(xtend yourself the compassion needed): *May I just give myself a break and relax.*

But this hasn't always felt right either. Because sometimes, like that one year, it could be more along the lines of the following:

> A(cknowledge): *This is a moment that feels like a complete mental squall.*
> C(onnect yourself to the human experience): *As humans, we have all experienced in varying degrees moments of such personal chaos.*
> E(xtend yourself the compassion needed): *And so, given that, may I be kind to myself in this moment?*
>
> *May I go into these challenges with neither high nor low expectations.*
> *May I enjoy the food.*
> *May we all get through this.*
> *May I allow the gratitude of this holiday to sink in.*
> *May I have the courage to ask myself and others for what I need.*
> *May my child and family be safe.*
> *May I see the suffering of others and the ways that manifests in their behavior.*

Ultimately, you must find the words and tone that work for you. What matters more than the words themselves are the sentiment and authenticity behind them. Trying to self-deceive only results in feeling worse (e.g., "*Just one more episode.*" "*Only one more slice.*").

> "*Do you have a wine that pairs with my dysfunctional family?*"

Blaming lead-based paint or your DNA is easy, but have you ever tried self-observation? The ability to observe ourselves objectively and compassionately is one of the most important skills for each of us to develop. The act involves observing and reacting to our own behaviors as if they were the actions of someone else – in other words, getting "woke," "red pilled," or "hip to."

Self-observation is like asking to speak to the manager within. This simple, but odd feeling tactic enables you to step outside of a stressful state and gain a new perspective to minimize damaging emotions and yield clarity and calm. We observe the antics and harmful behaviors of others constantly. Rarely do we turn this focus inward for our own pattern interrupts any positive redirection. There are concrete things that stand in the way of our own happiness that include living in the past, worrying about the future, and observing others.

### Behold, the Joy Thief (Is You)!

Upon self-observation we often realize that nothing external is to blame for our misery. Rather our reaction to things is most often the primary factor in our state of mind. Figure out the themes or patterns that trigger you. For example, she holds long grudges over trivial things, or he prattles on and on about guns and Camaros. Take a walk together, be on kitchen prep or cleaning duty, or give your mother-in-law's Bichon Frise a bath. Anxiety wanes in activity. And Bichons.

Stress is not a useful term in that, like humor, it's a highly subjective experience. But if you can't define stress, how can you possibly measure it? The term "stress" as used in modern times was originally coined in 1936 by Hans Selye as "the non-specific response of the body to any demand for change."[1] It likely began when your mom said she'll be "right back" when you were next at the checkout stand.

> *"Does this stress match my shoes?"*

Through much experimentation, Seyle found that laboratory animals exposed to acute, harmful physical and emotional stimuli such

---

1 Tan, S. Y., & Yip, A. (2018). Hans Selye (1907–1982): Founder of the stress theory. *Singapore Medical Journal, 59*(4), 170–171.

as glaring light, intense noise, extreme hot and cold temperatures, and continuous hindrances all showed the same pathologic changes of gut ulcers, shrinkage of lymphoid tissue, and enlargement of the adrenals.

Perhaps more fascinating, but equally unsettling, Seyle showed that animals under constant stress could develop similar maladies experienced by humans, to include heart attacks, stroke, kidney disease, and rheumatoid arthritis. It was believed back then that most diseases were caused by specific and separate pathogens. For example, tuberculosis was due to the tubercle bacillus, anthrax by the anthrax bacillus, syphilis by a spirochete, and so on. But Selye suggested the contrary: that various abuses could cause the same disease in both animals and humans. We really do have spirit animals.

### Good News! Stress Doesn't Cause Anxiety

If you are genetically predisposed to anxiety, a stress trigger or trauma may precipitate symptoms. It's like your anxiety is showing your stress around. Even the tension associated with positive events can affect anxiety. Just consider all the woes of a lottery winner. How does one spend all that money? More importantly, how does one hide their winnings from family and friends wanting to suckle at their money teat?

Everyone experiences stress and anxiety at one time or another. **The difference between the two is that stress is a response to a threat in a situation. Anxiety is a reaction to the stress.** We don't want to rid of all stress in modern society, as it acts as a motivational force in metered doses. It spurs college students to study and show up for an 8:00 a.m. statistics class. It signals us to honk at people sitting through green lights while texting. And it stimulates workers to join weekday video calls in their pajama bottoms and meet project deadlines to keep up appearances and maintain employment. Stress holds our feet to the syllabus, traffic, and management fires and inspires us to mediocrity or greatness – depending on our stress motivation and tolerance.

> Me: *Trying to be productive.*
> Stress and Anxiety: *I'm gonna stop you right there.*

However, there are just as many reasons why stress is bad. While mild stressors such as "where's the next gas station" on your road trip are motivating, major stressors can be debilitating. These include caring for loved one who has a chronic or terminal illness, financial insecurity, or having a horrible boss. Such stressors are harmful to the brain and body and can elicit depression, anxiety, and other mental and physical health issues.

### Set Physical Boundaries and Obtain Some Distance

Chris always recommends that people have a ready-made escape for any intense social situation. Have a "bug-out" plan ready to activate. Tell your family that you just took up walking each day and you *have* to get your steps in. Even if you don't. Or you could go into a back room and do some pushups and planking to clear your head from all the sitting and forced civility. I do this often, and it has kept my core strong and my body out of jail.

Gina, a client Chris works with, throws herself into cooking and cleaning during family gatherings to keep herself stable while having an outlet. When Uncle Jim grabs his phone and starts showing photos of his new model railroad blueprints, Gina simply excuses herself to go check on dinner or wash the gravy boat. When her mother-in-law starts her unsolicited commentary on Gina's parenting style, she heads to the kitchen to make cherries jubilee from scratch.

To avoid any *"Come at me bro!"* scenarios, her husband has a similar strategy, helpfully hauling laundry up and down from the basement for the cousins, taking an hour or two to fix the clog in the bathtub, or suddenly needing to check little Trina's diaper for a half an hour. Relatives will never complain about how helpful you're being, and you can duck out of any conversation under a real or assumed guise of familial dedication. Plus, you'll sleep better on the guest twin bed knowing you're not the black sheep of the family.

### If You Can't Lessen Your Source of Stress, Make a Literal Run for It

Running gives you that endorphin-generated runner's high and clears your head like nothing else. What's more, you immediately feel both the physical and psychological benefits. A 12-minute mile is just as far as a six-minute mile, so take your time and find your groove. Make sure you warm up and gently stretch, or you'll learn all about IT bands, plantar fasciitis, and shin splints.

*"Running helps me maintain my 'never killed anyone' streak."*

Chris had a client who talked about running as a way of coping with loss. She ran when her father died and said she felt she was running through the grief. She ran when she lost her job and talked about running toward her new future. She ran when she went through a divorce and shared how each stride felt like she was moving physically and emotionally away from her awful marriage and making herself stronger in the process.

She started one January, right when her husband had left for good after the holidays. She loved watching as the seasons changed, as she cautiously ran around snowbanks and over ice, then through rainstorms, and into the beauty of spring flowers, and finally through the summer. Your runs don't need to be as romantic or end with a medal and finisher T-shirt.

Joining a running group is a great way to challenge and inspire your exercise, while keeping your mind off the hurt you may still feel, and maybe even help you meet some spectacular people. If you're not sure where to find one, ask the staff at your local running shoe store. Grab a foam roller while you're there.

### HRV Sounds Like an Electric Vehicle, But It's About Your Electric Heart

Regular meditative practice is a powerful tool but greatly enhanced when coupled with direct biofeedback on how well you're doing it. **This is where heart rate variability (HRV) training comes in.** HRV is a measure of the variation in time between each heartbeat controlled by part of the nervous system called the autonomic nervous system (ANS).[2] Your ANS regulates heart rate, blood pressure, breathing, and digestion and is made up of the sympathetic (fight-or-flight component) and the parasympathetic nervous system (the relaxation response component). When it comes to your fight-or-flight response, be a penguin. They don't fly.

---

2 Shaffer, F., & Ginsberg, J. P. (2017). An overview of heart rate variability metrics and norms. *Frontiers in Public Health, 5.*

If Godzilla was rampaging toward a group of influencers, they'd take selfies until being crushed. When your own ANS is in a fight-or-flight mode, the variation between your heartbeats is low, versus when you're in a relaxed state and the variation between heartbeats is high. Chronic anxiety is like living in a constant state of fight or flight. The healthier your ANS, the quicker you're able to maintain a calm state and exhibit more resilience.

*"Hey, girl – are you my sympathetic nervous system? Cause you make my heart pound."*

Research has proven a direct correlation between low HRV and increased depression or anxiety.[3] A low HRV is also correlated with a heightened risk of cardiovascular disease and death.[4] In positive opposition, having a higher HRV is associated with greater cardiovascular health and better resiliency to stress. We are resilient by nature, and resiliency protects us from mental and emotional disorders. Resiliency is a choice with or without a TED talk. In short, if you want to track how your nervous system is affected by your thoughts, feelings, and emotions, consider monitoring your HRV.

### How to Check Your Heart Rate Variability

The simplest and most inexpensive way to check your HRV is to purchase a chest strap heart monitor and download a free accompanying app to review the data. It's the kind you see on skinny, shirtless dudes running through the park while looking all intense. Chest strap monitors tend to be more precise versus the finger or wrist versions. Check your HRV when you first awake and at various times during the week to monitor changes as you implement new tactics in stress and anxiety management. But do it on decaf days, or you'll be utterly disappointed.

---

3 Hamilton, J. L., & Alloy, L. B. (2016). Atypical reactivity of heart rate variability to stress and depression across development: Systematic review of the literature and directions for future research. *Clinical Psychology Review, 50,* 67–79.
4 Kubota, Y., Chen, L. Y., Whitsel, E. A., & Folsom, A. R. (2017). Heart rate variability and lifetime risk of cardiovascular disease: The atherosclerosis risk in communities study. *Annals of Epidemiology, 27*(10), 619–625.e2.

**Your Anxiety-Trigger Toolkit: Seven Tips for Coping With Family**

1. Always have a plan of escape, such as creating solid plans in the day to get out of the house and away from family and stressors, even if it's going to Target to sniff pillar candles.
2. Find space to yourself and gently place a hand over your heart, on your belly or cheek. This gesture instantly soothes and consoles, while releasing comforting oxytocin to achieve the level of chill to which you aspire.
3. Add the self-compassion ACE. A: Acknowledge what's happening around and within you; C: Connect yourself to the human experience; and E: Extend yourself whatever compassion you need in the moment.
4. Observe and react to your own behaviors as if they were the actions of someone else. In doing so, you will realize that your reaction to things is most often the primary factor in your state of mind. Be your own best boo.
5. Set physical boundaries and obtain physical distance when needed. Have a ready-made escape for family holidays or any intense social situation. Always have a getaway car and "bug-out" plan ready to activate.
6. Running provides a high and clears your head like few other things. Consider joining a running group as a great way to challenge and inspire your exercise and meet some like-minded people. Become an apex predator chasing serenity.
7. Leverage HRV to track the physiological effects of meditation and relaxation. The greater the variation between your heartbeats, the healthier your ANS, and the quicker you're able to maintain a calm state and exhibit more resilience.

# 13 Toxic People

DOI: 10.4324/9781003345350-17

Sometimes it feels like the whole world is permeated by selfish jerks pursuing their own agenda. It only takes one idiot out of every 1,000 decent people to taint our outlook. The quickest way to a better mood is redirecting your thoughts toward gratitude; for example, aren't you thankful *you're* not a jerk?

The biggest mistake many of us make in life is letting people stick around far longer than they deserve. Toxic people would rather stop speaking to you than apologize when they're wrong. They do not thank you, compliment you, listen to you, or give you credit. Whether a friend, partner, colleague, or family member, toxic people feel entitled to be disrespectful and it's not okay.

*"Judge me by the people I avoid."*

As I pen this chapter, I think of the decades-long, childhood friendship I recently ended on the basis of the negative effects it had on me for years. Sadly, I let it go on far too long. "Alex" had a heart of gold, and he's someone with whom I share more outlandish memories than anyone else. However, he also drinks more straight, cheap vodka than anyone I've encountered, to the detriment of all his relationships. He lost his wife, friends, and the respect of his two teen daughters who will long suffer the brunt of his selfish vice.

Countless times I approached him one-on-one and shared my love and concern for him, and each time he became defensive and aggressive. I pleaded with him to consider quitting for the sake of his kids and his health, while offering to attend weekly A.A. meetings with him. I later tried an intervention with his family. Much to my dismay, they turned on me for it. It was easier for them to enable him than to receive his scorn for speaking up. There ain't no party like an enabler party.

I let the guilt of severing the tie keep me involved for a decade longer than I should've. The hardest part of leaving toxic people isn't ending things; it's the ensuing guilt for doing so. Currently, Alex still calls me every few weeks and leaves long drunken messages with no insight or memory that we're no longer friends. Due to severe alcoholism, he suffers from "wet brain," which has impacted his cognition and memory. It's a self-inflicted dementia.

As much as I miss him and the friendship we once had, I'm not willing to continue watching him live recklessly, selfishly, and descending toward certain death. The only way to accommodate a friendship with him would be to condone the intolerable substance abuse and somehow endure hearing the exact same stories every time we talk, knowing we'd have an identical conversation the next time due to his booze-soaked brain.

*"Some of the most poisonous people come disguised as friends and family."*

Toxic relationships can be controlling or manipulative, negative, self-centered, or narcissistic, dishonest, insecure, abusive, blaming or demanding, secretive based, and drama filled. Abusive people are extremely defensive and averse to change. By remembering and accepting that you are *choosing* to be in the toxic relationship, your distress is reduced, although it may not improve the experience of being in a toxic relationship. And don't mistake something for abuse because it's not physical. Words and lack of respect leave permanent damage. You can heal broken bones, but it's harder to heal a broken mind. And no, it's never your fault.

## Honor Your Instincts; They're Usually Right

The moment that you start to wonder if you deserve better, you do. Normal people don't go around destroying other humans. Most abusers are also narcissists. This means that, like a car with shag carpet for a windshield, they lack the ability to see the impact of their own behavior on others.

---

**Anxiety Safety Briefing: 11 Subtle and Overt Signs of a Toxic Relationship to Help You Identify the Noxious**

1. They often exhibit exceptionally alluring and "too good to be true" behaviors.
2. They use the silent treatment as a means of control.
3. They force you to mind-read and guess and then act vindictive when you're wrong.
4. They ask you to do something for them because they (deceptively) can't do it for themselves, but whatever you do is met with harsh criticism and damnation.
5. They constantly correct you.
6. They lie to you.
7. They treat you as if you did something wrong, and if you deny it, they confirm your behavior as justification for the accusation.
8. They use sexual manipulation.
9. They bask in the tactic of denial to convince you their actions are to help you become a better person.
10. They treat you poorly and justify it by blaming you for their own poor conduct because "*No one else makes me act this way*" cites the toxic.
11. They can hit you right in the childhood.

---

## Tactics for Relief: How to Break the Toxic Ties Holding You Behind

### *Make Sure Everyone in Your Boat Is Rowing and Not Drilling Holes When You're Not Looking*

Some people will hold grudges against you for things they did to you. Toxic people strive to control the speech, thoughts, actions, or daily living patterns of another person secretly or overtly. If the abuser is very adept at being abusive, he or she may be withholding in nature, or generally insult you in subtle, hard-to-spot ways.

When toxic people can no longer manipulate you, they try to control the narrative of how others think about you. This is a scorched Earth, last ditch effort to punish you for rightfully casting them aside. Do not feel guilty if this happens. It's proof that you did the right thing. Other people will ultimately see the truth, just as you did. You can't run from your problems unless your problem is another person.

An interesting facet of removing someone toxic from your life is to mistake the peace of their absence as them no longer being toxic. That's when we tend to reengage only to learn that peace exists only when we leave conflict, not because the other side changed. Don't allow loneliness to make you reconnect with toxic people. You shouldn't drink poison just because you're thirsty. The loneliness will pass, I assure you. So many victims are in therapy learning how to deal with people who should be in therapy.

> Parent: *Do you think I'm a bad mom, Timmy?*
> Child: *My name is Travis.*

Third wheeling with a toxic couple is the most damning when it's your parents. It's not necessary to return to your parents for approval or reconciliation. By radically accepting and releasing the past, it's possible for you to alter the way you look at potential partners in a way that allows you to achieve romantic success with a person who empowers you.

> *"Not all toxic people are scary monsters. Hurt people hurt people. Psychologists know that 100% of the world's worst-behaved humans are the most fragile."*

Patterns are great and familiar but interrupting them is even better. Try a pattern interrupt and execute some kind behavior toward
the toxic person. A pattern interrupt is an effective tactic to break
an unwanted or automatic habit or response you've developed over
time.[1] It's "deconditioning." The tactic is designed to break your
focus or commitment to a certain task or mindset. Most importantly,
it can be used to eradicate any negative tendency you may want to
stop. And once you succeed, a good habit is just as hard to break.

A simple pattern interrupt example is breaking the feeling and
need to respond to a text as soon as you receive one. Unless you're a
cardiothoracic surgeon, responding to an Amber Alert, or a super-
hero summoned via text to save humanity, it's likely that 99.99%
of your text responses can wait. Indefinitely. This is an easy behavior on which to practice.

### Recognize That You Are in a Toxic Dynamic

It is common to be in a toxic relationship without being aware that
the relationship is toxic. In a toxic marriage or romantic relationship people are often told that the reason their partner is so angry,
upset, unloving, or abusive toward them is because of something
they did to cause it. It's similar within a toxic work environment,
where their boss will imply or outright state, *"The reason we are
treating you this way is because you are not doing a good enough
job."* And yes, a micromanager is a toxic manager. A bad job with
a good boss is better than a good job with a bad boss.

A particular type of toxic relationship of concern is the parental
bond from childhood that repeats in adulthood. Bringing you into
the world is not a privilege you need to earn. The effects of your
childhood upbringing extend into adult relationships, where you
find lovers who fill the void your parents created. And like your
parents, never make you a priority, or always leave you feeling like
you need to work harder to gain approval. Do not return to the
toxic roots.

I have family members that remain in my heart and regular
prayers but out of my life. Rolling nude in poison ivy is less harmful

---

1 Theodore. (2020, October). *Pattern interrupt (definition + examples).* https://practicalpie.
com/pattern-interrupt/.

than any time spent with them. The distance between you and toxic family is directly relative to the amount of harm they cause. In a toxic family setting, the black sheep is often just the person who sees through everyone else's crap. If you can stand up to family, you can stand up to anyone.

**And never assume that just because someone is family, they are allowed to mistreat you.** All relationships need boundaries. Oftentimes, *especially* family as they can exert the biggest influence over you. You specifically may not realize that you are being abused if you grew up in an abusive, alcoholic, or dysfunctional family as we tend to seek out familiar family patterns.

Within toxic romantic relationships, a key indicator is the marked difference between how your partner speaks to you in public versus private. Having a toxic partner is the quintessential "lipstick on a poison pig" scenario. There are over eight billion people on the planet, yet we often want the worst ones. This says more about us than the other person. Leave the toxic relationship before you end up a motivational speaker.

> Them: *Do you want to try and make it work for the 37th time?*
> You: *Have you changed?*
> Them: *No.*
> You: *Okay, let's try.*

### Strive for Independence From the Toxic Source

You have options in addressing the toxic person's improprieties while gaining independence. If the abuser is emotionally stable, you can simply say, *"This relationship is not working out for me. I have decided to withdraw and ask that you respect my boundaries by not contacting me."* Toxic people never think they're the toxic ones. And you don't need to show them.

If, however, the abuser is emotionally unstable, it is best to simply withdraw from the relationship without further discussion to avoid a dangerous conflict. Many relationships that are toxic, including those with family, remain toxic because of financial control. Family members have less control over those who have their own independence financially and in all aspects of their life. With financial independence, it's much easier to live life on your terms. Another person is not a financial plan.

### Create Boundaries and Electrify Them

Setting boundaries and limits isn't rude; it's an act of self-care. Most toxic people derive their influence because they prey on the difficulty that kind people have in setting boundaries in both platonic and romantic relationships. For some toxic relationships, it's best to set boundaries that prevent you from having anything to do with the other person; especially for people who are dangerous and those who have shown disregard for your well-being. Treat these people like the Chernobyl Exclusion Zone.

*"I don't say 'no' a lot. Did I pronounce that right?"*

Healthy boundaries are upheld with action. If you're able, it's best to subscribe to a zero tolerance for idiots paradigm and create boundaries for anyone that has shown repeated disrespect toward you. Such limits often come with age, experience, or a general aversion to jerkingtons.

Consider placing personal limits whenever dealing with toxic people. For example, rather than allow a person to extensively vent their problems or opinions while you attempt to work, let them know you are not available right now. Craft an unwavering and repeatable phrase and have it ready like Chapstick or nunchucks, because the moment you slightly change the wording you are likely to let that person back in. Toxic people feed off insecurity, self-doubt, and fear.

### Prepare for the Counterstrike

Toxic people thrive on power through the manipulation and control of their subjects. When this control is threatened via healthy limits or calling them out, they will either try to "punish" you by avoidance or redouble their efforts to keep the dynamic going. If you deviate from the role of the easygoing, boundary-less being that the toxic subject needs you to be (aka, you have needs, rights, feelings, limits, or opinions that are not gratifying to the toxic person) you are penalized. Stay resolute in plans to extricate yourself. Anne Lamott said it concisely: " 'No.' is a complete sentence."

### Go Gray

But if you *must* be around the abuser, try to stay neutral and unreactive. Abusers thrive on intensity and drama, so making yourself as boring and disengaged as possible can be a surprisingly helpful measure. This response is called the Gray Rock Method and is another pattern interrupter. It might initially frustrate the abuser and escalate things, but usually leads to them disengaging out of their own confusion and failure to get a rise out of you.

Be like the "b" in "subtle." The idea is that you keep your head down and blend into your setting, like a gray rock. The toxic person will move on to someone else to get what they need instead. It is important to not divulge to the toxic person what you're doing, however. Even the fact you're using this tactic should remain subtle and "gray."

### *Regularly Delete Your Brain's Browser History*

You've mastered the selfie; now master the self. There are truly never bad times for contemplative meditation. And it can be done most anywhere when you're trying to be Zen but there's too much real life.

---

### Modify Your Mindset: Meditation for Beginners

- ✓ Sit or lie comfortably in a quiet setting.
- ✓ Close your eyes.
- ✓ Make no effort to control the breath; just breathe naturally.
- ✓ Maintain your focus and attention on your breath and on how your body moves with each inhalation and exhalation.
- ✓ Each time your mind drifts to your thoughts, refocus back to your breaths.

**All it takes is one conscious breath in and out to be a "meditation."**

---

### *Limit Contact*

"*Hello. I'm at my mental threshold at the moment. Can we connect at a later date?*" There are circumstances that require us to remain connected to a toxic person, like toxic co-workers, a narcissistic boss, or the ever modern "sharing custody of children with a toxic ex." You may choose to remain married to a toxic spouse to protect your children from having to endure the toxic relationship alone were you to split custody. This is a topic for an entirely separate book. In such cases, it's best to minimize the toxic person's access to you and their ability to affect you.

Setting clear parameters such as "*I don't answer emails on vacation*" or "*Let's discuss the kids Sunday evenings*" can limit the toxicity spilling into the rest of your life, which abusers count on. While I hope you won't need a lawyer to enforce it, informal agreements like this, with boundaries set early on, can limit the mental and emotional chaos.

Understanding that you will never feel loved or supported by them and that they are not emotionally safe people (and *never will be*) can be liberating in that you stop feeling upset or hurt when they behave the way they do. Read that again.

### Don't Discount Rude Behavior

**Rudeness is the weak person's imitation of strength.** Many of us ignore adverse behaviors simply to avoid confrontation, or because using reason and rationale with the irrational is futile. Speak up confidently and state that you do not condone the disrespect directed toward you – particularly in instances of verbal abuse, physical abuse, and the like.

In such situations, a reply isn't even necessary but immediately leaving is. You can't change toxic people into non-toxic people. That will happen only if they want to change (a rare occurrence). But you can work on being less reactive. When you change yourself, the person creating issues in your life will either change with you or go away. A shift within you will shift everything around you. Otherwise, forgive them and revoke their social access.

### Seek Outside Help

It often takes an outside perspective of a therapist or insightful friend to help you understand that you're not actually at fault. If you suspect you're in a toxic relationship, the best thing you can do is to find healthy, supportive relationships with other people to help strengthen you, shift away from blaming yourself, and help you plan your escape strategy. You can't change the people around you, but you can exchange the people around you. We surround ourselves with people that reflect our self-worth, and we even date our self-esteem in what can turn into a woemance. An appropriate professional, such as a clinical psychologist, can help you learn how to challenge and reshape your unhealthy core beliefs. Vibe high and avoid becoming a toxic liability.

### Start a Digital "Fire Sale"

Manage your online and offline relationships the same way. We often fear unfriending or blocking toxic people on social media because we have seen how they respond when others do not behave the way they demand. But they need to be both daylight and digitally dumped.

"Done" is also an emotion. If the person is difficult and you want/ need to make a clean break and remove them from your life, don't overlook this crucial step. You don't have to tell them a thing. Just unfriend, unfollow, remove connection, delete, block, and sever ties. They don't deserve or warrant an explanation. They'll figure it out. Or they won't. Either way, it doesn't matter. If you're not ready to remove someone from social media completely, you have privacy options such as unfollowing or muting. They'll never know.

*"Not my pigs. Not my farm."*

Not everyone you lose is a loss. Don't chase people. Be you and do your own thing. The right people who belong in your life will come along and stay. It's remarkable how quickly things improve, and inter-personal peace returns when you remove toxic people from your life.

If you or somebody you know needs help for emotional or physical abuse, please call your Domestic Violence Hotline.

---

**Your Anxiety-Trigger Toolkit: 14 Tactics to Keep Your Contacts Non-Toxic**

1. Never allow loneliness to cause you to remain or reconnect with toxic people. There are worse things than being alone.

2. If you experienced emotional neglect by your parents, radically accept and release the past and surround yourself with people who empower you. Consider that most superheroes lost all parental love early on (e.g., Superman, Spider-Man, Batman, the Hulk, the Punisher, Deadpool, Thor, Hellboy, and Willie Nelson).

3. In dealing with a toxic person, try a pattern interrupt to break your focus away from a certain mindset.

4. Identify when you are in a toxic relationship. It's common to be in a toxic relationship without being aware that the relationship is toxic. Awareness is half of your escape.

5. Work toward independence from the toxic source. If the abuser is emotionally unstable, leave the relationship without further dialogue to avoid a dangerous conflict.

6. With financial independence, it's much easier to live life on your terms and become your own "finfluencer."

7. Create boundaries. Healthy boundaries require action. If they get upset, it's because they benefited from your previous lack of limits. Lean into it.

8. Never assume that because someone is family, they are allowed to mistreat you. All relationships need boundaries.

9. Anticipate a counterstrike and stay committed to removing yourself. It's uncanny how much toxic people love playing the victim.

10. If you can't avoid the abuser, try to stay neutral and unemotional (aka, go "gray"). And don't disclose that you're using this tactic, or the point is lost. Keep it gray all the way.

11. Regularly train your brain for rewiring via contemplative meditation.

   ✓ Sit or lie comfortably in a quiet setting.
   ✓ Close your eyes.
   ✓ Make no effort to control the breath; just breathe naturally.
   ✓ Maintain your focus and attention on your breath and on how your body moves with each inhalation and exhalation.
   ✓ Each time your mind drifts to your thoughts, refocus back to your breaths.

12. In those cases where you must remain in contact with the toxic person, minimize their access and ability to affect you. Play "the toxic person is lava."

13. If you suspect you're in a toxic relationship, an appropriate professional, such as a clinical psychologist, can help you learn how to challenge and reshape unhealthy core beliefs.

14. Manage your online and offline relationships the same way. You don't have to tell them a thing. Greater bliss is one click away.

# 14 Relationship Conflict

DOI: 10.4324/9781003345350-18

Conflict theory, developed by Karl Marx, asserts that due to society's never-ending competition for finite resources it will always be in a state of conflict. Conflict exists wherever two or more living entities exist. Because it's universal and inevitable, it's best to learn to address it on your own rather than rely on a third party such as litigators or juries. No amount of "Coexist" bumper stickers will get us to a life of peace.

## Without Conflict There Is No Plot

Conflict exists at work, home, within friendships, and between lovers, sports teams, animals, governments, and at every level in between. The repercussions to any conflict range from passive-aggressive side-eye and mild tensions to nuclear bomb drops from a B-29 Superfortress and decades of armed occupancy by foreign invaders. A lot of people like conflict. That's why there are cage matches, pay per view, and "Real Housewives of <name your favorite city>."

Even if you somehow avoid conflict between yourself and others, that doesn't mean conflict won't arise elsewhere, if only an inner moral conflict as in "I need to save money, but #YOLO." Conflict resolution skills are an essential life skill and are appropriate for any relationship or interaction you might have. It helps to remember that conflict is not inherently good or bad, but an inevitable result of humans relating to one another.

There are benefits of conflict. Rather, there are benefits to facing conflict by learning to effectively engage with conflict when it arises. Otherwise, problems will grow and communication will break down. Some of the benefits related to conflict resolution include developing an awareness that a problem exists; improved problem solving; improved relationships; better results via debating differing views; and conflict alerts us to what is important to those involved. It also gave us dance-offs and Rochambeau (aka, "rock, paper, scissors").

There are, of course, downsides to attempts at conflict resolution that can include the emotional toll from the conflict itself; escalation of the conflict while attempting to resolve it; the creation of a winner and a loser with the resulting resentments; and limited effect, whereby the resolution of a conflict may only be temporary, and the situation may arise again in the future (e.g., marriage, internet trolling, etc.).

## Conflict Often Arises When Someone Does Not Respect Boundaries, Whether Overt or Implied

Your different responses to boundary violations are often rooted in your upbringing. You might feel guilty when you say "no" because at one time you feared a caregiver's or peer's response. Or there may have been fear that if you said "no" it would lead to more anger from that person or that they would take it as a rejection and become more depressed, more anxious, or fall harder into a worrisome addiction or behavior for which you would feel responsible.

Others have been conditioned by the larger culture to be less assertive in certain contexts including women, people of color (BIPOC), LGBTQ people, and other groups. All these play into our emotions, which include fear and shame about being more assertive in the face of potential conflict. When you're not used to being confident, confidence can feel like arrogance.

When you're used to being passive, assertiveness can feel like aggression. And when you're not used to getting your needs met, prioritizing yourself can feel selfish. Don't use your comfort zone as a reliable benchmark.

## Tactics for Relief: How to Rise Above the Conflict in Conflicts of Interest

Managing the difficult emotions associated with conflict can fill book volumes that rival those between the allegorical frescoes within the Bibliothèque de la Sorbonne in Paris. The focus within this section is to cover a few of the most common, beginning with how to conflict mediate. Conflict resolution is nothing more than a tactic for two or more parties to find a peaceful solution to a disagreement among them. The disagreement may be personal, financial, political, or emotional.

### "That's a 'no' from me, dawg."

If any of these life influences are a part of your background, you can practice saying "no" and setting boundaries in general. You can add some simple exposure therapy to saying "no" to things by saying the word out loud several times, as you notice how awkward or challenging a word it can be to say, and gradually becoming more comfortable as you practice. It can be fun to say "no," and it immediately lowers the recipient's enthusiasm. Oftentimes I'll blurt out a *"nope!"* before someone even finishes asking something. Then I'll say, *"I'm just kidding. But, let me think about it,"* which buys me time till I feel more comfortable seriously telling them "No."

### Normalize Saying "No"

The things you say "no" to are often more significant than those you say "yes" to. Learn to say "no" from a place of strength, rather than saying "yes" from a place of insecurity. You can make a deliberate habit out of saying "no." One tactic Chris suggests is to practice saying "no" to everyone for a solid week. Or maybe a day. Or even an hour. It's like the Jim Carrey movie "Yes Man," but in reverse. If you fall mostly into the *appease* or *avoid* categories, this is a great technique to try. You can start on your stylist after they cut your hair and ask, *"So, do you like it?"*

---

### Anxiety Safety Briefing: Fifty Shades of "Nah"

There are many polite forms of "no." Consider some of the following:

1. *No, thanks, I'm all set.*
2. *I'm slammed and simply can't take it on right now.*
3. *I don't think I'm the right person for that.*
4. *I sincerely appreciate the invite, but I have a conflicting engagement.*
5. *I must respectfully decline.*

---

If someone pushes you further, you can simply provide a general *"I'm sorry. It's something I can't get into right now."* If that's not enough for them, bear spray.

### *We Repeat What We Don't Repair*

It's fun to repair things just enough so the next person using it thinks they broke it. Relationships are more complicated, however. Chris created the following acronym to guide the repair of your relationships damaged by conflict.

---

### Modify Your Mindset: REPAIR a Relationship

Follow these steps in order, beginning by recognizing your part in the fray:

As an example, consider a blow-out with your partner over their constant tardiness to events that you attend together. They reply to your frustration with rationale like "*We're already late, so we might as well take our time. You can't be late twice.*"

Recognize that you must communicate early and often regarding expectations.

Engage them in the process by asking what you can do to help them better prepare and to improve their time management.

Present yourself as willing to assist and support them in jointly reducing late arrivals.

Amend anything you've done or said to contribute to the issue and Apologize if necessary.

Inquire about how you don't want to repeatedly criticize them over this and ask how it feels to them when you do.

Remind them that you value the Relationship.

### Use Some LOL: A Time-Honored Strategy in the Repertoire of Nonviolence

Back in the day, we used duels or jousts to "resolve" conflict by ending the other person. People still do this, but it's illegal now. Today when conflict and disagreement arise anywhere, humor can help lighten the tension and restore a sense of connection. Used respectfully, humor can quickly turn conflict into an opportunity for common ground. It allows you to get your point across without raising the other person's defenses or hurting their feelings. Humor isn't an instant fix for conflict, but it's a worthy tactic in assuaging tensions and shifting perspectives.

Humor can help neutralize conflict by:

- Disrupting the power struggle, creating a long-enough pause to regain perspective.
- Facilitating spontaneity allowing everyone involved to see the problem in a new way and create a solution.
- Dropping defenses to allow each person to accept learning things about themselves they might otherwise overlook or ignore.
- Lowering inhibitions for members to freely express thoughts and feelings.

Humor should be beneficial for everyone involved. Before you unleash your mic-dropping material, first consider your motive and determine the pulse of the group. Know your audience. If you're unsure, assume it's comprised solely of grandmas and Girl Scouts. #CYA

### Don't Use Humor or Mascara to Cover Sadness

Humor helps you stay resilient during tough times. But humor is unhealthy when used to avoid rather than cope with painful emotions. Knowing when and how to humor is half the humor heuristic.

As much as possible, avoid letting your emotions rule the conversation, especially about challenging topics whether it's co-workers, kids, or couples. In considering romantic conflict, couples researcher John Gottman describes the "Four Horsemen of the Apocalypse" of divorce in couples' communication styles, which also apply to other conflicts in our life.[1] Because neither a ring, threesome, baby nor boat will save a relationship.

Gottman's "Four Horsemen of the Apocalypse" divorce indicators to watch out for:

1. **Criticism:** Watch the critical accusations, especially when paired with black-and-white thinking distortions and phrases like "you always" and "you never." Counter such sentiments by responding with "I statements" and "feeling statements." If you do criticize, focus on the *behavior*, not the *character* of the other person. "*When you criticize your partner, you are implying that there is something wrong with them*," says Gottman. Even if you're a Virgo, to whom sharp wit and criticism come naturally.
2. **Defensiveness:** It's natural to defend ourselves and our position, and you should. But falling into "whataboutism" when you throw back on the other person every past mistake is detrimental to potential resolution. "*Defensiveness keeps partners from taking responsibility for problems and escalates negative communication*," stresses Gottman. "*The antidote to defensiveness is to examine your part and acknowledge it before and during the time you are engaging with the other person*," Defensiveness escalates the conflict.

---

1 Gottman, J. M. (1993). *What predicts divorce?: The relationship between marital processes and marital outcomes* (1st ed.). Psychology Press.

3. **Contempt:** Contempt is displayed by verbal and nonverbal behaviors that downplay or degrade your partner's position. It's any statement or nonverbal behavior that puts yourself on a higher ground than your partner. It can include name calling, mocking, or demeaning gestures. Of Gottman's four horsemen, this one is considered the worst due to the irrevocable damage it can cause. You can reverse this slide by reminding yourself and the other person of what you appreciate about them and their positive contributions to the relationship. Hold each other, but not in contempt.

4. **Stonewalling:** This evasion tactic includes cutting off communication altogether, ghosting the other person, or taking a "screw them, screw their crap" attitude. It can be considered toxic behavior or emotional abuse. "*The stonewaller may look like he doesn't care (80% are men) but that usually isn't the case,*" says Gottman. Regrettably, stonewalling rarely works because your partner will mistakenly assume you truly don't care. The opposite approach is to tenderly reengage after asking for a specific amount of time to cool off, and letting the person know exactly when you are ready to talk (note: It can't be "when hell freezes over").

### *"I Am the Captain Now"*

My cat, Thelma, asserts dominance by not covering her crap in the litter box. It offends her sister, Louise, and me while one of us – either me with a small, plastic shovel or Louise with a paw – buries it in litter like she owns us, as Thelma looks on with an air of pompous disdain. She lacks decorum. For many of us who aren't cats, asserting ourselves can be a challenge.

Chris attended an assertiveness group, which he found incredibly helpful. One of the tactics they used to help attendees regarding interpersonal style was what they called the "Four A's" (not to be confused with the Four F's or the Four Horsemen).

Whenever we find our boundaries being tested, we often unwittingly respond with one, or a combination, of the following:

- **Attacking**
  Like the fight response, this can be helpful as a last resort, but often we use it too early and end up damaging important

relationships in the process. Or we must walk back our attack, but in a weaker position because we've possibly embarrassed ourselves. People end up writing us off and we don't get our needs met from them afterward.

- **Avoiding**

  Like the flight response, we run away and pretend everything is fine, not ever bringing up the fact that we're aware our boundaries are being violated or dismissing it altogether as too much trouble to bring up. Avoidance can also be perceived as weakness.

- **Appeasing**

  This response is somewhat like denial in which we try to make the other person happy, despite feeling violated. Sometimes we need to give in or choose which battles to fight and which ones to let go. However, oftentimes when we do, we come away feeling resentful. This creates more stress, depression, and shame, which we take out on ourselves, or we passive-aggressively undermine the other person. Winston Churchill once said, *"An appeaser is one who feeds a crocodile, hoping it will eat him last."*[2]

- **Asserting**

  Assertiveness is a balance of the first three. It's neither aggressive nor passive; it's showing up for and standing up for ourselves. We know it when it's happening, and often the other person does too because it's also the most effective approach to a boundary violation.

*"I'm going to start being more assertive . . . if that's okay with you."*

*Do you speak body language?* You can deescalate tensions by adjusting your body language to communicate to yourself and to the other person a willingness to be open, flexible, and reasonable. Stand confidently, but not aggressively. You don't need to get into a menacing T-pose or karate crane stance. Think self-assuredness, not double leg sweep. Avoid crossing the arms, face

---

2  Sir Winston Churchill (1954, December) *Reader's Digest*.

scowling, angry or dismissive tones of voice, shouting, and literal finger pointing.

### Let Me Hear Your Body Talk

Another physical tactic Chris often recommends to couples, families, and co-workers to lower conflict stress is to do something together and talk side by side, rather than face to face. Often when we are sitting or standing across from one another, we are routinely in physically defensive positions with our bodies in opposing placement. Such positioning serves to heighten and escalate feelings of threat. But *feeling* threatened is not the same as *being* threatened. The distinction lies in your perception or if you're a Vaquita or a Red Panda.

Nonetheless, talking while taking a walk or driving, for example, facilitates a more relaxed arrangement that is non-aggressive by default. Riding a tandem bike through the park with your enemy allays any chance of hostility merely by physical arrangement.

When we are in a conflict over text, email, or someone's DMs, it's easy to misinterpret the motives of the other person without hearing their tone of voice or viewing their facial expressions and body language.

When we are anxious, we automatically assume the worst and act accordingly. When we are in person, however, taking a walk or doing something side by side allows the threat to dissolve. Take a stroll with that difficult colleague and see if the conversation doesn't go much better. Have the talk you've been avoiding with your kids in the car rather than at the dinner table. Raise a challenging conversation with a friend while you're next to them cooking at the grill or walking the golf course and watch as the conversation eases compared to sitting or standing across from each other. The efficacy of this simple tactic goes beyond modern science.

### The Prescription for Angst Is More Kettlebell

A self-defense class, whether traditional martial arts from Asia, Krav Maga from Israel, the Afro-Brazilian Capoeira, CrossFit, or self-defense classes can leave you feeling physically more confident and assertive, while also helping you defend your lunch money from the office park bullies.

Online classes (live or archived) or working out at home can help create more confidence, especially before you need to set a tough boundary. Keep in mind that you're training to develop self-confidence, not to bench-press your rivals.

If you want to learn self-defense skills and don't have a frying pan or know where to begin, look for videos of people practicing on YouTube and see which one appears the most fun and empowering. Then find a nearby studio, and maybe get a friend to sign up with you. Cut your toenails before class. Many courses emphasize not just physical self-defense but assertiveness, conflict avoidance, and verbal de-escalation techniques because they know that's often part of why people attend. And you gotta stay right with the Lord.

**Your Anxiety-Trigger Toolkit: Ten Tips for Coping
With Modern Times or the Roman Empire**

1. Conflict resolution is a tactic for two or more parties to find a peaceful solution to a disagreement among them. Since agreeing to disagree is still a disagreement.
2. Practice simple exposure therapy to saying "no" to things by saying the word out loud several times to gradually become more at ease saying it.
3. Say "*no*" to everyone for a solid week. Or even a day. Consider the many polite forms of saying "*no*," and alternate their usage. "*I would not like to say 'yes.'*"
4. You repeat the broken processes you don't fix. Refer to the REPAIR acronym as a technique to mend relationships. Even Androids and iPhones communicate.
5. Use appropriate humor to diffuse tensions and turn conflict into an opportunity for common ground. If you're not funny, skip to #6.
6. Regarding romantic conflict, stay mindful of Gottman's "Four Horsemen of the Apocalypse" divorce indicators: criticism, defensiveness, contempt, and stonewalling. You never really know someone till you meet them in court.
7. When you feel your boundaries being tested, be conscientious to not respond with the first three of the Four A's: attacking, avoiding, or appeasing. Go with the fourth A: asserting. Assertiveness is a healthy mash-up of the first three.
8. Deescalate tensions by adjusting your body language to communicate to yourself and to the other person a willingness to be open, flexible, and reasonable. Uphill situation? Take the de-escalator.
9. To lower conflict stress do something together and talk side by side, rather than face to face. Saber-rattling feels silly with no one in front of you.
10. Keeping fit can help you feel more confident and assertive. Self-defense classes, not TED talks, can leave you feeling physically more confident in the world.

# 15 Pandemic

Here's an alarming trigger we had not seen since 1918 until 2020. And despite epidemiologists, virologists, and Bill Gates sounding the alarm that one was looming, we had better things to concern ourselves with – like anything else that would distract us from the idea of imminent plague.

If you were to ask the public as to what specific outbreak might wreak mayhem within our lifetimes, you'd likely hear flu, locusts, boils, frogs, athleisure wear, or something similar from social media prophetics or the Book of Revelations.

Even when news of another coronavirus hit, it was in a faraway land impacting only "other peoples." It would seem hyperbole that cruise ships would become the vector ferrying tiny, spiky, murder spheres to our own shores. Our sole defense was keeping the potentially contagious temporarily adrift on floating petri dishes, while they enjoyed 24-hour buffets and sequined Bon Jovi and NSYNC tribute bands.

But we'd soon be worried over parents, grandparents, and ourselves as we came face to face with our vulnerability and the interconnectedness of our planet. Moreover, we realized that nothing was ever "under control," an illusion most had believed and subscribed to for a generation. And we became angry at the thin veil through which life was sewn.

Didn't someone's omnipotent God assure us we'd never be given more than we can handle? Actually, no. This guarantee isn't in the Bible, Quran, Torah, Guru Granth Sahib, Vedas, Tripitaka, or Kojiki. It's a motivational quip we like to keep next to those *Live, Love, Laugh* prints from TJ Maxx.

The media loves to scare you, whether about pathogens thriving in your kitchen sponge or the carcinogens in your mattress. I saw online images of barren store shelves and heard tales of people having to wipe themselves with socks because Cottonelle became a controlled substance. Yet somehow, I did not join the Costco Fight Clubs or subscribe to the mania.

## What If . . . ? → Worry → Anxiety (Hoarding) → Demoralization and Exhaustion

Taking precautions is sound practice. But thieving McDonald's napkins and one-ply toilet paper from Starbucks is unhealthy paranoia. Fear is contagious. Fortunately, so is normalcy. The anxiety seed-planting by the media was the biggest contagion of all. It's reckless of news outlets to create a culture of fear through biased reporting, thereby sustaining an anxiety continuum that frays our nerves.

### Anxiety's Muse Is Worst-Case Scenarios

Those of us prone to anxiety have been mentally (if not physically) prepping for disaster, chaos, and contagions all our lives. When one occurs, we're in our element. Finally, everyone else moves into our irrationally dysfunctional lane. Except that most people aren't career worriers, and they did it all wrong.

By way of example, I have *always* worn 6-mm-thick black nitrile gloves at the gym on each visit. I also have a legacy of using hospital-grade Sani wipes at cafes, hotels, and in rental cars, all while fully cognizant that it was excessive and likely why I have little immunity to the common cold or children. But I finally had justification for my compulsions and appeared less neurotic to the neo-anxious.

**The problem with living such a comfortable existence for so long is the depth of the fall to a life of discomfort.** Thankfully, we were buoyed by the frontline workers in healthcare, at nursing homes, behind badges, delivery personnel, pharmacists, grocery employees, and agriculture workers.

Anxiety is rooted in a fear of the unknown. And the pandemic was exacerbated by a "looming vulnerability" as it got closer to our own doorstep. The media-fueled paranoia created a culture of hoarding that wasn't commiserate with the reality. Hoarding is a natural human reaction in times of high anxiety. Hoarding toilet paper made us feel like we were doing something, while fulfilling a need for control. Even if only over anal hygiene.

Mid-2020 saw the indoctrination of millions of newcomers into the anxiety and depression clubs. Their steep dues were paid with inner chill and peace of mind. Though many of us (e.g., the anxious) had been mentally prepping for a lifetime, we too found ourselves ill-equipped for an epidemic. You can't train for a contagion that exists only in one's mind (another reason why worry is a useless endeavor). But suddenly it wasn't so weird to clean an apple with a bleach wipe.

## Tactics for Relief: How to Respond When a Virus Goes Viral

### Humor Abounds

Find the humor. It's *always* there. Read humor. This might not be the best time to ponder Dostoyevsky's *Poor Folk* or *The House of the Dead*. A pandemic calls for some light and cheery reading to facilitate laughs and levity. Consider something from Issa Rae, Dave Barry, Tiffany Haddish, or Judd Apatow.

Mark Twain knew it best: "*The secret source of humor itself is not joy but sorrow.*" Studies confirm that laughter lowers blood pressure and releases beta-endorphins, a chemical in the brain that creates a sense of joy. Moreover, humor is clinically validated to reduce stress long term by improving the immune system through the release of neuropeptides, relieving pain, increasing personal satisfaction, and lessening depression and anxiety.[1] The simple act of smiling causes the brain to release dopamine, which in turn makes us feel happy. This includes smiling under a mask or while autoclaving yourself.

### Humor = Tragedy + Time

Humor will change your relationship to the problem of stress, worry, or anxiety. And it reduces stigma. The stigma aspect is of particular interest, as clinical literature has consistently documented that men seek help for mental health less often than do women, although they suffer from mental illness at comparable rates.[2] This is particularly troublesome as depression and anxiety in men are more likely to manifest in substance abuse and suicidal behavior. Sad men often present as angry men.

Austrian neurologist, psychiatrist, and Holocaust survivor, Viktor Frankl, sourced and used humor as one tactic to survive German concentration camps, and he highlighted humor as "another of the soul's weapons in the fight for self-preservation." "*The attempt to develop a sense of humor and to see things in a humorous light is some kind of a trick learned while mastering the art of living,*" said Frankl.[3] Humor produces endorphins that soothe the body and allow a responsive brain to take charge. Even if it's otherwise confused by CDC and regulatory pivots.

### *There Never Was and Never Will Be a "Normal" in an Unpredictable World*

We used terms like "new normal" to instill an element of control over things. Control is an illusion. I started to think about the term "new normal" and how we ever acquiesced on an "old normal."

1 Louie, D., Brook, K., & Frates, E. (2016). The laughter prescription: A tool for lifestyle medicine. *American Journal of Lifestyle Medicine, 10*(4), 262–267.
2 Call, J. B., & Shafer, K. (2018). Gendered manifestations of depression and help seeking among men. *American Journal of Men's Health, 12*(1), 41–51.
3 Frankl, Viktor, E. (1962). *Man's search for meaning: An introduction to logotherapy.* Beacon Press.

I observed the rampant OCD taking place nearly everywhere by those not accustomed to OCD'ing. To be fair, courtesies such as shaking hands during cold and flu season or in general, have always been an archaic practice in the transmission of filth. *Have you seen what you do with your hands?*

And consider a University of Arizona study that found that cell phones carry ten times more bacteria than most toilet seats.[4] Yet we don't hesitate to pinch zoom a pic when someone hands us their toilet phone.

And how many times have you eaten birthday cake blown on by someone you didn't like or barely knew? They might as well forcefully exhale directly into your mouth. A study in the *Journal of Food Research* determined that blowing out candles over that sweet, sticky icing resulted in **1,400%** more bacteria compared to icing spared the puff. The study was aptly titled "Bacterial Transfer Associated with Blowing out Candles on a Birthday Cake."[5] "Hep-C birthday to you."

> *"Blacklight most any hotel room and it will look like a Jackson Pollock painting."*

Hotels will charge $250 for smoking in your room, but you can leave behind biologicals for free. Most of us make that room as cozy as our own, in full denial that few people tip the maids upon checkout. Hotels are where people go to cut their toenails, trim body hair, or bleed. The mattresses are literal smut sponges. But we gladly pay for the privilege of rubbing our faces into the pillows and bleach-infused towels.

Humor is ever present in your world. You just have to peek through the dank mental hues of your angst and ask yourself, "*What's funny about this?*" and brainstorm a list. Sourcing the lighter side of your emotions is vital, particularly at a time when so many people worldwide are exhibiting signs of clinical anxiety or

4 Kõljalg, S., Mändar, R., Sõber, T., Rööp, T., & Mändar, R. (2017). High level bacterial contamination of secondary school students' mobile phones. *Germs, 7*(2), 73–77.
5 Dawson, P., Han, I., Lynn, D., Lackey, J., Baker, J., & Martinez-Dawson, R. (2017). Bacterial transfer associated with blowing out candles on a birthday cake. *Journal of Food Research, 6*(4), 1.

depression. COVID created a massive wake of mental health issues across the globe, along with new phrases like "immunity privileged," "coronacations," "the before times," "walktails," "vaccine nationalism," and "covidivorce."

During the initial stages of the pandemic, I felt that I spent most of my time hiding from humanity to avoid the contagion. My core activity was sterilizing everything I ordered via Instacart and Amazon with disinfectant wipes. I wondered who else wore protective eyewear in public to block microscopic viral spheres from entering their bodies via corneal adhesion.

When the first wave of COVID hit, most hospital procedures, elective surgeries, and even much-needed chemotherapy were halted for millions of cancer patients, including for my mother's late-stage cancer. My anxiety spiked as the weeks passed where the risk of infection outweighed her treatment regimen. She was eventually allowed to restart, as my angst shifted away from a resurgence of the cancer and back to potential infection.

My mental health was worsened by the dawning recognition that I had moved to their region 25 miles outside of Sacramento in hopes of being of assistance to them. But I have Boomer parents who are stalwarts of stubbornness, and who hide injury, falls, and personal adversity from me. They would sooner take Tums for chest pain than admit a heart attack.

Consequently, I grew increasingly frustrated, depressed, and miserable in my new climes as they shunned most aid from me and temps reached the 100s. It was time to reprioritize my mental well-being and move. Again. It would be my fourth major move while writing this book. By the time you read this, I could be living most anywhere, including in a camper van. Maybe you could leave a bag of Sani-wiped fruit by my bumper.

### Activities to Manage Your Anxiety During a Quarantine

One of the most vital tactics I leveraged during quarantines was the distraction afforded by Netflix binges. But I also read a lot. At any given time during the pandemic, I concurrently read four to five books depending on my mood. I also attended live, online church and men's group sessions to feel connected to others. This is where I learned specific Bible verses that also helped to carry me through the salty times. Isaiah 41:10–13, Isaiah 53, Psalm 23, Psalm 40:1–3, Psalm 91, and particularly Philippians 4:6–8 were pivotal in soothing the frayed nerves. Memorizing any scripture is also a form of meditation. And it helps train the brain for other things, like remembering to brush your teeth, wear pants, or learn to cut your own hair.

A good chunk of my COVID coping time was spent on building an in-home gym once my fitness center closed. This was exceptionally challenging as millions had the same idea, and every dumbbell, kettlebell, and old-school vinyl-covered cement prison weight was sold out online and in stores. But over weeks, I slowly accrued a Frankenstein gym of mismatched heavy things. I converted my living room into a carpeted fitness studio where I performed calisthenic feats of athleticism, such as 3,000 burpees and push-ups per month and press-ups against the wall. I also fast-walked 120 miles per month like I was trying to beat the virus in a walk-a-thon.

Anxiety and/or depression can peak in the absence of coping skills. When you assign value or validity to intrusive thoughts and fears, it's like mental Miracle-Gro. Talking to a therapist via phone or teletherapy is a measurably effective adjunct tool during stressful times.

### There Is a Little-Known Dichotomy About Mental Health Issues That Makes Seeking Treatment Difficult

When you're feeling anxious or depressed, it's often hard to do what's best for your welfare. This includes seeking help. My anxiety doesn't want me to pay bills until I'm getting hate mail from creditors, fold laundry until I have no room on the bed to sleep, get groceries until I'm down to cereal and a jar of encrusted mayo, or wash my car until strangers finger-write profanities on the windows.

Mental health disorders like anxiety or depression will cloud your mind and fill your consciousness with a perverse volume of thoughts, noise, feelings, and stressors that have no validity. Meanwhile, the things that matter get buried in a cerebral ruckus. Next thing you know, you're feeling apathetic, missing deadlines, and arriving late to work, and everyone's wondering why you can't get your act or matching socks together. But if they saw the thought carnival in your mind, they'd surely understand.

Sitting with a stranger in talk therapy may feel awkward at first. But if you think of a therapist as a soundboard and proponent who has your best interests in mind, it'll put you more at ease. It's a definite advantage to have an impartial third party in your life.

Therapy is like strength training in that you get out what you put in. Everyone can benefit from talk therapy. Most of us regularly bounce ideas off friends and seek advice from those closest to us anyway. A therapist is a 100% dedicated professional resource to provide objective help and advice. The most powerful and successful people on the planet have professional advisors guiding them. So should you.

---

### Anxiety Safety Briefing: When to Seek Help

There are two instances when you should absolutely seek out a professional:

1.  If you are in danger of hurting yourself or others, or if you are having passive thoughts about hurting yourself or others (even if you don't have a plan or any real intent to follow through with these thoughts), then you should see someone. Depending on the intensity of these thoughts, calling 911 and asking for help might be your best option.
2.  The second incident where you should consider seeing a professional is if your symptoms are starting to interfere with your daily life. Such symptoms could include suddenly not getting along with friends or family, difficulty with sleep, problems eating, doing poorly in school or work, or starting to use alcohol or drugs to cope or feel better.

---

### How to Choose a Therapist

There are many different types of talk therapies available, and many types of therapists to choose from. So which therapy and therapist is right for you? When it comes to treating all mental health issues, especially anxiety or depression, you want to make sure you choose a therapist who uses an approach that is evidence based or empirically validated. This simply means that they say and do things to treat your symptoms that have been proven by research to be effective.

> Client: *What should I do?*
> Therapist: *What do you think you should do?*
> Client: *Alright then, keep your secrets.*

When choosing a therapist, there are various types of therapy degrees. They include psychiatrists (MD), psychologists (PsyD.), and masters-level therapists (LCSW, MCSW, etc.). Make sure the person is licensed. If they are licensed, this means they went to a school that was accredited, received training that was accredited, and have passed both a national and state licensing examination to prove they know what they are talking about.

*In addition to the accreditation, you want to see someone that you like. The quality of the relationship is key. If you don't like the therapist, then the treatment isn't going to be as effective.* So if you are going to see a therapist, the type of degree is less important than making sure they are licensed, practice using techniques that are supported by research, and are someone you can trust and get along with.

### How Long Will You Need to Attend Therapy?

The duration of therapy needed is unique for everyone. Many people experience improvement within only a few sessions, while others reap benefits through months or years of seeing a professional. There's no commitment, and your therapist works for you, with the goal of helping you achieve measurable improvement. If you don't like or work well with one psychologist, choose another. It's that simple. They won't take it personally. And if they do, they should see a therapist. Not every therapist should be one.

Come away from this knowing that you have options. You never need to white-knuckle things alone. Your state of mind can make it hard to reach out, which is precisely when you should.

### No Need to Ask What Chapter of Revelations We're on Today

*"When this pandemic is over . . ."* started to sound like, *"When I win the lottery . . ."* Despite the societal dumpster fire, we collectively learned there is hope beyond future variants and future pandemics. And humankind finally started washing their hands, even if it's not for a full 20 seconds. Humanity has accomplished immeasurable things since COVID began as an overused name – from fast-tracking safe and efficacious

vaccines via a global database of development, to furthering mRNA vaccine development for other indications, and largely unifying as an entire planet for the greater good. We've never been better prepared for a future that's never been known.

Additionally, hundreds of millions of dollars poured into mental health companies and resources to identify and connect those who need help with more timely assistance. We learned to better commune with nature, to have more empathy for others, to effectively work remotely, and we discovered what we look like without regular dental visits, haircuts, and Botox. It turns out our inner beauty was what mattered most all along.

**Your Anxiety-Trigger Toolkit: Seven Tips for Coping With a Pandemic**

1.  Humor will change your relationship to the problem of stress, worry, or anxiety. Laugh with your anxieties till you can laugh at them.
2.  Look past the dark mental hues of your anxiety and ask yourself, *What's funny about this?* and brainstorm a list.
3.  There are specific religious scriptures that can provide peace of mind through uncertain periods. Memorizing any scripture is also a form of meditation while helping to train the brain for other things – like brainstorming that preceding list.
4.  Talking to a therapist via phone or teletherapy is a measurably effective adjunct tool during stressful times. They can help restore you to factory settings.
5.  There are two instances when you should contact a professional: (1) if you are in danger of hurting yourself or others or having passive thoughts about hurting yourself or others. (2) if your symptoms are starting to interfere with your daily life.
6.  When choosing a therapist, make sure the person is licensed and it's someone that you like. Shop around; they work for *you*.
7.  On the basis of human compassion and ingenuity, there is much hope for the future despite the risks of future variants, pandemics, and people who have conversations in doorways.

# 16 Starting a New Job

DOI: 10.4324/9781003345350-20

Many of us leave a job we hate for a job we hate that pays more. If the best part of your job is a chair that swivels and 5:00, then you're due for some workplace diagnostics. Our stress often begins at the sound of the alarm and ends only when we can stifle the internal chatter long enough to doze off at night.

*"A poem about work: Coffee blah blah blah. Drive home. Wine."*

Few of us ever dreamt of working hunched over in a cubicle under fluorescent lighting. Sometimes jail seems better than 40+ hours in a cubicle. Jail includes onsite healthcare; an outdoor gym; hot meals; a TV room; a library; pick-up basketball games; cookies; and conjugal visits. At work you might get free fruit, foosball, and Folger's.

Many of us are forced to sit catatonically in an onsite or home office for 40+ hours per week. According to research, sitting is the new smoking. And we've known the risks for decades. Consider the still relevant 1953 British study that compared the occupations of bus drivers and trolley conductors. Though the roles appeared similar in scope, the bus drivers sat for most of their day, while the trolley conductors ran up and down stairs and aisles of the double-decker trolleys for much of theirs. The bus drivers were nearly twice as likely as the conductors to die of heart disease.[1] Yet if a conductor died while driving, they became a projectile with a healthy heart.

## It's My Desk of Regret

According to Julie Schlosser of *Fortune* magazine, the modern-day cubicle was denounced by its designer, Robert Propst.[2] Cubicles were created in 1968 as a way to increase office productivity. But prior to his death in 2000, Propst regretted his unintentional contribution to what he called "monolithic insanity." Preach, Bobby. Propst's original plan included adjustable desks so workers could sit or stand. But due to increasing office space costs coupled with maximizing efficiencies of space, his flexible cubicle design became unhealthy and unproductive cage rows to crush human souls and potential. It's hard to think outside the box when you're stuck in one.

There are, however, many business-critical positions such as the Presidency or being a prolific, email spamming Nigerian prince that requires a desk. And many people are perfectly suited and happy at desk-based careers. But if you have a sedentary job – within a cubicle, corner office, cockpit, or couch – there is growing research to support that the more

1 Morris, J., Heady, J., Raffle, P., Roberts, C., & Parks, J. (1953). Coronary heart disease and physical activity of work. *The Lancet*, 262(6796), 1111–1120.
2 Schlosser, J. (2006, March 9). FORTUNE: Trapped in cubicles. *CNN Money*. https://money.cnn.com/2006/03/09/magazines/fortune/cubicle_howiwork_fortune/

hours a day you sit, the greater your likelihood of dying an earlier death regardless of how lean you are or how much you exercise.[3] The slower we move the faster we die.

Though job satisfaction tends to increase as earnings increase, those with higher earnings are not necessarily happier at work. The increased job satisfaction that follows a pay increase is temporary, and the effect fades over time.[4] According to behavioral economic theory, workers do not evaluate their income in absolute terms, but against their previous income. And people adjust to their new income level over time, so a salary increase becomes the new benchmark of comparison. The American dream has left my body.

## Tactics for Relief: How to Manage the Anxiety of a New Gig

### Make Day One a Day Won

We are evolutionarily hardwired to respond with anxiety to new situations. This feeling of heightened alertness is to protect us. As you go into the new job, meet with your supervisor and make sure you are clear about what is expected of you: stated working hours, performance expectations, quantifiable objectives, and understanding what a fax machine is. And if you still don't know what you're doing, walk around quickly and look worried.

At the same time, list some of your own learning goals for the job that matters to you. This will help you to feel less like a cog in the machine. You already know the reasons you were hired and competent to do this job. If Nicolas Cage can still get work, you can do anything.

Being new means you're allowed to ask questions, make mistakes, and screw up the little things. Take advantage of those first few weeks. Find allies and mentors who can help you through. Learn from HR what the benefits are for employee assistance programs (EAP) in case you ever need the extra assistance. It turns out HR does more than overseeing auto-generated rejection letters.

3 Edwardson, C. L., Gorely, T., Davies, M. J., Gray, L. J., Khunti, K., Wilmot, E. G., Yates, T., & Biddle, S. J. H. (2012). Association of sedentary behaviour with metabolic syndrome: A meta-analysis. *PLoS ONE, 7*(4), e34916.
4 Diriwaechter, P., & Shvartsman, E. (2018). The anticipation and adaptation effects of intra- and interpersonal wage changes on job satisfaction. *Journal of Economic Behavior & Organization, 146*, 116–140.

Companies increasingly have programs where people can present challenges they're facing or mentor employees who might be facing them, whether it's caring for a sick parent, struggling with mental health issues, or buying a home. Such programs foster a happier more supportive workplace for everyone. Because "happy Monday" doesn't need to be an oxymoron.

---

## Modify Your Mindset: Quick Tips to Manage the New Job Shakes

- **Risk Is Scary. Regret Is Scarier.** Be willing to sit with the anxiety caused by the thought that you may not be committing to the ideal job if it wasn't your first choice. Nothing is permanent, and all work is noble. Once you stop pursuing a futile quest for certainty, you can move forward. Seeking assurances is a compulsion that increases obsessive thinking patterns.
- **Thoughts and Feelings Don't = Facts.** Remind yourself that all anxiety is rooted in irrational fears and that anxiety lies to you with baseless thoughts, feelings, and ruminations. Just because you think it or feel it, doesn't mean it's true. And if you have experienced past anxiety symptoms, a new job can easily become the new focus. Anxiety is an opportunist that can lie dormant and flare like gout.
- **Practice Self-Care.** This includes simply taking time for yourself. From a mental health perspective, anxiety and stress are exhausting. However, you also need to honor your intuition and feelings. If you don't want to attend a happy hour with new colleagues because you're not "feeling it" and won't be on your "A-game," then heed that instinct. You gotta nourish to flourish.
- **Nurture with Nature.** A Stanford study found quantifiable evidence that walking in nature can reduce stress and lead to a lower risk of depression.[5] Through a controlled experiment, participants who went on a 90-minute walk through a natural environment reported lower levels of rumination (repetitive thought focused on negative aspects of the self) and showed

---

5 Bratman, G. N., Hamilton, J. P., Hahn, K. S., Daily, G. C., & Gross, J. J. (2015b). Nature experience reduces rumination and subgenual prefrontal cortex activation. *Proceedings of the National Academy of Sciences, 112*(28), 8567–8572.

reduced neural activity in an area of the brain linked to risk for mental illness compared with those who walked through an urban environment. Nature is also the best place to untether from electronics and imposter syndrome.

- **Give Yourself the Present of Presence.** Mindfulness is a skill that is practiced and perfected little by little – like using chopsticks. Mindfulness meditation encourages the practitioner to observe wandering thoughts as they drift through the mind. The intention is not to get involved with the thoughts or to judge them, but simply to be aware of each mental note as it arises. With practice, an inner balance and peacefulness develop until you become the spitting image of Siddhartha Gautama (aka, Buddha).

## It's Important to Define What Job Satisfaction Means

Job satisfaction is largely about your attitude toward a particular job. Not only does job dissatisfaction damage employee performance, but it can damage company performance. Beyond salary increases and free snacks, it doesn't appear that many corporate leaders strive to ensure their companies are truly great places to work. So *what does that mean?* Job satisfaction and your overall happiness are up to *you.* The right job can make a Wednesday feel like a Friday. Almost.

Since we often associate our self-identity with work, our sense of self-worth is greatly impacted by what happens at work. If we lose a few rungs on the socioeconomic ladder, we are left to reflect upon what is really important. "*Happiness comes to us when we dedicate our lives to something greater than ourselves – a path of service in the world, the raising of a loving family, the creation of beauty through art, or any passion that inspires one*" (*Listening to Your Inner Voice*, Douglas Bloch).[6] Having lived in this manner, you can look back over your life with a genuine sense of fulfillment.

Job dissatisfaction leads to anxiety, unhappiness, and a harmful disposition. There is no upside to negative thinking. It does not

6 Bloch, D. (1994). *Listening to your inner voice: Discover the truth within you and let it guide your way – A new collection of affirmations and meditations.* Hazelden Publishing.

prep you for life events, ward off salty mojo, or prevent worrisome outcomes. It does the opposite. It also causes face furrows, addictions, mental disorders, insomnia, and heart disease.

### Distorting Reality Is Fun but Naive

Most of us unknowingly use automatic thought distortions (aka, mental filters) to subvert ourselves. When we stop, we become marvels of happiness, positive energy, and efficiency. A mental filter is one type of cognitive distortion. It is a biased way of thinking about ourselves or the world around us. The core issue lies within the troubling emotional states and behaviors yielded by these irrational thoughts and beliefs. These include unpleasant mental states and behaviors like anxiety, depression, and conflict.

---

### Anxiety Safety Briefing: Failing to Recognize Your Own Cognitive Biases Is Also a Cognitive Bias

There are dozens of common mental filters we use within our daily lives. In the case of starting a new job or taking on a big, new "something," the mental filters you most likely use may include any of the following:

- **Negative predicting** involves foretelling the future in a negative light. There are typically just as many reasons your new job can go right. Assuming you will nervously botch an upcoming presentation is just a thought steeped in pessimism. Channel that nervous energy into poise and a standing O when you arrive for that first-day introduction.
- **Unrelenting standards** is the mindset that extremely high standards are required to avoid calamity. There are often no measurable benefits of doing a task beyond a basic acceptance level; and many such tasks exceed opportunity costs.
- **Must-erbation** involves having steadfast rules about how you and others should or must behave in a situation, such as at a new job. The emotional consequence when expectations are not met is anger, frustration, resentments, and guilt. The road to hell is paved with shoulds and oughts.

- **Underestimating coping ability** to handle a new job or negative events is a mindset of many who have not previously been held to the fire. This isn't your first challenge. And what doesn't kill you gives you coping mechanisms.
- **Overthinking** is a mindset that worry and rumination will lead to solutions. Overthinking your new responsibilities can impair your problem-solving ability and is a direct route to unhappiness. If you question the answers too many times, you will never answer the questions.
- **Catastrophizing** is being extremely well educated about all the things that could go wrong while always expecting the worst. A person who is catastrophizing might lose a sale and instantly think he or she will be fired and live in a Dodge Caravan with a bucket for a toilet.
- **"I can't change my way of thinking."** Lastly, rather than convincing yourself that changing mentalities is too hard, aim for small reductions in your negative automatic thoughts at 10%, for example. You will immediately obtain benefits, while working toward the goal. You can still see the glass as half-full. Just not half-full of hemlock.

### Harness Your Physics

Both confidence and insecurity reside in the brain and within the body. You can concurrently build up our mental *and* physical resiliency to handle challenges like a new job. Consider how your body often holds itself when you are lacking confidence and feeling scared or overwhelmed. Oftentimes we "turtle" and shrink in and withdraw into ourselves, which signals back to us that we are as timid and helpless as we feel. It can be so bad that a compliment from someone feels like a prank.

I stress the importance of movement and exercise often throughout this book due to the wealth of mental, emotional, and physical benefits. But the type of physical exercise you use also matters. For example, during times where you feel weakness or helplessness, strength training makes a noticeable difference in how you stand and physically feel, in turn changing how you feel emotionally and project yourself outwardly. Look no further than the confidence-exuding poses of the Power Rangers.

### *You Never Know How Badly You Chafed Until You Shower*

One of Chris's clients who's had a string of life misfortunes, in addition to frustrations related to graduate school, was left feeling helpless overall. Running became her primary coping activity, largely because she had been too broke in grad school to afford a gym membership. Running, while boring to her, had always helped her manage mood, stress, and anxiety. She would later graduate and land a job with benefits that included a gym membership, which isn't boring because you can watch other members hit on each other.

But what most shifted her feelings of helplessness was beginning a strength training regimen at the gym. The psychological results for her were immediate. She defined her workouts as a measurable confidence boost to walk into the office feeling strong and steady, saying:

*When I use the pull-up machine, I feel like I'm clawing back my confidence. When I do the bench press machine, I feel like I'm shoving all the anxiety off of my body, while the leg presses make me feel like I'm getting strong enough to stand my ground, and nothing can mess with me or knock me down. And when I increase the weight a few pounds each week, I feel more and more confident.*

Anxiety is the best pre-workout.

*"Can you send an ambulance? I just killed my workout."*

You can order weights online or find great deals on refurbished equipment like spin bikes, rowing machines, ellipticals, dumbbells, barbells, and kettlebells at fitness outlets. Or you can join a fitness center and ask a friend or employee at the gym for instructions on some of the weight machines. See which ones feel the most powerful for pushing away weakness, pulling in strength, and pressing away panic. Refusing to workout does not qualify as resistance training.

### *When Your Emotional Membership Is Anxiety Prime*

Chris has another client that was a former actor who used an actor's trick for managing pre-performance jitters. Chris shares this tactic with clients for new, anxiety-provoking social scenarios. *And scene.*

It's a simple hack in which you simply pretend the anxiety is excitement and trick your brain before it can dupe you into panicking. Include this technique for that first day on the job when your nerves are heightened. It's also great for walking into a new room, going to a job interview, a first date, or when tripping on flat carpet and acting like it's the floor's fault.

### Woot!

Think about a roller coaster going up, up, up, ticking and clicking as you ascend. Your brain might be thinking, "*Why did I do this?*" while flashing to news bytes of ghastly amusement park mishaps where people lose a limb or worse: a cell phone. Your hands grip the bar, your heart pounds, and your stomach rises into your throat as you rip down the first drop screaming with terror. By the next slope, that scream of fear is more a shriek of excitement. And by the end, it's a scream of elation. That's proceeding with conquest.

Afterward, your heart is still pounding. *Why?* Because your brain went from deciding those were signs of dread and anxiety, to determining they were feelings of fun and excitement.

**Therein lies the secret: As far as your body is concerned, excitement and anxiety are fundamentally the same thing.**[7]

The next time you feel anxious as you walk into a job interview or the first day in a new role, tune into your bodily sensations and reactions. Rather than trying to turn off any anxiety, change your vantage, and think of the emotions as signs that you're genuinely excited. Remarkably, over time you start to rewire your brain to reinterpret once scary situations as thrilling, if not fun. Now when you start a new job, you won't feel like the new character on season eight of a show.

### The Trouble With Your Curve

In many situations you need an amount of stress to keep your performance edge. The Yerkes–Dodson law (aka, Stress Curve), originally developed in 1908 by psychologists Robert M. Yerkes and John

---

7 Brooks, A. W. (2014). Get excited: Reappraising pre-performance anxiety as excitement. *Journal of Experimental Psychology: General, 143*(3), 1144–1158.

Dillingham Dodson, states that performance increases with physiological or mental arousal, *but only up to a point.* When levels of stress become too high, performance decreases. It sounds like physics, but let's not use labels.

*"My stress level is this many."*

The process is often illustrated graphically as a bell-shaped curve, which increases and then decreases with higher levels of stress. The research tells us that you want to be at a **60 to 80%** physiological stress arousal rate for optimal performance in most situations.[8] You likely already know what a 100% stress arousal rate feels like, so back it off from there to achieve a motivational target level. Anxiety is just hyperactive motivation.

8 Błońska, E. (2013). Motivation – Yerkes-Dodson law. *Linguodidactica, 17*, 35–40.

**Your Anxiety-Trigger Toolkit: 11 Tips for Starting a New Job and Acting Your Wage**

1. Meet with your supervisor on the first day to ensure you're clear about what's expected of you, while conveying your own learning goals for the job, even if you embellished your resume. Ask questions, make mistakes, and play the "new" card as needed.

2. Be willing to sit with the anxiety caused by the thought that you may not be committing to the ideal job if it wasn't your first choice. Nothing is permanent, except income tax.

3. From a mental health perspective, anxiety and stress are exhausting. Take time for yourself and honor your intuition and feelings.

4. There is quantifiable evidence that walking in nature can reduce stress and lead to a lower risk of depression. It's the antidote to *"Can everyone see my screen?"*

5. For a few minutes each day, practice staying in the present, moment to moment. Observe wandering thoughts as they drift through your mind without judging or attaching to them. The moment is always right now.

6. Job satisfaction and your overall happiness are up to *you*. Work is not indentured servitude, and you always have options, even if it doesn't feel that way.

7. Avoid the most common mental filters related to starting a new job. Turn on your mental "spam" filter to avoid mindsets like catastrophizing.

8. Build your mental and physical resiliency to handle this challenge via strength training. You don't need abs of iron or to become "quadzilla." A simple but regular strength training regimen helps to work worries away.

9. To your body, excitement and anxiety are fundamentally the same thing. Instead of trying to turn off any anxiety, think of the emotions as signs that you're genuinely excited. Channel it, repurpose it, and use it as positive energy.

10. You need an element of stress to keep your performance edge. Strive for a 60 to 80% physiological stress arousal rate for optimal performance. Stress enough to impress.

11. Don't forget to send a "Sorry for your loss" card to your former manager.

# Part IV

# Panic Disorder

A panic attack (aka, anxiety attack) is a sudden rush of physical symptoms that include chest tightness, shortness of breath, sweating, heart palpitations, and muscle spasms, paired with intense anxiety and often with a shot of imminent doom. ER visits and desperate phone calls to clinician offices are often the result, as are test results such as EKGs that reveal . . . nothing.

Panic disorder is a form of anxiety characterized by reoccurring unexpected panic attacks. Researchers have found that several parts of the brain, as well as biological processes, play a key role in this ailment.

If you panic at more places than the disco, there is some no-fail hope for you. You can begin by doing "opposite brain," and instead of thinking of all that could go wrong, think of all that could just as well go right. There is also some little-known wisdom about mitigating panic attacks, like the importance of allowing one to happen when it surfaces.

> "New study shows that people with panic disorders respond poorly to being locked in underwater elevators."

Panic disorder is diagnosed in those experiencing spontaneous panic attacks and are fixated with the fear of recurring attacks. Some people experience only one or two lifetime panic attacks, which end with the triggering situation. But if you've had chronic, sudden panic attacks with long periods constantly fearing additional attacks, you may have panic disorder.

DOI: 10.4324/9781003345350-21

# 17 Chronic Illness or Pain

DOI: 10.4324/9781003345350-22

When you were young, you wanted to date a doctor for money. Now, it's for the advice and prescriptions. Being alive can be painful and expensive. But one can be both chronically ill and chronically epic. For those of us with voluminous medical charts, there is still much hope.

## On Burning Bridges and Being in Cancer Remission With Mom

As an adult adoptee, the older I get the more mannerisms I see in myself from my parents. If there's any question regarding the nature versus nurture debate, I can tell you firsthand that it hardly matters if you're birthed or bought.

By way of example, my brother (Jeff) and I are from separate families and not related beyond sharing a new last name, yet we both exhibit considerable features of our parents. If you were to meet Jeff your first thought might be, "This guy's nothing like his genteel, Midwestern parents." Though, he is fiscally responsible and likes khakis and hotel robes as they do. Whereas I'm overtly kind, drop all my money on feral animals, and have an aversion to chinos and monogrammed shared clothing.

Though I've gleaned countless positive characteristics from my parents, there are two traits I wish I never shared with them: anxiety and cancer – conditions that abscond heredity or lack thereof.

My dad, a victim of indecision, often had me second-guessing my own choices or not making one at all. To this day, I'm often paralyzed by an Applebee's lunch menu. With mom, I currently share the mixed blessing of cancer remission. I'm remarkably gracious to be in remission with her, but uncertain how as a former athlete and lover of kale I succumbed to a smoker's cancer. Or far worse, how she was hit with an exceptionally rare stage IV breast cancer. I would take hers on if that was ever an option in my regular fantasy where some omnipotent entity grants us the power to switch maladies.

### *Mammogramming Your Boobs Is More Important Than Instagramming Them*

Being in this unique position, I've learned that the only thing worse than your own pain is helplessly watching a loved one suffer – the first being purely physical, the latter crushingly emotional. Yet it does not stop me from trying to will health and strength upon her.

I also have the perspective of 13 prior orthopedic, sports-related surgeries to keep me chronically swaddled in discomfort. In fact, as I write this section, I'm immobile due to a torn tendon in my foot. My physician's response was to put me in a half-leg cast for 4 weeks. But at 1:00 a.m. on day five, I had an itch-turned-full-blown-claustrophobic-panic-attack, and I sawed off the black, fiberglass cast in my bathtub with a dull, serrated kitchen knife. Patient compliance has never been my attribute. By the time I freed my leg at 3:00 a.m., the panic and itch were gone. I'm just not a cast person.

There is always an upside or takeaway to every hardship, though it often takes time and distance to source it. In my instance, I am much closer to my parents through our shared experience caring for my mom. Adversity also gave me the incentive to leave a dead-end job and justifiably demote many family members and friends to the "acquaintance pool."

## Tactics for Relief: When You Want to Do All the Things, But Your Body Doesn't

Pain lets you know that you're still alive. Some of us are hella alive. Chronic illness or pain can make you solitary and chronically irritable–even depressed. You may feel like you're 15% water and 85% pharmaceutical. But your worth is not measured by your productivity or body composition.

### Redirect Your Thoughts Away From What Is Being Taken From You, and Toward What You Do With What's Left

We come into this world with bodies that get sick, experience pain, and eventually die. We do anything to resist these truths. Let go of asking "*Why?*" and instead focus on "What can I do that's useful?" You need a plan that includes not taking it out on other people or yourself.

### Write Your Own Obit

"*Here lies <your name>, a lover of renaissance fairs, monster trucks, and brunch . . .*" Consider the effective but gloomy exercise of writing your own obituary or eulogy. Yes, it's grim. But when you look back on your life, what will you have wished you did, and more importantly, who will you have wanted to be? It's never too early to start beefing up your obit. Note: If this feels a tad too morbid, think instead about what you would want people to say about you at your retirement party or a toast you'd like to hear at your 90th 4:00 p.m. birthday dinner.

1. Take some time now to think on what really matters to you. Then, for about a paragraph or more, write out your obituary

or eulogy. I don't just mean what material wealth, promotions, or public recognition you might have acquired, but something more intimate than that. What do you want the people who love you to say? Maybe you're known for your empathy, resilience, positivity, confidence, bear hugs, wit, or an ability to stomach mini-mart rotisserie hotdogs at 2:00 a.m. on weekends. Everyone has a gift.

2.  As you look it over, reflect on your values. In what ways did this clarify or sharpen your values? Where did they come from? Are you living in accordance with them now, today, this past week? If not, how can you course correct and redirect yourself toward them?

What unnecessary obligations are you saying "yes" to? What other habits are getting in your way? As you work toward your goals, are there people that might be holding you back? Are there others who can help you move toward your goals? What does each day look like as you move toward your goals? In the words of author Gayle Forman, "*We are born in one day. We die in one day. We can change in one day. And we can fall in love in one day. Anything can happen in just one day.*" The time is nigh.

### A Bad Attitude Is a Disability, and a Disability Can Cause a Bad Attitude

An attitude shift can go a long way. What are you grateful for, and what's going well? The late Zen master Thich Nhat Hanh describes gratitude and appreciation in an unexpected way: "*When you have a toothache, all you think about is the toothache and suffer. When the toothache is gone, you don't remember to enjoy the 'non-toothache.'*"

What preexisting physical or emotional pain in your life is more at ease right now, and can you lean into and enjoy that pain absence in this moment? Even in the smallest of ways, what "toothaches" are not present? These aches can take various forms. It could be the easing of grief from a prior loss, such as a death or divorce. Or it could be the fresh absence of low back pain. As a brief guide, ask yourself:

*   What's not here physically in terms of pain and discomfort?
*   What's not here emotionally in terms of unpleasantness?

- What's no longer here in terms of past bad habits and self-defeating coping strategies?
- What's not here in terms of people who brought you down or held you back?

Write these down. Notice your internal response to each one as you read them over. You can also practice what Chris's friend, Jessica Morey, calls a bit of "AWE." Even when there is an unpleasant sensation, emotion, or situation in which you find yourself, you can simply ask:

> And . . .
> What . . .
> Else . . . is here besides the anxiety, frustration, and discomfort in this moment?

Anxiety challenge accepted. To lessen the anxiety associated with illness or injury, first recognize and accept that you are feeling anxious. Anxiety ebbs and flows. Receive it as it waxes and wanes over and through you. Then ask yourself, "And what else?" Remember, anxiety is the bully of emotions. Embracing it robs its unilateral power over you.

---

**Anxiety Safety Briefing: When You Live in Spain but the "S" Is Silent**

- **Don't accept every invitation pain-related anxiety offers.** Contest your fears related to your condition. What is the evidence? What is the worst case? What is likely? Remember this important chain: Thoughts precede feelings, which precede behaviors. Negative thoughts lead to negative emotions, which lead to negative behaviors. *Nip it at thoughts.*
- **Put the "I" in Desensitize.** Practice desensitization related to your current fear and anxiety. You can oppose your greatest doubts and worries or placate yourself to them. If you fear driving on the freeway, then get on the freeway. In a car.
- **Calm your chakras.** Practice mindfulness and summon your internal peace. Ground yourself in the present moment, accepting it without judgment or looking to the past or future. As

Buddha once said, "*When you walk, just walk. When you eat, just eat.*" Some say that Buddha ate more than he walked. But the real Buddha wasn't fat. "Fat Buddha" is actually Budai, a deity in Chinese folklore.

- **Water the grass you're standing on.** Stop comparing your physical status to the health or well-being of others and stay fixed on your own grandeur. Take solace in knowing that you're right where you need to be at this moment. No one is you. Therein lies your power.

- **Get ducks. Get a row.** Get organized. Messy was cute when you were little. But clutter in your physical environs will cloud your mind and spirit. And it's a tripping hazard. The first things people tend to avoid when anxiety escalates are routine tasks.

- **Get Your "Om" on.** Use meditation rather than anxiety or pain medication when and where reasonable. Scientists are discovering[1] that meditation increases the amount of gray matter in the brain, essentially rewiring the body to stress less. Incense optional.

- **There's nothing stronger than the heart of a volunteer.** Helping others has the dual benefit of (1) getting you out of your head and off your own problems (2) and feeling good about it in return. No matter what your physical state, there are ways you can help others.

- **Replace "what ifs" with "hell yeahs."** What-iffing fuels anxiety and saps power by projecting your focus into an unknown future. Change the "what ifs" into positives: "What if I *can* do it?" "What if I *don't* get worse?" "What if things turn out much *better* than I think?" The goal is not to overload yourself with positive self-talk, but to reduce the negative internal chatter and nix your inner naysayer.

- **Decaffeinate.** Caffeine is anxiety nectar and jacks up your central nervous system. Worse, caffeine can trigger panic or anxiety attacks, especially if you have an anxiety disorder. Eat healthfully. This includes reducing sugar and processed foods. Trail mix isn't health food; it's M&M's with obstacles.

- **Set goals, insert effort.** For each day, set at least these two goals: (1) a productivity goal (something from your to-do list) and (2) a pleasure goal (something from your fun-to-do list). Nothing changes if nothing changes.

---

1 Tang, R., Friston, K. J., & Tang, Y. Y. (2020). Brief mindfulness meditation induces gray matter changes in a brain hub. *Neural Plasticity*, 8830005. https://doi.org/10.1155/2020/8830005

### Show Me Your War Face

Mindfulness research finds that turning toward your pain can make a measurable difference.[2] When you lean into the pain, it doesn't change your pain exactly, but it changes your relationship with the pain, and you can then better tolerate it. I'm not trying to say "mind over matter" here, or not completely. Before you fire off scathing hate mail my way, hear me out. I know that chronic pain can be all-encompassing. My greatest recurring fantasy isn't sexual or financial; it's mugging a younger, athletic man and swapping out my wrecked joints for his.

Living with chronic pain is like trying to get comfortable on a bed of nails. But your mindset can greatly contribute to making it worse. Alleviating some of the suffering that goes with pain, especially chronic pain, is the part over which you have some power.

### What's Better Than an X-Ray or MRI? A Self Body Scan

The body scan was built on the pioneering work of Jon Kabat Zinn, who has helped thousands of people with chronic illness and pain and the stress that goes with it through practicing mindfulness.[3] The key is not letting the issues in your tissues overwhelm the signals of pain to your brain.

What people often notice with the body scan is that the pain isn't as constant or as bad as they think. It certainly sucks, but sometimes it's not constant throbbing. Sometimes it's diminishing. Sometimes it's not pain, but it's actually burning, or tingling, or something maybe less painful depending on our mindset.

*"Pain-free days? I've heard of this. Is it like Bigfoot?"*

For a video tutorial, search "Jon Kabat Zinn Body Scan Meditation" on YouTube. The body scan technique allows you to guide your focus thoroughly and purposefully throughout the body, while noting sensations within each part. Without firing a single muscle, you can place your mind anywhere in the body with intentional awareness of any sensations present in the moment.[4]

2 Zeidan, F., & Vago, D. R. (2016). Mindfulness meditation-based pain relief: A mechanistic account. *Annals of the New York Academy of Sciences, 1373*(1), 114–127.
3 Kabat-Zinn, J. (2003). Mindfulness-based interventions in context: Past, present, and future. *Clinical Psychology: Science and Practice, 10*(2), 144–156.

**Exercises in Fulfillment: How to Perform the Self Body Scan**

For a body scan, take anywhere from ten minutes or up to an hour, depending on time and what you can tolerate. Find a comfortable place to lie down where you won't be disturbed.

1. Allow your eyes to close if you wish, and bring attention to your breath and the sounds and sensations of your in-breath and out-breath.
2. After a few moments, direct your attention down to your feet. Notice sensations there and your emotional reactions to them: frustration, sadness, fear, and so on. Also notice any stories you tell yourself related to pain in your lower extremities such as *"I'll never run again because this pain will always get in the way." "Why didn't I listen to the doctor?" "And, what's a bunion?"*
3. Whatever thoughts, emotions, or stories are entering your mind, simply notice and set them aside and return to the sensations. Name the physical sensations as you notice: *pulsing, swelling, rubbing, stinging, on fire* . . . or whatever descriptors arise.
4. After spending about a minute on your feet, move up to your shins, and repeat the process – from there your calves, knees, thighs, and all the way up through the rest of your body. Scan it like you're the TSA.
5. Once you've mentally scanned each part of your body, you might revisit some of the more difficult parts, particularly the aching and painful areas. Just try being with the pain for a few moments, and imagine yourself breathing some healing energy into those places and exhaling some of the pain. See if anything changes for you.
6. Practice this technique regularly and notice if your relationship to the pain doesn't start to shift after a few weeks or months.

While practicing the body scan, it's common to feel some bodily sensations more acutely, to include noticing more pain in certain

---

4 Kabat-Zinn, J. (2022). *Coming to our senses: Healing ourselves and the world through mindfulness* {Paperback} 2006. Hyperion Books; Kabat-Zinn, J. (2005). *Coming to our senses*. Hyperion Press.

areas. Kabat Zinn explains that your awareness adapts to allow less emotional reactivity and rumination.

That said, *"The body scan is not for everybody, and it is not always the meditation of choice even for those who love it,"* says Kabat Zinn. You can also scan your body quickly, depending on your schedule and where you find yourself. You can do a one in-breath or one out-breath body scan, or a 1- to a 20-minute body scan, for example. With time and practice, you will increasingly appreciate the parts that don't hurt – the "non toothaches."

**Your Anxiety-Trigger Toolkit: 13 Tips for Coping With Chronic Illness or Pain**

1. Steer thoughts away from what's being taken away from you by your condition and toward what to do with what's left. In the words of Ice Cube, "*Today was a good day.*"
2. Write out your own obit, eulogy, or retirement toast. Review what you wrote and reflect on your values to ensure you're adhering to them. If not, make tweaks.
3. Regularly contest your fears related to your chronic condition to achieve desensitization to your fear and anxiety. Go ahead and call it bravery.
4. *Your presence has been requested.* Ground yourself in the present moment, accepting it without judgment or looking to the past or future.
5. Don't compare your physical status to the health or well-being of others. Your uniqueness is your power. Happiness begins where comparisons end.
6. Clutter within your physical space will increase stress. Messy might be a sign of genius, but organized is blissful.
7. Use meditation rather than anxiety or pain medication when and where reasonable. Your peace should feel like going to Target without kids.
8. No matter what your physical state, there are ways you can volunteer and help others. You've just been voluntold.
9. Change your "what ifs" into positives: "What if I *can* do it?" "What if I *don't* get worse?" "What if things turn out much *better* than I think?"
10. Decaffeinate. Decaf may taste like lies and betrayal, but caffeine measurably intensifies your central nervous system and palpably increases anxiety.
11. For each day, set at least these two goals: (1) a productivity goal (something from your to-do list) and (2) a pleasure goal (something from your fun-to-do list).
12. Turn toward the pain to change your relationship with and better tolerate it. You're still young, even if you feel 126.
13. Until we all have tattooed QR codes, use the body scan technique to guide your focus throughout the body with intentional awareness of any sensations present in the moment.

# 18 Birth of a Child

DOI: 10.4324/9781003345350-23

Don't fear childbirth. It's parenthood they don't give drugs for. While other parents are talking about honor roll, dance recitals, baseball, and gymnastics, you're excited that your infant latched on to a breast and wore socks longer than ten minutes. You used to be cool and do cool things. Now you're under house arrest with a tiny, angrier version of you.

## Sibling Smackdown: Anxiety Doesn't Fall Far From the Tree

If moments of parenting ever get you down, consider what my hapless folks unwittingly signed on for. The turmoil began the day I was adopted at a year old from the Children's Home Society of Oakland, CA in a Pontiac station wagon by two Midwesterners. Upon arriving home, I was stalked about the premises by my brother, Jeff (also adopted). As a toddler my only hobby was annoying the hell out of Jeff. I had no reason, but hobbies are like that. I was quite eager to kick down, or otherwise destroy, his latest LEGO or Lincoln Log engineering marvels, and he soon lost all patience while harboring ill-will toward his shelter-baby brother.

> *"The realization that I'm as related to the Easter Bunny as my own mother is unsettling."*

By the time we entered junior high, our sibling arguments had escalated into furniture-obliterating brawls. My dad was soon out of options, so he did what any man at his breaking point could legally do in the 80s: He dragged us to the front yard one evening for a suburban meltdown fight night. Our family life was moments away from detouring into a white-trash sideshow, as Jeff and I laced up our Ked's to release a fury of middle-class angst.

The twisted irony was that we were never allowed to play, or even walk, on our front lawn. We didn't have a normal lawn; we had dichondra. Dichondra was most popular in Southern California during the 50s and 60s as a "lawn substitute." It does not consist of a blade, like regular grass, but takes the form of a tiny stem with a leafy top.

We were never permitted to mess with our nouveau lawn. This included mowing. Jeff and I were the only kids raised in the suburbs who never mowed their own lawn. This would be a blessing to most children, but it deeply troubled Jeff, and he regularly mowed neighboring lawns like his own GoFundMe.

Our fake turf was simultaneously my dad's retreat from life and his biggest source of anxiety. He never took vacations, except for the mental retreats he visited while tending to this small parcel. When he was painstakingly weeding and caring for it, he was no longer subject to the tyranny of family life.

> *"I fought the lawn and the lawn won."*

He was obsessed and meticulous about every tender sprout while crouched over, scrupulously removing any petite stem of grass not matching the others. And yet Jeff and I were about to not only step upon the turf, but smother it altogether in a contorted rage.

It's not like I would routinely beat Jeff down at the age of 13. Quite the opposite. But I believed I was furious enough to destroy him Hulk-style on that particular day. He was much larger and more athletic than me, and had not yet begun his pack-a-day Marlboro 100s habit. But I did have a monster temper. When agitated, I possessed super-human strength, with the ability to hurl my brother into the air and then batter his body with fists and nearby objects.

I made nearly everything in our house a weapon at one time or another. Book ends, candlestick holders, extension cords, and even the large family Bible, until everything was locked away. Our house became a large, child-safe playroom.

As our one-on-one battle in the front yard ensued that day, the dichondra was pummeled along with my boy-band body. It wasn't long before the neighbors noticed our familial collapse. People began peeking out their awning-covered tract home windows. Slowly, neighbors filed out of their homes to view firsthand what appeared to be my father's beleaguered attempt at parenting us.

## Raising Teens Is Like "Caligula" Meets "Dateline"

Mom would have nothing to do with our lawn fracas. This was unfortunate, as I could have used her sympathy and first-aid skills. Like my father, she was fresh out of ideas on how to deal with Jeff and me. The fight lasted only about 10 minutes, during which time I was tossed like a broken department store mannequin all over the yard. I'm sure this calamity bordered on child abuse somewhere. If I had a cell phone, I would have called Child Protective Services on my own behalf.

My dad's soft, cool, leafy grass alternative made for a more comfortable shellacking. The pubescent combat only ended when I admitted defeat for all to see. I returned to the house to nurse my wounds, with the evidence displayed as smashed dichondra indentations of my body in various mangled poses. But we finally got to be on the lawn.

### Tactics for Relief: What to Do When You're Still Tired From Yesterday's Tired, and You've Already Used up Tomorrow's Tired

The scariest hood you'll ever pass through is parenthood. The list of parental worries is long. Remind yourself that anxiety puts you in a constant state of overestimating danger and underestimating your ability to cope. Tell your partner or family how you're feeling. Leverage family and other friends with kids to trade favors and assistance. Find a network of parents to build support. If you're still feeling stressed, talk with your healthcare provider.

The joys, challenges (or, surprises) of conceiving, birthing, or adoption make you wonder whether you're not just qualified, but if you're even ready. Additionally, you may find yourself seemingly punished at random with frustrations and setbacks throughout the process. Parenting was much easier back when you were raising hypothetical kids.

Just as every well-meaning but intolerable friend or stranger has already told you, nothing can prepare you for parenthood. There's no perfect time to become a parent, and there's no straight path to child-rearing. Like folding a fitted sheet, no book or technique is going to yield a failsafe parenting strategy that leaves you with a happy, healthy, well-adjusted adult in 20 years who might gently usher you into senility.

> *"Don't be so hard on yourself. The mom in "ET" had an alien living in her house and didn't notice."*

### Don't Plant Anxieseeds

While part of anxiety is genetic, a larger component is learned. It's learned by our kids in terms of what they see us do, and how they see us respond to and talk about things.[1] Whether that's crossing the street after looking both ways 16 times, driving our children across the street because we don't want them to risk walking (as one anxious parent Chris worked with did), or in the well-meaning ways telling your kids how you might've struggled with math anxiety. It all tends to backfire via anxiety seed planting. Strive not to sow such seeds in your quest to protect them.

#### Anxiety Me = Anxiety Mini-Me

Mentally you want to be able to regulate your own anxiety so that your kid(s) learn to distinguish between real versus perceived

---

1 Affrunti, N. W., & Ginsburg, G. S. (2012). Maternal overcontrol and child anxiety: The mediating role of perceived competence. *Child Psychiatry and Human Development*, 43(1), 102–112.

danger. In study after study, kids look to adults for a clear under-standing of what is safe and what isn't. So the more you regulate yourself, the better off your kids will be.[2] A lack of said advice has generated reality TV shows like "Toddlers & Tiaras," "16 and Pregnant," and "The Bachelor" series.

Chris was working with a patient named Dustin, an Ivy league graduate in his early thirties. He and his wife, Lena, were trying to get pregnant. The first in his group of friends, he was feeling pressure from his sick and aging in-laws who desperately wanted grandchildren. Dustin and Lena cleared their work travel calendars and set aside 6 months to try to conceive. To Dustin's delight and shock, she was immediately pregnant, expecting a baby girl nine months from their first attempt. Getting pregnant should be harder than making a pregnancy board on Pinterest.

Chris found Dustin pacing outside his office ten minutes before his appointment one day. He invited Dustin in, and after congratu-lating him, Dustin paused for a few moments, lip quivering before tearfully confessing he felt completely unprepared for the looming and drastic lifestyle change. Over time he settled into the new truth, grateful that biology offered all that time to prepare for parent-hood. Chris admits that his first mistake was congratulating him before asking him how he truly felt about it. Some guys prema-turely congratulate.

Dustin and Lena spent the next few months physically and emotionally preparing for the baby. They made lists of what they wanted to do before the baby arrived, such as doing a yoga retreat in Mexico. Six weeks before Lena was due, Dustin found himself tossing and turning every night. He was scratching himself to sleep and waking to tiny bloodstains on the sheets, which can mean only one thing to the modern urban dweller.

With a month to go before the baby was born, it appeared they had somehow acquired bedbugs in their apartment. *Perhaps from the yoga retreat travels?* they wondered. They frenetically located an exterminator, rented out a short-term apartment, and moved all of their own and the baby's belongings, and had the place fumigated.

2 Eley, T., McAdams, T., Rijsdijk, F., Lichtenstein, P., Narusyte, J., Reiss, D., Spotts, E., Ganiban, J., & Neiderhiser, J. M. (2015). The intergenerational transmission of anxiety: A children-of-twins study. *The American Journal of Psychiatry*, 172(7), 630–637.

After a week, they moved back into their original apartment, hauling all the additional baby regalia.

But the next morning, the bloodstains were back. Dustin's legs were on fire with the itchiness. Once more they moved out and called the exterminator. And this time the bedbugs seemed to hitch along. Dustin tried scratching himself to sleep at the Airbnb, while pondering if they should discard everything they owned, including the generous gifts from the baby shower. Meanwhile, Dustin happened to casually ask his prescribing psychiatrist if there was any lotion or cream that could help the itching, as the doctor looked closely at the bites, "*Dustin . . . these aren't bedbug bites,*" the doctor began. "*These are hives.*"

> "*You're not a real millennial until you mistake stress hives for bedbug bites.*"

There were no bedbugs and never were. There were never even allergies. Dustin had intermittent stress hives about the coming baby. This is a rare but real side effect of anxiety.[3] It's not hypothetical that worry, stress, and anxiety can mess with your body in intrinsically related ways. For some, hydrocortisone is an adjunct anxiety med.

Months later Dustin told Chris, "*I feel like such a jerk. I wanted to have my baby, Leah. But it's also like my body told me I didn't. I love being a dad now, but every time I get an actual bug bite and scratch it, I worry that it means I don't really want to be a dad and hate myself for that.*"

Chris acknowledged Dustin's feelings, including how scary it is being a new parent. He also stressed to Dustin that it wasn't his body betraying him, rather sending him a message to take care of his own well-being in the process. Once Dustin learned that it was anxiety and talked about it, both the anxiety and the manifestations faded. Once you *name it*, you can *tame* it.

Dustin didn't have any more outbreaks. Instead, he found the words to say whenever he was anxious and feeling panicky and offered himself some compassion, while laughing at his own crazy story. He had discovered the healthy balance of realizing the upsides

3 Tat, T. S. (2019). Higher levels of depression and anxiety in patients with chronic urticaria. *Medical Science Monitor: International Medical Journal of Experimental and Clinical Research*, 25, 115–120.

of fatherhood, rather than predicting it as solely chicken nuggets and destruction.

### Insomnia: A Transient Condition Transmitted From Babies to Parents

We can land a rover on Mars, but we can't get a baby to sleep through the night. Take solace knowing that poor sleep doesn't last forever with kids. Unfortunately, for the non-morning types, by the time your kids are teenagers and sleeping half days, they'll have rewired your internal clock so that you'll still be waking at sunrise and eating dinner at 4:00.

Adequate sleep is not always a priority or even a possibility for new parents, especially in the early years. But inadequate sleep will measurably intensify anxiety. It is said to "sleep when the baby sleeps," which is as realistic as "iron when the baby irons."

### Practice Shiftwork

Early parenting is like a 24/7 unpaid internship where there are no sick days, holidays are mandatory, and you go to bed by 9:00 p.m. Chris can tell you firsthand that both parents don't need to get up every time your baby winces or cries. He and his wife would get up together to check on their son every night for months and jointly change diapers and sing him back to sleep. Then they'd both have pudding for brains the next day. Instead, split the night into two shifts and alternate who gets up to change diapers, feed and burp, or consider alternating nights altogether.

### The Strawberry Icing on a Pop-Tart® Is Not Fruit

There are few things more difficult than trying to eat healthfully when you're exhausted, stressed, and permanently time constrained. But your cheat meal shouldn't be 3 months long, or you risk once forgiving sweatpants becoming inappropriate.

With childbirth often comes an abrupt halt in exercise while trying to adjust to a new lifestyle. There is also an inability to sit down and enjoy full meals, like your childless friends take for granted. Instead, you graze on whatever is left in the fridge or pick at your kid's unfinished mac and cheese and Cheerios.

### Abs Might Be Made in the Gym, But They're Exposed in the Kitchen – the 70/30 Rule

The 70/30 rule refers to weight management being 70% the foods you eat and 30% exercise. Anything other than healthy eating is not normal. Not according to your body anyway. You can start by avoiding most canned food and anything in a bag or box (cookies, crackers, chips, emotions, etc.). When you're hungry, open the fridge, not the freezer or cupboard.

If you don't already have one, consider a smoothie blender. Smoothies are a nutritious and epic time saver. But make them with fruit, vegetables, and protein powder, not peanut butter and Kahlúa. As moments permit, prep for meals as you're able; that way you're more likely to stay on track.

Stick to the perimeter of the grocery store where you will find fresh produce and meats, and avoid the processed and shelved foods in the middle. Consider chicken, turkey, and fish for proteins, and round these out with many dark-colored vegetables, avocadoes, raw nuts, Greek yogurt, sweet potatoes, and an embarrassing number of fruits for snacks.

> *"Catching your kid eating an entire bag of Cheetos for dinner and realizing you don't have to cook sends the wrong message."*

Even if you're bad at math, if you consume more than you burn, the calories will count themselves and convert to adipose tissue (i.e., fat). Focus on vegetables, lean proteins, and minimal starches/carbs for dinner and lunch, and leave the good fats for breakfast.

Consider using a website or downloading a simplified food and exercise tracking and logging app. There are apps that track your calories simply by taking photos of your food. It's a quick and easy way to know where you're at calorically on a given day. And you become truly aware of what you're eating without having to count the calories yourself. You want to be aware of what you're eating and not become a hostage to it. That said, doing "crunches" is not chewing potato chips.

Parenting requires moving quickly and efficiently while performing feats of multitasking (i.e., doing many things at once, all poorly). For example, while grilling salmon for 3 to 4 minutes each side, you now have a total of 6 to 8 minutes to start the laundry, sweep the floor, catch up on texts and emails, or get in some push-ups, crunches, or pull-ups. If nothing else, parenting teaches you to be hyper-efficient.

### When It Feels Like You'll Never Mentally or Financially Recover

As a new or prospective parent, be good to yourself; forgive yourself when you fail or fall short; and leverage resources in the form of friends, family, support groups, agencies and nonprofits, counselors, and churches and religious support affiliations. You can start by running an online search on "parenting support" or a similar search string. As anxious and ill-equipped as you might feel about becoming a parent, there will never be an ideal time to start. You will learn on-the-fly as every parent since Adam and Eve has. And everyone's still talking about their screwups.

**Your Anxiety-Trigger Toolkit: Eight Tips for Coping With the Birth of a Child**

1. Lean on family and friends with kids to trade favors and build a network of support. If you're feeling chronically stressed, talk with your healthcare provider. Try not to snap at your childless friends who compare pet ownership to parenting.
2. Regulate your anxiety so that your kid(s) learn to distinguish between real versus perceived danger to avoid anxiety seed planting. Cool teen angst can turn into chronic adult anxiety.
3. Practice nighttime shiftwork as new parents to maximize on rest. Also consider alternating nights altogether.
4. When choosing between shaving your legs/face and feeding your child, always feed.
5. Strive to adhere to the 70/30 rule. Until Oscar Meyer makes a less-processed, insulin resistant, adult Lunchable with steak and wine, meal prep ahead of time as you're able.
6. Focus on the perimeter of the grocery store where you'll find fresh produce and meats, and avoid the refined and shelved foods in the middle.
7. Consider using a simplified food and exercise tracking and logging app. The goal is to become aware of what you're eating without the laborious calorie counting.
8. As a new or prospective parent, be good to yourself, forgive yourself when you fail or fall short, and leverage available resources. If you pick them up to smell their butt, you're doing it right.

# 19 Death of a Loved One

DOI: 10.4324/9781003345350-24

We can't all have the DNA of Wolverine or Deadpool. At some point, most of us will deeply mourn profound losses. And no matter how unfathomable the sense of grief, we are inherently designed to reflect and recover.

There's no way around it; the death of a loved one is awful. Platitudes from others fall woefully short and run the gamut to include *"I'm sorry for your loss," "Everything happens for a reason,"* and *"At least he died doing what he loved"* (even if he was eaten by a shark). As a therapist, countless people come to Chris's office with grief issues, wanting to feel better. But there's no shortcut through grief, which lasts far longer than the sympathy received. It takes the time it takes, and the more you try to rush or shortcut it, the worse it can get.

## The World Doesn't Stop for Your Grief

Chris lived a relatively sheltered life up until college when he struggled with his own mental health and substance use issues. When he returned to college after a few years off, most of his friends had already graduated. That first year back was particularly tough for him. And only hours after he submitted his final college paper, a friend shared some awful news. Chris's closest friend, Chuck, who'd stuck by him before, during, and after all his challenges, had died in a freak natural episode while sleeping.

Chris was devastated and reached out to other friends and family for support. Everyone was kind, but no one seemed to fully "get it." In a sense, it was a moment that felt deeply defining as he began adult life because no other person could take away the pain. Nor could any substance negate the pain. And by that same time, Chris was trying to get sober.

He got through graduation, and to this day there is a bittersweetness forever associated with the end of college and the beginning of his adulthood.

## Tactics for Relief: How to Ease the Impact of Life's No. 1 Stressor

Despite how fast you might be, you can't run from grief forever, nor fight it, nor drown it in whatever substance or behaviors you turn toward. You have to be with it. You've got to practice self-care and obtain some companionship, because the only thing worse than mourning the death of a loved one is mourning alone. The good news is that despite the intense mental, emotional, and physical pain associated with the loss of a loved one, you were created and built to adapt and endure it.

Things to do today:

1. Get up.
2. Survive.
3. Go back to bed.
4. Know that it was enough.

Be the things you loved most about the people who are gone. This is but one of the ways you never truly lose the people that you love, even in death. The people you lose stay with you in the stories you tell, in aspects of your personality, in the skills and strengths you've developed over the years, and in the paths you follow.

### On the Myth of Anticipatory Grieving

At the time of this writing, I watch my mom decline from the ravages of chemo and stage IV breast cancer that spread to her brain and largely paralyzed her. I am constantly filled with anxiety wondering how much time she has left, while futilely trying to emotionally prepare for the loss. With every health setback she has, my anxiety spikes wondering if this is the physical sign that will be her end.

It's an odd feeling to try and live normally while death looms to take a loved one away. Our brains stop working as they usually do when we think we're going to lose someone we love. Conversely, the death of a loved one often comes without warning, where you don't get time to mentally prepare or brace for the emotional impact. It's like being awakened from a peaceful dream to find your bedroom ablaze.

> "When I die, I hope it's early on a weekday so I don't go to work for no reason."

What I've learned through this unwelcomed life lesson in anxiety triage is that you cannot emotionally prepare for the loss of a loved one. You can mentally prepare to a degree. And you can physically work out your fear and sadness in various ways. But you cannot pre-process a loss. We must all deal with it on the backend in roughly the same manner.

Grief and loss are indiscriminatory and inflict their pain equally on all. And no matter how much time has passed, there are still times when it suddenly becomes harder to breathe. These are called "grief attacks." But they're not setbacks; they are a fundamental part of the grieving experience.

### Identify Your Negative Thoughts

Every emotion is valid during times of grief. But there are times when your harmful thoughts can become inundating, such as during a breakup/ divorce or loss of a loved one. Fortunately, you can change thought patterns through a process called cognitive restructuring or reframing.[1] Don't be distracted by the jargon. It's simply adjusting to how you respond to your automatic negative thoughts. Here are a few examples:

**Negative Thought Pattern**

| | | |
|---|---|---|
| Nothing seems to be going right for me | I'm worthless | Depression |

**After Cognitive Restructuring/Reframing**

| | | |
|---|---|---|
| Nothing seems to be going right for me | I fought and survived for so long, will continue to fight, and will make things better | Less or no depression |

How an abridged reframing looks regarding the loss of a loved one:

**Negative Thought Pattern**

| | | |
|---|---|---|
| My mom died | I cannot handle the pain of her loss and absence | Inconsolable grief |

**After Cognitive Restructuring/Reframing**

| | | |
|---|---|---|
| My mom died | Her lifetime of love and support forever remain and what I will reflect upon | A shift toward more adaptive thinking |

1 Shahane, A. D., Fagundes, C. P., & Denny, B. T. (2018). Mending the heart and mind during times of loss: A review of interventions to improve emotional well-being during spousal bereavement. *Bereavement Care: For All Those Who Help the Bereaved, 37*(2), 44–54.

It looks wildly simplistic, and I'm not asking you to con yourself into feeling better. But everything begins with your thoughts. Know that Chris and I get it. Throughout the creation of this book, he and I have regularly commiserated about our terminally ill mothers. Our related anxieties were parallel.

But much to our sorrow, Chris lost his mom to cancer over Mother's Day weekend of 2021. "*As I reflect on my mom's death, I feel both sadness and white-hot anger at her life ending before her time, and relief that her death saved her from the ongoing pandemic, and the humiliations of a rapidly deteriorating body and mind,*" reveals Chris.

Reframing takes regular and intentional action, starting with identifying each time your thoughts begin to harmfully spiral. It might help by talking it out loud to yourself. This might take the form of "*I miss him/her so much that I have an aching hole in my chest and stomach, and will never function again or live up to what s/he wanted.*" Your feelings and emotions are justified and universal.

But the narrative is not necessarily truth, and you can change your maladaptive internal beliefs by gently reframing your thoughts to telling yourself something like "*I have to grieve for as long as it takes before I can function how I used to. I can remember the wonderful times, love, and bond we shared that will sustain me through the pain I'm feeling now.*" In the meantime, as the author Yumi Sakugawa conveys, "*Sometimes it's okay if the only thing you did today was breathe.*"

Perhaps you experience guilt for feeling like you should have visited your lost loved one more when they were alive. Or maybe your last interaction with them wasn't a good one or worse. These and an infinite amount of other self-inquiries and thought loops are exceptionally common during instances of loss. The key to successful reframing is first noticing and then changing how you talk to yourself about what is happening. You can then shift the narrative to a more helpful, and likely more realistic, scenario. Here too, the self-compassion I've previously imparted is crucial.

### What Concrete Evidence Is There to Support Your Negative, Unhelpful Thinking?

More often than not, there is no evidence. Try to identify the basis for your subjective thoughts and then challenge them. What actual evidence do you truly have to support these beliefs? This is where talking to a professional can help. If you're suffering with guilt over something related to your lost loved one, challenge your feelings of remorse in knowing that no genuine or loving relationship can be defined by a lapse, failure, miscommunication, fight, and so on. Our relationships are the sum of many parts. This skewed thinking can cause you to blame yourself for things outside your control. By way of perspective, in a moment of panic, the Australian quokka will throw their own babies at a predator just to escape.

If you truly believe that you fell grossly short in some capacity, refer to a few trusted peers for objectivity. Those who know you and knew your loved one can impart much-needed and redemptive feedback. Moreover, peers are also great for sharing how they navigated similar losses of this magnitude.

When it comes to losing a loved one, we often fall prey to the "fallacy of fairness" trap where we measure things on the basis of fairness and equality, when in reality things don't work that way. Your loss can feel overwhelmingly partial and undeserved. But life's fairness is purely happenstance for every one of us.

> Life: *The existence of an individual human or animal.*
> Fair: *A place where you eat deep-fried Twinkies and ride a Tilt-A-Whirl.*

### Embrace Your Powerlessness

Life consistently reminds us that none of us are in control. As soon as you identify a situation over which you are powerless, economize by turning down your stress response. Call a friend or fellow survivor and share your feelings of loss and helplessness. No one can feel another person's grief. What is important is to grieve and keep moving by connecting with others and taking good care of yourself. There are no rules on grieving. And you don't know how you will handle it until you're in the grip of sorrow. "*It is the peculiar nature of the world to go on spinning no matter what sort of heartbreak is happening*," shares writer Sue Monk Kidd.

Some people fall to their knees unable to breathe at news of a loved one's death. While another – equally close in love and relationship to the same person – appears to go about their days largely unmoved. The difference is nothing more than what and how they externalize their grief. If you don't allow yourself to grieve at some point, your grief will make other plans for you.

> *"The difference between promises and memories is that we break promises, and memories break us."*

Weeks after the funeral, Chris started a job, and Chuck's huge absence wasn't as vast. It still hurt, but moving forward with his life helped. So too did honoring Chuck's legacy by focusing on what mattered and Chris staying sober ever since. The biggest accomplishment of Chris's young life was publishing his first book, which he dedicated to Chuck. For Chris, keeping Chuck's memory alive helped him, and he built new friendships and deepened others in the wake of Chuck's early death.

### Emotions Serve a Purpose Other Than Distinguishing Us From Sociopaths and Artificial Intelligence

Emotions motivate and organize us to action by reducing our reaction time in critical situations. Emotions communicate to and influence others. But they also communicate to us. For example, when you're experiencing a bout of anxiety, you may not initially recognize your current frame of mind as "anxious." Instead, you interpret and feel the sensation as restlessness, agitation, or irritability.

### There Is Good Grief, Just Ask Charlie Brown

In the case of a death and the related grief, your emotions signify to yourself and others that you need care, communion, and support. Distracting or otherwise disregarding such feelings can put you in peril. Research on avoidance indicates that suppressing and avoiding the pain ensures that the pain will continue. Avoid prolonged pain by avoiding avoidance.

There are, however, times when it's healthy to distract yourself from pain, such as when you're simply unable to process the loss, or if you're in a time and place where your ability to efficiently function is required. In such instances, you can decrease the emotional intensity for your own well-being and immediate efficacy.

### Put Your Sleep on Restriction

In the instance of loss, sleep is elusive. That's where the tactic of sleep restriction can prove helpful.[2] It sounds aggressive, but it's fondly self-kind. Sleep restriction is a behavioral therapy for sleeplessness that works by decreasing irregularity in the timing of sleep, while increasing the intensity. The goal is simple: reduce time spent in bed in order to consolidate sleep. Sort of like an "absence makes the heart grow fonder" take on sleep.

Me: *I'm going to bed early tonight.*
Me: *Is that the sun?*

Not only does sleep restriction work as well as medication, but it also has a longer-lasting effect.[3] The hitch is that it takes several weeks of diligence in altering your sleep schedule to reap the results. You may feel sleepier and experience more disrupted sleep *initially*. Let that not dissuade you, my puffy-eyed sheep counter. Stick with it and your insomnia will improve.

### Exercises in Fulfillment: The Sleep Restriction Technique

**Step 1:** Determine your allowed time in bed. Begin by staying in bed for only the average amount of time you are actually currently sleeping. This can be calculated by keeping a sleep log for 2 weeks. **Total up the average number of hours you slept each night, and this is your average total sleep time (ATST).** I'm getting mathy but stay with me.

**Add 30 minutes to your ATST.** This may mean that you are only allowed to stay in bed for 5 hours a night. **Time in bed = ATST + 30 minutes.**

2 Maurer, L. F., Schneider, J., Miller, C. B., Espie, C. A., & Kyle, S. D. (2021). The clinical effects of sleep restriction therapy for insomnia: A meta-analysis of randomized controlled trials. *Sleep Medicine Reviews, 58*, 101493.
3 Morgenthaler, T., Kramer, M., Alessi, C., Friedman, L., Boehlecke, B., Brown, T., Coleman, J., Kapur, V., Lee-Chiong, T., Owens, J., Pancer, J., & Swick, T. (2006). Practice parameters for the psychological and behavioral treatment of insomnia: An update. An American Academy of sleep medicine report. *Sleep, 29*(11), 1415–1419.

Step 2: Set a wake time. Wake up at the same time **every** morning no matter how much sleep you got the night before. Feel the snooze but deny it.

Step 3: Set a bedtime. Your bedtime is determined by counting back from your wake time following the amount of time in bed you were allowed in Step 1. For example, if your time in bed is 5.5 hours and you have set your wake time to 5 a.m., your bedtime is 11:30 p.m. You should not get into bed before 11:30 p.m. even if you are sleepy and think you could fall asleep. You got this, weary warrior.

Step 4: Stick to this sleep schedule as closely as possible for at least 2 weeks. If you are sleeping relatively well for most nights and you feel good during the day, keep this sleep schedule. If you are feeling tired during the day, add another 15 minutes to your time in bed. **You can increase the time in bed by 15 minutes per week until you are sleeping better at night *and* feel good during the day.**

Step 5: Use bright light in the morning and dim the lights in the evening. Bright light is the most powerful controller of the sleep/wake cycle. Using light will help you return to a normal sleep/wake pattern, and trying sleep restriction therapy without bright light is not nearly as successful. **Using light for 30 minutes upon awakening is sufficient to regulate the sleep/wake cycle.** You can go outside into natural sunlight or purchase a light box or light-based alarm clock.

Step 6: **Avoid napping.** Despite the longing, napping will only decrease nighttime sleep drive.

A cautionary note: Regardless of how long you think you sleep, it is suggested that you **begin by spending a minimum of 5.5 hours in bed** so that you are able to function during the day. If you have significant difficulty staying awake, do not attempt this method. It's not for everyone. If you have any concerns or questions, please talk with your doctor.

## Grief Support Resources

There is no right or wrong way to grieve. But there are healthy ways of coping with painful emotions to facilitate healing and recovery. For example, most companies have an HR person that can point you to resources for bereavement counseling, at least short term. And you can walk into most any place of worship and find that they have regular grief support meetings held year-round. The coffee and snacks alone are worth going. I didn't start drinking coffee until I joined a support group. It was the best, worst coffee and powdered creamer in Styrofoam cups ever because it came with unsurpassed fellowship and learned coping skills.

For further assistance, do an online search of **"grief support, <your city/county>"** and you will find a list of resources and groups in your area. Local hospice care professionals often have resources as well. You can also contact your doctor and ask what bereavement support services they offer.

We must all walk through the valley of the shadow of death, but we don't need to be afraid or alone. Remember to clear your internet browser history first.

### Your Anxiety-Trigger Toolkit: Nine Tips for Coping With Grief

1. Practice self-care and obtain some companionship. A friend will remind you to eat, wash your hair, and get you to laugh again.
2. Be the things you loved most about the people who are gone. This is one of the ways you never truly lose the people that you love after death. Love transcends death.
3. "Grief attacks" are not setbacks, but a fundamental part of the grieving process.
4. Change adverse thought patterns through cognitive restructuring or reframing by shifting your perspective to adjust automatic thoughts. The presence of pets is also remarkable in shifting perspective.
5. Lean on bereavement buddies. Peers are great for sharing how they navigated similar losses of such magnitude. Grief shared is grief lessened.
6. Embrace your powerlessness. There are no rules on grieving. You can't compare grief or losses. Sadly, people will try.
7. In the case of a death and the related grief, your emotions signify that you need care, communion, and support. Pay them mind.
8. When you're unable to process the loss, you can decrease the emotional intensity through distraction or short-term denial. It's okay to be selective in the reality you accept.
9. For grief-related insomnia, practice sleep restriction. Your sleep should be a pattern, not a freestyle.

# 20 Breakup or Divorce

DOI: 10.4324/9781003345350-25

Studies show that to the brain, quitting love and heroin are the same. Our brains cannot differentiate another human from smack. Take solace knowing that your ex's love longings are normal. To an extent.

A prominent study alludes to a physiological basis to cravings for an ex.[1] Researchers used functional magnetic resonance imaging (fMRI) to record the brain activity of adults who had experienced a recent unwanted breakup and who reported still feeling love for their ex. When viewing photographs of former partners, study participants showed brain activity in the areas associated with reward and motivation, specifically, the release of dopamine that is also seen in drug addiction. It is theorized that people experience cravings for their ex similarly to the way addicts crave a drug from which they are withdrawing. We become exaholics.

*"I'm sorry I annoyed you with my unconditional love."*

But there is good news! Just like the brain is hardwired to fall in love, it also has a mechanism that helps us fall out of love and move along.[2]

## Why Are Romantic Relationships So Hard?

You position your companion against idealistic projections of "real" love from episodes of *The Bachelor*, royal weddings, or Cialis ads. This is exacerbated by dating apps, which have created an atmosphere of seemingly endless options, short-attention-span dating, and the BBD (bigger, better, deal). We have literally commoditized ourselves, and dating has become transactional. It's no wonder that our anxiety surrounding relationships, commitment, and marriage has shot up, while the principles of love and marriage run askew.

Add to this the notion of "soulmates," which further ups the relationship anxiety ante. There's a fantasy that guides many into seeking idyllic partners or soulmates. If you could find that perfect match, you'll be guaranteed a lifetime of relationship bliss, right? Soulmate is what Satan puts in his coffee.

There is a persistent idea that when we choose someone to be a long-term partner, they will be an incredible lover, hold fireside chats about Tolstoy, and take long beach saunters while sharing hemp and flaxseed smoothies. Research has shown that this mindset leads to heartache and failed relationships.[3] What if you thought you met your soulmate and then discovered they clap whenever the plane lands?

1 Albert Einstein College of Medicine. (2010). *Study links romantic rejection with reward and addiction centers in the brain.* https://einsteinmed.edu/news/releases/546/study-links-romantic-rejection-with-reward-and-addiction-centers-in-the-brain/

2 Boutwell, B. B., Barnes, J. C., & Beaver, K. M. (2015). When love dies: Further elucidating the existence of a mate ejection module. *Review of General Psychology, 19*(1), 30–38.

3 Burnette, J. L., & Franiuk, R. (2010). Individual differences in implicit theories of relationships and partner fit: Predicting forgiveness in developing relationships. *Personality and Individual Differences, 48*(2), 144–148.

## There Is No Single Effective Cure for the Anguish Associated With Heartache

Although the emotions surrounding a breakup can affect both males and females, they are far less socially acceptable in a man. This is the primary reason there are so few books available to men regarding breakups. Look no further than the breakup book covers and titles to validate this claim: *He's Just Not That into You*; *The Smart Girl's Breakup Buddy*; and *Breakup Girl to the Rescue*, for example. The list is long, and each cloaked in pink, pastel, and effeminate covers.

> *"The exhausted brain loops re-enactments of the severed bond piece by piece in some macabre relationship forensics."*

You painstakingly dissect past conversations, events, and nuances of the bond while cerebrally clawing toward a personal salvage strategy. You become a pariah to friends and family who look upon you with pursed lips of empathy while avoiding sustained eye contact or dialogue at the risk of triggering an emotional flare.

People make tired comments like *"There are plenty of fish in the sea,"* *"You're better off,"* or *"How long were you together?"* so they can quickly determine if the number justifies your level of distress.

How long will the pain last? What is considered acceptable by friends? By society? Is the recovery period half the time you were together? There is no mystical breakup algorithm to determine your fixed emotional penance. It takes what it takes. And for everyone this is different. But everything you need to heal is already within you.

## Tactics for Relief: How to Handle "Goodbye" and the Flashbacks That Follow

The pain of rejection works on the same neural pathways as our physical pain. And oddly, the same painkillers shut down the intensity on that pathway. Over the counter headache medicine seems to help with breakups.[4] But there are plenty of other tactics to usher you to the other side.

---

4 Dewall, C. N., Macdonald, G., Webster, G. D., Masten, C. L., Baumeister, R. F., Powell, C., Combs, D., Schurtz, D. R., Stillman, T. F., Tice, D. M., & Eisenberger, N. I. (2010). Acetaminophen reduces social pain: Behavioral and neural evidence. *Psychological Science, 21*(7), 931–937.

*Don't Ask Them to Sleep With You One More Time in
the Hope It Will Somehow Woo Them Back*

If you pose this question, you will be denied even a sliver of dignity
upon which to rest. It is imperative to limit self-humiliation and to
avoid further contact with your ex. An effective technique to implement at this early stage is deleting the object of affection's number
from your phone contacts list.

Even better is turning off the phone and keeping it somewhere
out of reach. If the number is permanently etched into your mind,
however, change it in your phone to something more appropriate
like "Toxic," "Drama," "Go-away-tionship," "Satan," "Do Not
Call," and the like. This will limit moments of nostalgia and the
certain romanticizing of their name.

*Perform an Exorcism of All Relationship Mementos*

This includes emails, cards, photos, half-used massage oils, candles, concert tees, and so on. Despite how expensive, memorable,
or impressively crafted, they must all be discarded or stowed away.
Change all venues you regularly frequented together such as gyms,
bars, naughty shops, theaters, cafes, Pottery Barn, and so on. You
could probably use the change of scenery right now.

*Skip Rebound Dating for Now, Under the Presumption
That "the Quickest Way Over One Is Under Another"*

This is a brief distractor and, invariably, turns into date-therapy
and sound-boarding your sorrow and anxieties on to some inno-
cent philanthropist kind enough to be with this woeful version of
you. Your sole focus is healing while limiting any carnage to yourself or some unsuspecting prey from dating apps.

---

**Modify Your Mindset: Additional Proven Tactics to
Hasten Your Heal**

1. **Therapist? You mean Tinder?** A breakup can lead to depression, isolation, self-accusation, or worse. You don't always

need to make grief clinical, but it's imperative to know when to seek outside professional help. The easiest index to use is if your emotions are starting to interfere with daily life functioning, including sleep.

2. **Only the strong forgive.** Forgiveness is simply giving up the hope for a different past. They may not deserve your forgiveness; but you deserve peace. It's about letting go of the outcome, rather than condoning any actions by someone who inflicted the pain. Forgiveness takes only one person: you.

3. **The magnanimous power of giving thanks.** Not only does gratitude increase how much positive emotion you feel, but it also just as importantly deprives the negative energy that is the driving force of why you feel so badly. There is omnipotence in gratitude. Focus on three gratitudes daily, no matter how small.

4. **Better than an FWB is a BUB.** *"He's only ignoring my texts because I haven't sent enough."* Utilize the exceptionally helpful camaraderie of a breakup buddy (BUB) to remediate poor decisions when reacting from emotions. These are dangerous moments of relapse; hence, the importance of someone who will think for you until logic is reengaged. Refer to them often.

5. **Change small behaviors to change your moods.** If you change small post-breakup behaviors, it will change your thoughts, feelings, and emotions. This is paramount in helping you to feel less anxious, worried, depressed, or experiencing an intolerance of uncertainty following a split. For example, if you do the opposite of what your emotions are driving you to do – such as checking out their social media or driving by their home – your anxiety, worry, and pain will subside.

6. **Cowabunga! Ride those thought waves.** Harness the technique of urge-surfing, which is nothing more than riding an emotional wave and not responding to any part of it, but letting it swell and then wane. This is an extremely helpful tactic to use in dealing with the impulsivity associated with a breakup because you are observing your emotions, rather than acting on them. And it prevents regretful actions.

## What good are emotions?

Emotions are signals within the body that tell you what is happening. Anger is an emotion. Anger is love disappointed. Some proselytize that feeling anger during the recovery process is good. Like a scab that itches, it means healing is taking place and is viewed as a sign of forward motion.

Depending on how long you stew, however, anger can be a toxic bog and a point of extended limbo. The potentiality for anger is a primary reason to avoid drinking and lowering inhibitions during breakup recovery, since it short-circuits rationality, yielding mean texts or rocket-propelled grenades, both with similar results. And drinking before noon does not make you a pirate.

### Why Do Breakups Have to Hurt So Badly?

If we all spooned and forked everyone we saw with no consequences, the world would spin off its axis. There must be societal checks and balances. Evolutionary biologists conclude that post-breakup pain and reflection is required for us to learn from loss.[5] The agony that comes with heartbreak leads us to scrutinize future attempts before we hit on the next thing we see in yoga pants or an Armani suit.

The pain of rejection is exacerbated by how we view and treat ourselves after it occurs. But rejection also causes physiological pain with an evolutionary purpose.[6] Back in early times, being rejected by your people meant lone survival and imminent death. Now we have HBO and DoorDash and being alone for a period is an under-utilized indulgence that too few learn to relish. Once you do, you'll realize how truly self-sufficient you are.

### Contrary to Widely Held Beliefs, Closure Is Not Necessary

In the throes of pain, the shortest route to ending heartache is seemingly with the source. It is not. It is within you and not with your defector. Countless people never gain closure yet still move forward and heal. When you are broken up with, your ability to reconcile who you are is upheaved. But you're still in there . . . somewhere. You are whole. And you are grand. Despite what you might be

5 Kansky, J., & Allen, J. P. (2018). Making sense and moving on: The potential for individual and interpersonal growth following emerging adult breakups. *Emerging Adulthood (Print)*, 6(3), 172–190.
6 Perilloux, C., & Buss, D. M. (2008b). Breaking up romantic relationships: Costs experienced and coping strategies deployed. *Evolutionary Psychology*, 6(1).

thinking, you never need to know why your ex did anything they did. Your ex was never the reason you thrived.

> *"Don't come off as desperate and chase your ex. Wait a while. Meet someone else. Get married. Start a family. Keep them guessing."*

### In Breakups, for Every Action There's an Unequal and Opposite Overreaction

One of the ways you can change your emotion is to reverse the loop. You start with an opposite action, and the emotion starts to subside. Change the emotion by changing your action. This opposite action technique is a mindfulness skill used to reduce unwanted emotional responses and increase positive emotions. Opposite action helps regulate emotions by intentionally going against what the specific emotion is driving you to do.[7]

---

**Modify Your Mindset: Change Your Emotion by Changing Your Action**

**How to do Opposite Action**

1. Use mindfulness to notice the emotion, the action it is urging you to do (and, if possible, the prompting event and the interpretations of the prompting event).
2. Do not suppress the emotion, or it will get bigger. Emotions are not the problem – urges and/or intensity are the problems.
3. Ask yourself if the emotion is justified and if the intensity of the emotion is justified or helpful.
4. If the emotion is not justified or the intensity of the emotion is not helpful, do the opposite of the action the emotion is urging you to do.

> *"Just gonna send him a message. . . . And I'm blocked."*

---

7 Linehan, M. M. (2014b). *DBT skills training manual* (2nd ed., Available separately: DBT skills training handouts and worksheets). The Guilford Press.

In the case of a breakup or divorce, for example, a primary opposite action is to "go ghost." Going ghost includes not responding to your ex's "*Hey, stranger*" text. Conversely, an "*I miss you*" doesn't equal "*I want to get back together and adopt Haitian toddlers.*"

Going ghost is one of the most sagacious devices for self-preservation. Most breakup sufferers greatly add to their angst by not following this one, basic tenet. If you're going to be friends with your ex, it'll happen organically and when you're long over them. If you must see your ex, keep it cool and make it fast. Otherwise, ignore them so hard they doubt their own existence.

*"I see your silent treatment and raise you one ghosting."*

Going ghost is not a game; it's not about punishment or revenge or to make your ex jealous; and it's not about getting your relationship back. If you and your ex have children together, then you will inevitably need to discuss issues such as welfare and access. However, it is best to keep these interactions to an absolute minimum, and at a McDonald's Playland just off the highway.

### Breakup Recovery Isn't Linear, But More a Game of Chutes and Ladders

Reverting and plateauing are common throughout the entire breakup recovery process. Healing is rarely direct in movement, but setbacks are temporary and short term. You may feel stuck at the same low level for weeks, only to suddenly leap forward in your progress out of nowhere. Your adherence to tactics such as the aforementioned will accelerate your imminent healing. In life, you can let go or you can be dragged.

Though the only way over breakup pain is through it, there are healthy ways to care for yourself until the negative emotions subside. To counter the melancholic feelings inherent to any breakup, it's imperative to spend time outside, get regular sleep, exercise, and eat right. Wean off the Pinot and cookie dough and get some nutrients. Studies have shown that foods can directly influence the brain neurotransmitter systems that are related to mood.[8]

8 Prasad, C. (1998). Food, mood and health: A neurobiological outlook. *Brazilian Journal of Medical and Biological Research*, 31(12), 1517–1527.

## *After a Breakup, Some People Gain 20 Pounds While Others Get Into the Best Shape of Their Lives*

Consider taking a hike by water or in nature, while paying close attention to the sights, smells, and sounds around you. Go out for a meal or just dessert with a friend if possible. Pay special attention to the ambiance, the tastes, and the conversation. Even when you don't feel like eating, food goes down much easier under the distraction of conversation and solidarity.

**During a breakup or divorce you experience a broad disbelief of what occurred, to the point that might include a panic/anxiety sensation.** You may better know it as a nervous breakdown, freak-out, or panic attack. They essentially mean the same thing and involve about 15 minutes of symptoms that include increased heart rate and breathing, muscle tension, sweating, dizziness, tunnel vision, hot/cold flashes, out of body experiences, detachment from reality, and flailing about inappropriately. It feels like a power-hug by a Yeti. In life, safe hugs come from the front.

Consider practicing some relaxation techniques. This can include simple meditative breathing exercises or guided meditations available on YouTube or via smartphone apps. Add yoga, prayer (Psalm 34:18), or meditation daily. With practice, an inner balance and peacefulness develop. Negotiating a stressful or anxious period is the perfect time to spend in self-reflection and meditative prayer, even if your higher power is a doorknob.

### *It's Never Too Late to Leverage the Mystic Power of Boundaries*

When someone contacts me at *State of Anxiety* seeking breakup advice, they're often in the early stage of breakup pain, while experiencing an emotional cocktail of shock, disbelief, sadness, and a side of anxiety. You had an entire life before the pivotal day you met your ex at the bar/gym/traffic light. So why does it suddenly feel like you can't make a sandwich without them?

Boundaries can prevent you from weeks, months, or years of anguish because you allowed the wrong person into your life. Boundaries also prevent enmeshment. At the most basic level, enmeshment is a concept where your life becomes blurred with that of another. In this scenario, you don't know where you end and they begin. A healthy relationship consists of two whole entities who love and support one another, while remaining complete on their own.

### Enmeshment is "1 + 1 = 1"

He or she does not actually complete you. You need to remain complete on your own. *Why?* Two reasons: (1) You never want to complete anyone or vice versa. A fence post that leans on another makes a shoddy fence. And (2) if the relationship/marriage ends, you will need to be a whole entity again. So why not remain one in the first place?

Establishing boundaries, even after a breakup, strengthens resolve and helps to rebuild self-esteem following a breakup. Establishing boundaries will protect you with regard to all of your interpersonal relationships. The best breakup advice is the advice you won't need later.

### What Is the Zip Code in Your State of Denial?

Denial and the hope for a different outcome is a coping mechanism that gives you time to adjust to a distressing situation. Being in denial gives your mind the opportunity to unconsciously absorb shocking or distressing information at a pace that won't send you into a psychological tailspin.

When the reality hits that you've been relationally evicted, denial is a great tool; as in "*If I don't think about it, then it's not happening,*" or "*I can totally fix this, I just need another chance.*" A less obvious way denial presents could be as a denial of inner strength: "*I can't handle this!*" The issue with denial as a coping mechanism is that it's not a long-term solution. Remaining in denial is not healthy, and it's unnerving to onlookers.

### Your Milkshake Will Still Bring All the Prospects to the Yard

Following a breakup you miss having someone around. It's old habit to say "goodnight," or sext on a random weeknight to someone who won't call the cops. Now you stare thunderstruck at a silent phone, willing it to ding with a text, while feeling a dreadful void from losing that regular communiqué. But if you reach out it's akin to another hit of heroin for a recovering addict: It will satiate the cravings for a bit, but you're only resetting your recovery clock. Remember, "It's Called a Breakup Because it's Broken." I read that on a pink breakup book cover somewhere.

**Your Anxiety-Trigger Toolkit: 15 Tips for Perfecting
Your Post-Breakup Palooza**

1. Delete their number from your phone contacts list. If you have it memorized, then change it in your phone to something irreverent or repulsive.
2. Rid of all relationship mementos. There's no reason to preserve and display the memories like the Louvre.
3. The quickest way over one is not under another. It's a temporary fix.
4. Seek outside professional help if your emotions are starting to interfere with daily life functioning, including sleep or work. There's no shame in the therapy game.
5. Forgive. They may not deserve your forgiveness; but you deserve peace. Forgiveness is for you, not them.
6. Give thanks. Gratitude deprives the negative energy that is the driving force of why you feel so badly. Three gratitudes daily, no matter how small. **Thank you!**
7. Designate a breakup buddy (BUB) and refer to them often. *"Siri, call my BUB."*
8. Observe your emotions, rather than acting on them to prevent regretful actions. Textual healing is not a thing.
9. The shortest route to ending heartache is within you. Closure only matters on contracts and coffins.
10. Do the opposite of what your emotions are driving you to do, and your anxiety, worry, and pain will subside.
11. If you're going to be friends with your ex, it'll happen organically and when you're long over them.
12. Even when you don't feel like eating, food goes down much easier under the distraction of conversation and camaraderie with a friend.
13. Negotiating a breakup is the perfect time to spend in self-reflection and meditative prayer, no matter your religious affiliation and beliefs.
14. Establishing boundaries, even after a breakup, strengthens resolve and helps to rebuild self-esteem following a breakup. Fortify with 24/7 heartache militia.
15. Being in denial gives your mind the opportunity to better absorb shocking or distressing information. They're gonna regret leaving you when your mixed tape drops.

# 21 Moving/Relocating

DOI: 10.4324/9781003345350-26

For many of us, gone are the laid-back days of moving a futon and mini-fridge from a college dorm back to your trophy-adorned room at mom's. There is an analogous relationship to getting older and the resources to hire professional movers. And a maid. If you insist on ruining a friend's weekend, at least box everything beforehand and offer a charcuterie board and pushcart. No one wants to slip a disc for pizza and Bud Light.

I typically stay in any one home as long as possible, no matter what record-level loathing I feel for the place, parking, or neighbors. I'm like a turtle tucked into his shell skirting life's various stings. Interestingly, at the time of this writing, both Chris and I were buried by geographic moves – he into a house for humans, and me into a 700 square feet "cottage" – a term for a cute but fundamentally uninhabitable space for grown-ups. Our experiences were radically dissimilar as my move was festooned with anxiety.

Moving is a top two anxiety trigger for me, followed only by midnight earthquakes. I am disappointed to share that I train-wrecked this move at case-study levels. On the upside, the relocation served as the embodiment of this anxiety trigger chapter. I'm here to serve.

*Tip: Spice-up your moving panic with a harmonica or kazoo.*

The tiny home was situated in a quaint neighborhood within walking distance to my vibrant downtown in Campbell, CA, where I had spent the previous six years. I sold as much as possible via phone apps beforehand. The $2,400 per month, 700 square feet size appeased my trendy pledge to minimalism, until I moved a bed, 55" TV, and cat tree inside. With each item unboxed, I quickly grasped the limits of the space, and my anxiety. I'm also bad at math. I had 1,200 square feet of furniture and possessions in my previous two-bedroom condo. But even the small new fridge couldn't hold all my existing perishables or regret.

I believe that humans are getting bigger over time. Look at kids today. Whether the bovine growth hormones in milk, or GMO'd blueberries, 14-year-olds shouldn't be able to bench-press 315 pounds. But I'm middle-aged and built like a horse jockey, and was still unable to clean myself in the payphone-sized shower unless skipping anything below the waist. Moreover, the toilet was awkwardly tucked into a small corner opposite the shower, requiring some creative hygiene.

My anxiety and claustrophobia soon reminded me of what I had tried to squelch. I lasted only three days in the bungalow before emailing my new landlords Kathy and Merril that I needed to meet to discuss a dire "situation." We met at a nearby Starbucks where I tried to explain to non-anxious people that I would be unable to remain in the home, despite committing to a 1-year lease. This meant that my state of mind trumped the legal consequences of breaking a lease in California.

Kathy and Merril let me out of the lease, refunded my full deposit, and extended a level of kindness and empathy rarely seen today. My next move was 147 miles away to a suburb outside of Sacramento to be closer to my ailing mother, into a 2,100 square feet house for less than the price of an SF Bay Area tiny home. And from there, I did two more moves hours away within the same 24 months due to work.

## No Matter Where You Go, There You Are

Anxiety is energy. It's nervous energy, but energy, nonetheless. And it's unrivaled energy. The kind you get from tsunamis and unrelenting "unexpected item in bagging area" alerts at self-checkouts. And it goes wherever you go.

The lesson for you is that when things become their worst and anxiety peaks, you can channel the energy for negative or positive. When channeling the angst-vigor for good, you become focused, driven, resilient, and unrelenting. Stuff gets done. It's like throwing an AC/DC switch, where AC is "anxiety current" and DC is "dominance current." DC will get you where you need to go.

### Tactics for Relief: How to Stay Focused in the Presence of Bubble Wrap

*Move Over Tranquility, Here Comes Moving Day*

Moving is one of the top five stressors of life, preceded only by divorce and death of a loved one, and rounded out by major illness/injury and job loss. The anxiety of moving is largely triggered because you are adapting to a new environment. Change is hard, especially for those with anxiety, because it's a fondue of unknowns.

Rather than trying to eliminate your symptoms, plan ways to distract from or reduce their severity, like using an itinerary. Do everything you can to start the moving process as early as possible. If it's financially feasible, try to overlap your old lease and new lease by at least a week, so you can move at a more relaxed pace. Assemble your moving troops in advance, especially if hiring professionals. And expressly if it's in the spring or summer, as this is when the majority of big moves occur.

*"I'd rather make new friends than help you move."*

**Anxiety Safety Briefing: Engaging Your Four Limbs and Five Senses**

Remember that home is where you *feel* at home and when the environment signals safety and serenity. Engage the five senses to signal to your brain that you are indeed home.

- Play your favorite music as you start unpacking.
- Cook your favorite food at the new house, or use the realtor's trick of buying premade cookie dough to make the house smell cozy and delicious.
- Clean it with your cleaning supplies, run a cycle in the dishwasher with your favorite smelling detergent and use your own soap in the shower until it smells a bit more like home for you.
- Set up the lighting and place some pictures up on the wall right away.

*Perform Regular Mental Mine Sweeps*

Survey your mindscape. Being mindful of distressing thoughts may act as a form of exposure to feared obsessions. People who are chronic sufferers of anxiety keep themselves in a continuously heightened state of stress with only brief, unsatisfying intermissions between fears. Mindfulness helps us become less invested in our thoughts to create the realization that a thought is just a collection of words or images and is nothing to fear. Give yourself 5 anxious minutes in the day and then go be gangsta.

*"Yes, I'd like to report someone not living in fear."*

Your worst day facing your fear is still better than your best day surrendering to it. You have what is needed within you to meet life demands, thereby lowering stress and avoidance behaviors. Continuously observe and monitor your thoughts and behaviors until it becomes a regular and natural process. And whenever you feel anxiety arising, ask yourself what your thoughts are. Then take a single, deep mindful breath and root yourself back in the present moment. Sometimes we need to be unplugged and plugged back in.

Sadly, the anxiety of moving does not end when the moving truck pulls away. It may increase after you have settled into your new job or home, especially if you moved to a region that salts sidewalks instead of margaritas.

Set up the most important spaces in your new home first. Get your bedroom sleep-ready immediately because you'll need rest. If you have kids, pack their favorite stuff and other critical items and bring them in your car, unless you want to spend hours tearing open boxes looking for *Cubby the Curious Bear*. Get their toys unpacked and their bedroom set up or rue the day and night. If you cook, the kitchen should be next. A home-cooked meal can help you to settle in. Once you have shelter and food again, everything else will fall into place.

> *"It's irresponsible to make unpacking a drinking game."*

Maslow's hierarchy of needs plays an important role here. You might recall the seven-tier model of human needs depicted as hier-archical levels within a pyramid from psychology. Lower needs within the hierarchy must be met before the ascending needs. Sex appeal and democracy aren't on the pyramid.

From the bottom of the hierarchy upward in order of importance, the levels are biological and physiological needs, safety needs, love and belongingness needs, esteem needs, cognitive needs, aesthetic needs, self-actualization needs, and transcendence needs. Shelter, sustenance, and health fall under the "biological and physiologi-cal" and "safety" needs tiers.

First you need food and health, then shelter and safety, and then emotional comforts. As you build these into your new place, the more secure and less anxious you'll feel. Which is why you can feel like a hermit crab scurrying across an open beach in search of a new shell during a move. Make sure your new shell has coffee filters, Wi-Fi, and light bulbs.

### Suffering Is Adaptive, Which Is Why Pain Centers Use Coldplay as Hold Music

On a scale of "1 to person who just awoke in a new house and can't find the toilet paper," how stressed are you? You cannot develop resilience in the absence of difficulty. It's imperative not to abandon healthy habits you may have had before you moved. This includes engaging in physical and relaxation exercises to release stress hormones. Forge a lifelong friendship with your body and be its bestie by implementing small changes. You don't have to get up at 5:00 a.m. to work out. I won't even get up at 5:00 a.m. to pee. I'll just lie there awake in pain.

### Kids Are Better Shakers Than Movers

When it comes to moving, children often lack the ability to put problems into perspective. Let your child know it's okay to be anxious or miss their friends and previous school. Encourage your child to participate in decisions about activities, meals, and bedroom paint colors. And give them time to adjust while listening to and showing empathy for their sadness and frustrations.

Everyone seeks support differently. Verbalize your own needs during this time. You may find comfort by turning to friends and family back home for support more than you had anticipated. Ask a relative or close friend to visit you. Hosting them in your new setting will make it feel like home – especially if you hand them a paint roller and point to a wall. Home improvement is both a love language and a housewarming gift.

### What Are All Those New Things Going Bump in the Night?

Falling asleep in a strange house is like doing battle with your biology. This sleep struggle, called first night effect, is an evolutionary adaptation to keep you semi-alert and safe in an unfamiliar setting.[1] Only half of your brain enters deep sleep when you try to sleep in a new place. The other half is a night sentry keeping watch to protect you, while remaining responsive and vigilant to possible threats like rising interest rates and homeowner association dues.

This protective physiological mechanism seems to mostly occur on the first night in a strange place. By the second night, both sides

---

1 Herbst, E., Metzler, T. J., Lenoci, M., McCaslin, S. E., Inslicht, S., Marmar, C. R., & Neylan, T. C. (2010). Adaptation effects to sleep studies in participants with and without chronic posttraumatic stress disorder. *Psychophysiology, 47*(6), 1127–1133.

enter deep sleep. Researchers have determined that when sleeping in an unfamiliar place, the left hemisphere of the brain stays alert while the right hemisphere rests. They also point out that some birds and marine mammals always sleep with one brain hemisphere asleep while the other is active, to compensate for risks that they are vulnerable to when asleep.[2] The effect is similar to watching a horror movie or "Dr. Pimple Popper" before bedtime.

### Insomnia Has Many Side Effects Beyond Keeping Spiders Out of Your Mouth

Even one night of bad sleep can be an anxiety fire-starter. The following day, you use what little energy you have left to breathe and maybe blink. The most well-balanced people become chilling versions of themselves on sleep deprivation. If you are prone to anxiety, do not underestimate the importance of rest, at the risk of your and everyone else's peril.

Sustained insomnia and fatigue can make you feel like you're losing your mind. You might even find yourself analyzing your inability to fall asleep. *Am I stressed? Dehydrated? Counting my debts and mistakes? Wondering how many animals we had to jump on the backs of before discovering horses were cool with it?*

> Friend: *What time do you usually go to bed?*
> Me: *10ish, sometimes 4.*

Many sleep hygiene guidelines will help you obtain rest despite a period of anguish. They include eliminating caffeine and alcohol, exercising regularly, avoiding heavy meals prior to bed, following a standard wake time, using the bed only for sleep, getting out of bed when you can't sleep, and not napping. People with poor sleep have poor sleep habits.

A classic method used by the U.S. Army to help soldiers fall asleep in chaotic conditions (e.g., battlefields) recently resurfaced. According to *The Independent*, "the technique was first described in a book from 1981 called *Relax and Win: Championship Performance* by

2 Tamaki, M., Bang, J., Watanabe, T., & Sasaki, Y. (2016). Night watch in one brain hemisphere during sleep associated with the first-night effect in humans. *Current Biology, 26*(9), 1190–1194.

Lloyd Bud Winter."[3] It's believed the tactic was developed by army chiefs to prevent exhausted soldiers from making dire mistakes. With practice, it's supposed to get you to sleep within 2 minutes. The method is a hybrid of muscle relaxation, breathing, and visualization that anyone can do.

---

**Exercises in Fulfillment: How to Fall Asleep When the Battle Is Within**

**Here's how it works:**

1. Begin by sitting on the edge of your bed with only dim or no light on. Your phone should be silenced and the alarm set.
2. Relax your facial muscles by first tightening them up in a cringing or wincing motion like you just bit into a wasabi-covered lemon. Now let your face muscles slowly loosen and relax, including your tongue.
3. Once your face feels like putty, let your shoulders naturally drop toward the ground. Allow your arms to fall and dangle one at a time by your side.
4. While you're doing this, gently breathe in and out at a natural pace and rhythm while focusing on the sound of your breath. Let your chest relax further with each breath. Move down to relaxing your thighs and lower legs.
5. Once your body is completely relaxed, try to clear your mind for 10 seconds by detaching from your thoughts. Let any thoughts pass by focusing on your breath and not attaching to them. You can acknowledge them as thoughts and then let them go.
6. Now visualize one of the following two scenarios: You're lying in a canoe on a calm lake with clear blue skies above you, or you're in a velvet hammock, gently swaying in a pitch-black room. If you happen to be a person who isn't great at visualization, you can instead chant the mantra, "*Don't think, don't think, don't think*" for 10 seconds.

---

3 Staff, I. (2021, September 1). The military secret to falling asleep in 2 minutes. *The Independent.* www.independent.co.uk/life-style/fall-asleep-fast-sleep-trick-military-b1912422.html

*Disclaimer: I'm not sure if anyone in the army has seen a canoe, but let's assume it's a comfy, old-timey, dugout canoe filled with throw pillows and no crossbar seats. I'd also like to talk to the U.S. Army about their velvet hammocks.

These easy steps should take about two minutes. Upon completion, lie down and turn off any light. Ideally, you'll drift off to sleep within a few minutes. If not, you can join the army and get hands-on training. But you'll have to move again.

### To Have Memories Tomorrow, You Need to Start Today

Memories and mail are what made your last residence feel like home. Start with the friends who can help you unpack in exchange for wine and take-out eaten off of boxes. Move on to having people over for book club, movie or game nights, or something regular. Host a housewarming, even if just one friend can visit, as a reminder that people believe in you and that this is your home. Once people see your new digs as your home, you'll start seeing it that way too. What's more, a few good memories will contribute to a feeling of emotional attachment to the place. Reward their loyalty with your Wi-Fi password and extra bubble wrap.

**Your Anxiety-Trigger Toolkit: Nine Tips When You Miss Your Home and Your Homies**

1.  Rather than trying to eliminate your symptoms, plan ways to distract from or reduce their severity, like doing everything you can to start the moving process as early as possible. Only roosters should start the day screaming.
2.  Continuously observe and monitor your thoughts and behaviors until it becomes a regular and natural process. Label the feelings and then let them go.
3.  After a move, unpack quickly and resist the urge to hunker down. Set up the most important spaces in your new home first. Recall why you should've better labeled the boxes.
4.  It's essential not to abandon healthy habits you may have had before you moved. This includes engaging in physical and relaxation exercises to release stress hormones. It's never too late to get heavily meditated.
5.  You cannot develop resilience in the absence of difficulty. Pause and reflect on previous life circumstances that you have overcome in the past. What specific actions helped you through those times?
6.  Let children know it's okay to be anxious or miss their friends and previous school. Encourage them to participate in decisions about activities, meals, and bedroom paint colors. Show empathy and give them time to adjust.
7.  You may find comfort by turning to friends and family back home for support more often than initially anticipated. Ask a relative or close friend to visit you. Start with those who are handy or good interior designers.
8.  Try the U.S. Army sleep technique in your footed camo jammies.
9.  Make memories in your new home by engaging your five senses. Have people over for book club, movie or game nights, or something regular for those *"Felt cute, might delete later!"* social media post moments.

# 22 Job Loss/Unemployment

DOI: 10.4324/9781003345350-27

Losing a job is destabilizing at best. It can lead to feelings of anger, panic, and depression. For many, it's also a loss of identity in addition to income. With the majority of people in developed economies living paycheck to paycheck, it can be devastating, even if the work made you feel dead inside.

But that's the tradeoff for regular pay and a false sense of security. *Or is it?* Nothing breaks the spirit like poverty. And things get far more expensive with kids, as you need money for college or bail, depending on the kid. If you don't open the bills, you can enjoy the illusion of having more cash for other things, like books on anxiety.

Since the economy and employment are dependent on so many variables, you are likely to experience under- or unemployment at some point in your career. That's not always a bad thing, but it's usually an anxiety-triggering thing.

*"I should've stolen more office supplies."*

The easiest and most unfulfilling job I've had was working as a city government driver at 18. I would drive all over town in a white Chevy Malibu emblazoned with the city emblem on both sides and a "For Official Business" decal affixed to the back, while taking important municipal documents here and there. One mid-afternoon the hypnotic drone of wheels on pavement lulled me to sleep as I merged onto the freeway. Fortuitously, I dozed off toward the right shoulder unknowingly steering the car into a long row of tall and merciful, drought-tolerant shrubs financed by California taxpayers.

The branches and debris slashed the car with talons of sinewy bark. The mirrors, paint, and hubcaps were scraped off the sides, and the entire exhaust system was ripped from underneath before the car halted atop a woody bush, smoke wisping from the undersides. My heart pounded as I tumbled out the door to survey my unique freeway egress. Branches and limbs jutted from everywhere on the car. But I was alive and the engine was still running, though it now sounded throaty and rough.

I manually tore the branches from their strangleholds, jumped back into the disgraced civil service vehicle, and drove to my dad's house with the residual kindling and remaining exhaust pipe following behind in a trail of sparks. Having a dad with a mechanical skills and a welder saved the car and my gig. But he couldn't save me from my job narcolepsy.

## Cubicles Are a Consistent Reminder That Office Work Sucks

Cubicles are where companies harvest wasted potential. People adorn them with rear-view mirrors stuck to monitors, cliché "teamwork" and "motivation" posters, plants, candy dishes, serenity table waterfalls, and easy-listening music to provide the illusion they are anywhere but the insipid place we spend the bulk of our lives. Our cubicles become little museums of the things that used to bring us joy before we started the job.

*You're Not Gonna Want to Sit Down for This*

Not only do our jobs sometimes kill us, but sitting at our jobs is killing us. And sadly, we can't make up for it after work. A comprehensive life-style study found that those who sat for most of the day were 54% more likely to end up clutching their chests than those who did not sit for the majority of time.[1] The surprising aspect, however, is that the weight or exercise frequency of the sitters did not matter. If sitting is the new smoking, then sitting and smoking are some next-level stuff.

## Tactics for Relief: How to Get Back Into Work Clothes Again

*When You're Sitting at Home Wondering How Long You Can Survive Unemployment With $217 in Your Bank Account*

Two of the worst feelings in the world are not having a job and having a job you don't like. If your resume is a list of things you never want to do again, then talking with a career counselor is a valuable first step. Capitalize on any benefits that may be coming your way from the termination, including training, coaching, and resume services. And use your remaining insurance to get some free therapy while knocking out any medical and dental appointments you need.

Practice interview questions, thinking about how each of the skills you have could apply to a range of positions. Add to your LinkedIn network recruiters, hiring managers, and people with roles you're targeting, and join as many relevant trade or industry groups as possible. You'll want to ensure your social media profiles are set to private because recruiters and hiring managers love to surveil candidates. And if your email user ID is something like "partyhottie@aol.com" you'll want to create a more suitable title with a provider from this era.

*Expose Yourself*

If you fear something (e.g., unemployment), you can radically accept the situation as a temporary state and then plan objectives

---

1 Nolamedia. (2017). Why your office chair is killing you. *Ghgb*. https://ghgb.pbrc.edu/why-your-office-chair-is-killing-you/

to get back on a payroll at your desired company. By facing this fear of the unknown, your anxiety decreases until it's eliminated altogether. It helps to remind family and friends to stop asking how the job search is going and to assume it's going poorly until you tell them otherwise.

> Friend: *How are things going for you?*
> Me: *Don't worry. Things are good!*
> Narrator: *Things were, in fact, not good.*

Unemployment sucks. Rejection sucks. But being in the wrong job also sucks. Oftentimes, we stay in an ill-fitting role until we're forced out. Then it's a positive because you are more likely (hopefully) to do some personal discovery to learn where you'd most like to work. This in turn leads to a better fit, more job longevity, increased happiness, and less burnout.

Work is not just a matter of skill and resume fit, but temperament fit. As a psychologist, Chris is largely an introvert. He had a few early career positions that required doing consulting within classrooms. While intellectually stimulating on some level, it created too much anxiety for him. It was not the right job, as supervisor after supervisor kept telling him to "put yourself out there" with the teachers he worked with. It simply didn't work for him. Not every place you fit is where you belong.

Chris discovered the same poor alignment with the factory-like aspect of treating clients hour after hour with demanding "productivity standards" in a large health care system. By trial and error, he learned that he needed to work for himself, even if it was less stable. He leveraged the anxiety of becoming fully self-employed to motivate him to successfully make the leap. He's probably long forgotten the timeless skill of faking niceties to co-workers, and the value of replacing "*screw you*" with "*Okay, great.*"

While you're hustling to find humble work, you read stories of others quitting jobs to make millions on social media without leaving their house. Losing your job can feel like an identity crisis or an opportunity. Emotionally, a job loss is devastating. A job is often a huge part of your personality and meaning. Unemployment also wreaks havoc on any structure in your life. *Why get up in the morning if there's nowhere to go? Why go to bed on time? Why not watch murder documentaries all day?* As our structure and meaning fall away, depression sets in. Never leaving the house and sitting around all day is a symptom of depression. But it may well be the cause.

### Don't Worry About the Future, Take It One Panic Attack at a Time

Don't take your worries to bed. Take 20 minutes during the day to write a T-chart in the form of two columns. At the top of the left column write "worries." Label the top of the right column "solutions." When you write out a worry, think how about the steps you might take toward a solution. It does not need to *solve* the worry; just move in a direction *toward alleviating* it.

Your solutions can be broken into smaller steps to prevent them becoming overwhelming. The worry could entail a lack of viable interviews, for example. A possible solution might be to contact someone on LinkedIn at your company of interest and request an informational interview with them. Employees that genuinely like their company are typically eager to talk with interested prospects. Conversely, if they're indifferent or dislike their company, they'll either ignore you, warn you to avoid it, or you'll see them sprinting from the office when you go to interview.

### It's Not Actually Because You're Awake in Someone Else's Dream

Insomnia in a sense is an "insomniaphobia" – it's the fear of not sleeping that keeps you awake. Stress and insomnia are usually symbiotic. If you can't sleep because you're wondering if owls have knees or you're filled with negative thoughts like, "*I can't believe I'm unemployed*," or "*How will I pay the rent/mortgage/bills?*" take a matter-of-fact approach: "*It seems my mind is too active to sleep right now, and trying to force sleep is counterproductive. I'm going to read a book for a while.*" When you're exhausted, it's tough to pull an all-dayer without a nap.

> "*What came first, not being able to sleep because you're on your phone or being on your phone because you can't sleep?*"

To avoid depression, it's critical that you maintain a routine of some kind – sleeping and waking at around the same time; getting out the door to a library, cafe, or co-working space to job search; and having an exercise and healthy eating routine. Set up virtual or in-person informational interviews and networking sessions each week. The structure will keep you healthy and poised for your comeback. It's hard to appreciate time off when it wasn't your choice. Go easy on yourself and source the humor in your interim "person of leisure" status.

Since your schedule is flexible, you can job-search earlier or later, while hitting the gym, grocery store, trails, and roads when they're relatively empty. As tough as it might be, try to appreciate and enjoy your unintended sabbatical while it lasts. Once you're back to work, exercise, home cooked meals, and time with family often become neglected. Unless you're Santa Claus, pets and people never loved you for your job.

---

### Anxiety Safety Briefing: Sample Unemployment To-Do List

- Go to sleep and wake up at a reasonable and consistent time each day.
- Shower and get ready as if you were going out in public. What you wear doesn't have to have buttons or a zipper, but it shouldn't be satin or flannel and adorned with mermaids or dinosaurs.
- Leverage a professional resume writer or update your resume yourself. Create specific resumes and cover letters for each job title of interest.
- Determine a set number of jobs to apply to each day.
- Send a predetermined amount of new LinkedIn network invites each day, update your profile, and join as many online industry groups as allowable. And engage!
- Make a target list of informational interviews, networking coffee meet-ups, and phone calls to do each week.
- Get in shape physically and make exercise a priority.
- Meet with recruiters or job coaches for advice and feedback.
- Update your skills by taking online or offline courses of interest and those that will further your career goals.
- If anxiety or depression (or, both) are hindering you, book a therapy appointment. Most therapists can work out a payment plan with a sliding pay scale on the basis of your ability to pay.

- Seek volunteer opportunities that can sharpen your skills, teach you new ones, offer additional networking opportunities, and help to get you out of your head.
- Still a bad time for a neck tattoo.

### Daisy-Chain Your Obsessions to Their Not-So-Tragic Ends

Unemployment gives you time to focus on your new passion: worrying about money. If you revisit the tactic on thought-chaining in Chapter 2 and mentally play out the dreadful beliefs causing you distress, you will deny their power over you. For each obsession, ask "*And then what?*" or "*And then what's the worst that can happen?*" until you get to the end and see that the worst possible outcome is not actually devastating. Unemployment often includes irrational, dystopian predictions about your future. Keep in mind that on any given day everything can change for the better. That's why people buy lottery tickets and pregnancy tests.

Avoid comparisons with your former and existing peers. **Comparison is the fastest route to misery.** This includes comparing your real life with your former one, or the rehearsed versions that plague social media platforms. During low moments grab a pen and get scribey. Research has shown that journaling helps reduce stress, solve problems more effectively, and even improve your health.[2] Regular journaling strengthens immune cells, called T-lymphocytes. Writing about stressful events helps you to accept them, thereby reducing the impact of the stressors on your mental and physical health. Writing also allows you to share something with others when you don't want to make eye contact with anyone.

### How to Prepare for Interviewing and Related Presentations

An elevator pitch is a brief (not more than 30 seconds) and persuasive speech used to create interest in a product, service, idea, or person (you!). It's a basic tenet for all interviews. It's the succinct

---

2 Pennebaker, J. W. (1997). *Opening up, second edition: The healing power of expressing emotions* (2nd ed.). The Guilford Press.

reply you'll provide when an interviewer asks, "*So, tell me about yourself*," and you want to present a polished version, not a slippery Pandora's box edition where you've stuffed your self-doubt and torched bridges.

Practice your personal pitch until it comes naturally. Each round of practice further quells the anxiety and will help you be ready for an interview or assigned presentation. The more you can remain off-script, the better, so that you are talking and not reciting. This way, if you stumble over the exact words, different ones will come right to mind and be just as effective in the moment while conveying the same message. Oftentimes we start a sentence without knowing where it's going, hoping we'll meet up with it later in the conversation.

> "*For my presentation today, I'll be reading the slides word for word.*"

If you are using slides during an interview presentation, have just enough information on them to jog your memory with the talking points that accompany them, either by connecting the images or a few words to the next idea. Don't word-murder your audience while lulling them into a trance. Be notable, not narcotic.

Practice standing tall and confident. Research shows that standing tall and upright before doing a task may change our body chemistry by boosting hormones that give confidence (testosterone) and lowering those that create stress (cortisol). Think Wonder Woman or Superman, not TLC's "Sister Wives."

A study by researchers from Columbia and Harvard Universities showed that using body language that symbolizes power can subconsciously affect our decision-making.[3] The researchers found that open, expansive postures (widespread limbs and enlargement of occupied space by spreading out one's body), compared with closed, constricted postures (limbs touching the torso and minimization of occupied space by collapsing the body inward), increased feelings of power and an appetite for risk.

> Interviewer: *So where do you see yourself in five years?*
> Me: *In your chair but asking better questions.*

---

3 Carney, D. R., Cuddy, A. J., & Yap, A. J. (2010). Power posing. *Psychological Science*, *21*(10), 1363–1368.

Your body language, whether confident or otherwise, communicates externally to your audience but internally to you as well. Practice as you imagine yourself being fully commanding with your interviewers completely enthralled. And pierce their soul with your sustained eye contact.

Be aware of the speed at which you're speaking. Anxiety leads to fast talking, which results in mid-speech panting to catch your breath. If anything, speaking slowly and putting in pauses to breathe draws the audience in with suspense while wanting to know what comes next. It also helps eliminate the "ums," while setting a controlled pace for you. There is great power in the pause. Wield interspersed momentary silences as a tactic. A great presentation happens between the words. That's when your audience will reflect on the significance of what you've said.

### Make a List of Things You Are Good at to Boost Self-Esteem Before You Interview

Spend time thinking about past successes with interviewing and speaking in front of others. Have you ever noticed how musicians, comedians, and speakers banter a little with the audience pre-show? That's to settle everyone down and build the performer's confidence. Asking questions of your panel or audience engages and relaxes everyone quickly and can get you through that initial anxious spike and to where you can begin to speak more naturally. It turns out small talk has meaning. In America when you ask someone how they're doing, and they actually start to tell you, you're still allowed to walk away mid-sentence.

### "Hello, My Name Is . . ."

When we meet someone new we always ask, "*What do you do for work?*" It's one of the first things we ask, as if this is the sole defining trait of a human. Work is what you do, not who you are. That's why they have to pay you to do it and watch you while you do. Work is a means to an end, where the end is not starving.

*So who are you?* Please try this: Take out some paper or a journal and write a list, starting with "*I am . . .*" and write as many self attributes as you're able. No negative adjectives allowed (e.g., "*I am an unemployed loser*"). Remember, thoughts and feeling don't equal facts. Write out who you are at the core – your true identity.

For example, maybe you're a parent and an aunt or uncle. You're a novice gardener, a best friend, a runner, a wine connoisseur, a bicyclist, or a great listener.

Now reflect on who you truly are and what genuinely matters to you. If you're able to find work that aligns with this, all the better. In the meantime, I hope you don't have to retype your entire work history after uploading a resume.

**Your Anxiety-Trigger Toolkit: Ten Tips for Coping With the Absence of Occupation**

1. To avoid depression, it's critical that you maintain a routine of some kind, to include sleeping and waking at around the same time. Wearing pajamas all day, showering at 10:00 p.m., and then putting on clean pajamas is the wrong regimen.
2. Turn your attention to things you can control during unemployment, such as learning new skills, writing a great cover letter and resume, volunteering, and asking for raving LinkedIn profile reviews.
3. Radically accept the situation as a temporary state, and then plan objectives to get back on a payroll at your desired company. By facing the fear of the unknown (e.g., involuntary "van life"), your anxiety decreases until it's eliminated.
4. Don't take worries to bed. If you're worried that your debit card is starting to feel more like a depleting gift card, use the T-chart (worries/solutions columns) to identify core anxieties and then move toward alleviating them.
5. Thought-chain negative beliefs and worries. For each anxiety, ask *"And what's the worst that can happen?"* until you get to the end and see that the worst result is not catastrophic. Anxiety is fear immaterialized.
6. Avoid comparisons online or IRL with your former and existing peers. During the low moments journal to problem-solve and improve health. If it's good, you may have found a way to pay the rent.
7. Craft an elevator pitch that doesn't end in, *"That's me in a nutshell."*
8. Your body language communicates both internally and externally. Practice as you imagine yourself being fully commanding.
9. Leverage pre-meeting banter and the power of the pause within interviews and presentations. If you can leave the building during your pauses, that's too long.
10. Write down your core ingredients, starting each with *"I am . . ."* and write as many self attributes as you're able. No negative adjectives (e.g., *"I am a hobo"*). Marinate on your core merits.

# Conclusion

We covered 22 of life's most anxiety-provoking scenarios. However, we could've written about 222, as each week seems to present the world with another unexpected trigger. Remember: Your brain clings to the negative as an evolutionary self-preservation feature. It wants you to pay attention to potential threats to keep you safe. But in modern society you don't need to concern yourself with the majority of perceived threats approaching at the speed of your data plan.

This book was written as a triage guide versus life's greatest anxieties. And we certainly put the content to the test. The tactics herein are some of the most appropriate tools to utilize on the basis of proven clinical efficacy and peer reviews. We did not foresee, however, having to use so many of the techniques ourselves in relation to anxieties we experienced individually while writing the book. Between Christopher, me, and our illustrator, Peter, we faced a combination of divorce, loss of parents, job loss, terminal illness of loved ones, parenting challenges, and serious illness, while all three of us experienced at least one large geographic move. We absolutely practice what we've presented. This material is road-tested firsthand.

You're certainly not expected to remember all the tactics in one or two passings. Dog-ear the pages, insert tabs or post-it® notes, or highlight it like a paper rainbow and go back to it as needed. Our objective is that on an initial review of the book you'll come away with a handful of techniques to use regularly (i.e., radical acceptance, 7/11 breathing, half smiling, being mindful in the moment, the exposure hierarchy, etc.). You will find your favorite "go-to" tools and then add to them as you practice and with additional readings.

Keep in mind that the anti-anxiety skills taught can be used for multiple anxiety triggers. In other words, don't concern yourself with trying to recall which tactic to use against which specific anxiety trigger. Just practice as many of the aids as you're able. The more you repeatedly practice using the techniques, the better you'll manage overall worry, stress, and anxiety in general. Think of it like a "square hole, many square pegs" problem and solutions set.

DOI: 10.4324/9781003345350-28

Lastly, contact me anytime directly at Jon@StateOfAnxiety.com with feedback or to share your experiences on what helped, what did not, or what you'd like to see in a follow-up book (e.g., calming lavender scented pages, and momma's comfort food meatloaf recipe, etc.). Until then, Chris and I wish you discernible internal peace and a sustained hopeful mindset in this uncertain, wild, and (mostly) wonderful world.

# Index

Printed in the USA
CPSIA information can be obtained
at www.ICGtesting.com
LVHW050543011224
797961LV00003B/587